Field Notes from Elsewhere

◇ ◇

Columbia University Press | **New York**

Field Notes from Elsewhere

REFLECTIONS ON DYING AND LIVING

Mark C. Taylor

Columbia University Press
Publishers Since 1893
New York   Chichester, West Sussex
Copyright © 2009 Columbia University Press
All rights reserved

Library of Congress Cataloging-in-Publication Data
Taylor, Mark C., 1945–
    Field notes from elsewhere / Mark C. Taylor.
        p. cm.
    Includes bibliographical references (p.).
    ISBN 978-0-231-14780-4 (cloth : alk. paper) — ISBN 978-0-231-52003-4 (ebook)
    1. Death.   2. Taylor, Mark C., 1945–   I. Title.

BD444.T355   2009
191—dc22
[B]
                                                                    2008054314

Design by Lisa Hamm
c 10 9 8 7 6 5 4 3 2 1

References to Internet Web sites (URLs) were accurate at the time of writing. Neither the author nor Columbia University Press is responsible for URLs that may have expired or changed since the manuscript was prepared.

Title-page spread: *Pinhole portrait of Mark C. Taylor* by Ann Hamilton

Contents

Field Notes from Elsewhere

ONE

A.M.

Day

DAWN ON STONE HILL, IVY FROM MELVILLE'S GRAVE

The world, ancient myths teach us, did not originate once and for all at a moment in the distant past but is created anew every time dawning light reveals changing patterns. This endlessly recurrent event almost makes it possible to believe that rumors of death are nothing but idle gossip. Eternity is neither the infinite extension of time nor its negation; rather, eternity and time meet in the paradoxical moment when creation repeatedly emerges as if from nothing.

As I write these words, dawn is slowly breaking on the Berkshire Mountains. For more than two decades, I have begun each day in silence, watching first light gradually dispel lingering darkness. The most intriguing moment in this ritual process is not when the sun's rays first touch the mountain but the instant just before dawn when all of what will be creation hovers on the edge of emergence. I am never sure whether light makes the mountains appear or the mountains make light visible. In the twinkling of an eye, betwixt and between not appearing and appearing, reality remains virtual and all things seem possible. But this moment never lasts, for it appears only by disappearing. As soon as light falls on the mountaintop, it begins a gradual descent to the valley. If you are patient, the eye can glimpse the sun's movement in the steady withdrawal of shadows. Light, however, is never merely light, for illumination creates a residual obscurity more impenetrable than the darkness it displaces but does not eliminate.

Annual rhythms repeat this daily cycle. On the evening of the summer solstice, the sun sets directly in front of my study window and then immediately starts its southward journey. The first day of summer marks the end of increasing light and the beginning of enveloping darkness. By the winter solstice the sun has moved so far south that I can no longer see it set. But then, in an instant, everything is reversed yet again—on the longest night of the year light begins to wax and darkness wane. Darkness in the midst of light and light in the midst of darkness. I never appreciated these rhythms until I moved to this hillside overlooking the valley.

What is most remarkable about each dawn is that the light is never the same—it changes with the seasons, by the day, even in each moment. There is a texture to light that allows—no, requires—the tissue of vision to be constantly woven anew. Scrims settle on the eye like a mountain mist that creates sensibilities no word or deed can disperse. Colors become moods, moods colors: the blue and gray of winter, the green and lavender of spring, the red and yellow of summer, the umber and amber of fall. In the mountains of New England, light is most remarkable during the early morning and late afternoon on sunny autumn days. The play of shifting light and the astonishing color of the hills creates an aura that is at once ethereal and palpable. The subtleties of its hues are reminiscent of northern light in Scandinavia. I never really understood Kierkegaard until this light absorbed me.

Around 4:00 in the afternoon on warm fall days, something very strange happens: I no longer simply see light but hear it as a tangible presence pressing on my eardrums, creating a resonance that lingers long after darkness falls. This autumnal light is always tinged with the melancholy that comes with the sense of an ending, which every beginning harbors. To see this sound is to understand that silence is truly golden.

P.M.

Night

There is not one night; there are two. The first night is the night that is the opposite of day and is familiar to all of us. At the end of a long day, we welcome this night and look forward to the renewal it brings. Night after night day dawns in the darkness refreshed, reborn, resurrected. At the end of the day, this night beckons like a lover with open arms: "Come, linger till first light."

NIGHT ON STONE HILL

The other night is different; it is, paradoxically, within as well as beyond what we ordinarily know as day and night. Far from familiar, it is forever strange; never reassuring, it is endlessly fascinating. If day marks the beginning in which light dawns ever anew, the night beyond night is the origin from which day and night, as well as all the differences and oppositions that structure our world and render it comprehensible, emerge and to which they return. Neither light nor dark but something in between, this other night is the realm of shades that wander and drift but never settle. The darkness of this netherworld cannot be dispersed. The light of reason tries but always fails to grasp the other night with strict oppositions and precise combinations: either this or that … both this and that. But shades always slip away—every light, we discover, casts a shadow. Shades of difference haunt our world and leave nothing clear or precise. If this placeless place that always appears by disappearing has a logic, it is fuzzy.

I am never sure whether I approach this night or it approaches me. It seems to draw near by withdrawing, leaving in its wake hints that provide no clues. The apprehension of shades can occur day or night, in light or darkness. Sometimes I glimpse this strange night as I lie awake in darkness, other times in the middle of the day when everything seems crystal clear. This night is inescapable—wherever I turn, it appears like a faint shadow I barely glimpse.

This night gives me no rest even when I am asleep. It is profound but without depth, utterly superficial yet fathomless, extraordinary because so ordinary. Through a synesthesia I do not understand, I hear the night beyond night as an endless murmur, something like white noise that is indistinguishable from silence. The patterns, rhythms, and routines of daily life seem fashioned to silence this murmur, but every strategy fails. The silence of this night can never be completely silenced and its echo lends every word an uncanny resonance. If someone asked me what is so disturbing about the night beyond night, I would reply, "Nothing, absolutely nothing."

TWO

A.M.

Beginning

It began—or so I thought—with two phone calls of which I have absolutely no recollection. In retrospect it seems fitting that the beginning was an event I cannot remember but know only through others. I have long insisted in my teaching and writing that life is always lived on the edge, along the elusive border between order and chaos. What we call normality is a narrow bandwidth—a fraction of a degree more or less, and everything spins out of control. Along this margin reason and madness are simultaneously joined and separated by a membrane so thin and porous that one inevitably bleeds into the other. No matter how hard I think or how much I analyze, I can never know myself by myself but must always come to myself in and through an other. This other bears many names—it can be a parent, teacher, or pastor whose gaze we flee or guidance we seek. The other can also be the enemy we struggle to destroy, the beloved in whom we long to lose ourselves, or a child in whose eyes we see our own reflected. There are, however, different others that are within rather than without. They might be ghosts of the departed or demons that possess us. The deeper I probe, however, the more I suspect that beneath, beyond, or within these uncanny spirits, both holy and unholy, there is an other other I can never fathom, that some name the unconscious and others name God. I am no longer sure where I end and these others begin, and thus the story I thought was my own is also the story of many others.

Almost two years after phone calls lost to memory, I learned that Dinny had dealt with the trauma by writing. This was unusual because her medium, unlike mine, is numbers rather than words. As I was gathering thoughts for what became the book you are reading, she hesitantly said, "You know, I wrote about what happened that day. It was not so much that I was afraid of forgetting—how could I *ever* forget?—rather, I needed to find some way to begin to make sense out of what seemed completely senseless." I asked if I could see what she had kept secret, and she agreed to show it to me and now is allowing me to share it with you. The following is what she wrote:

⁘

The fever began late Saturday. We had gone car shopping because the old one was breaking down and no longer was safe for late-night drives on the Taconic Parkway. I'd insisted that we go to several dealers because he had what the Danes call a special "round" birthday (60) coming up very soon. Tylenol helped and the fever came and went. On Sunday morning he didn't feel very well, and the fever was still up and down, so he called the doctor who had performed the biopsy on Friday. The doctor explained that infections sometimes occur—especially in diabetics—and upped the antibiotic dosage.

It was the last week of the fall semester at Columbia and, being a dedicated teacher for thirty-three years who had missed only one class in all that time because of illness, he was determined to go to NY and wrap up the semester. The book he was to teach that day had been written at his urging by his friend, the well-known and controversial French philosopher Jacques Derrida: The Gift of Death.

"Yes, I'd feel better if you stayed here," the doctor said, "but I understand how important it is to you to teach your class, so go ahead. Do you have any medical contacts down there in case you need intravenous antibiotics?"

"I'll ask our son who his doctor is." After he hung up, we collected the names and numbers.

"OK, here's what we're going to do," I said. "I am going to drive you down and if you seem stable, I'll come back in the morning and be late for work." He didn't resist, which is not like him.

The up-and-down pattern of the fever continued throughout the day and into the night. I started writing down the numbers. That's what I do.

Monday morning he felt better and called the doctor's office [from Manhattan] and talked with the nurse. He described the fluctuating fever. "Sounds like you will be OK with the additional antibiotics," she said confidently. Nevertheless, I insisted, "I am going to wait until you get back from class before I leave. I'll work from here." Once again, he didn't resist.

When he returned from class early in the afternoon, he seemed to be doing much better. His fever was down and he ate a good lunch. The class had gone well; he really enjoyed this group of students.

I kissed him good-bye and felt fine about leaving him now. As I drove north, I noticed a major traffic jam in the south lane of the Westside Highway just above the bridge to Manhattan. Fire trucks were by a building, and traffic was being diverted. "Good thing I'm going north," I thought.

We often stop at a spot about an hour north of the city for gas and a break. I was almost there when my cell phone rang.

"I think we may have made the wrong decision. My fever's spiked to 103 and I'm shivering like crazy and can't stop shaking. I just don't know. I don't know."

"I can't turn around here. I'll call you from the gas station and we'll decide what to do."

When we talked a few minutes later, he said repeatedly, "It's very, very bad, very, very bad."

"I'm turning around and I'll bring you home." The three-hour drive now would be five and he was concerned about that. "Doesn't matter. I'm on my way." I was worried, but at least we had a plan.

Twenty minutes later the cell phone rang again. "This is Mark Taylor. I called earlier this morning about my fever."

"Mark—this is Dinny!"

"Jenny?"

"No, Dinny. Your wife!"

"My wife? My wife is driving back down to get me."

Now I was really scared. I had voice-activated many of the family phone numbers in my contact list. "Aaron work," I said into the phone, hoping beyond hope he would answer.

"Aaron Taylor."

"Aaron, something is really wrong with Dad. Can you go up to his apartment immediately?"

"Um, yeah. What's going on?" I told him about the call.

RING—RING!

"Hello?"

"Mom, where are you?"

"I'm forty-five minutes north on my way back to the city."

"I called Dad to see how he's feeling and he's delirious!" The panic in Kirsten's voice was chilling.

"I just called Aaron. Call him and go up to the apartment with him. Make sure Dad has sugar in case it's an insulin reaction."

RING—RING!

"We just called 911. Dad came downstairs to wait for you, and he is wandering around sweating and incoherent. Kirsten is going in the ambulance, and I will follow on my own."

Traffic stopped. The fire. The detour. Have to call Aaron.

ST. LUKE'S-ROOSEVELT AMBULANCE

EMERGENCY ENTRANCE,
ST. LUKE'S-ROOSEVELT HOSPITAL

I spoke into the phone, "Aaron cell." BEEP! Name not recognized. "Kirsten cell." BEEP! Name not recognized. I tried again and again, but the phone no longer recognized my voice—it was shaking too much. I had to find the contact list to make the call.

We finally connected again, but the cell phone worked only on some of the calls. How did it know?

"Which hospital? Columbia-Presbyterian?"

"No, Saint Luke's."

"Where your baby will be born, near 59th?"

"No—wrong Saint Luke's. It's Saint Luke's–Roosevelt at Amsterdam and 113th. There's a garage across the street. It's one-way going east so drive up Broadway to 114 and turn right."

When I arrived, the emergency room was chaotic. Aaron and Kirsten were nowhere to be found. Eventually, a nurse's aide led me to where they were holding Mark for observation. We were allowed to stay with him. By this time he was coherent and the drugs they were pumping through his system seemed to be taking effect. Just as we were beginning to feel better, an attendant, who had been checking Mark's blood pressure every few minutes, abruptly dropped the machine and ran out of the room without saying a word. Aaron, Kirsten, and I looked at each other and rolled our eyes. What kind of place was this? Suddenly, he reappeared with several doctors, who explained that they were moving him to another ER cubicle for more critical cases, where they could monitor his blood pressure constantly. They asked him, "Can you walk up a hill or up stairs without losing your breath?" I saw where this was going. "He runs four to five miles a day," I said. All the doctor replied was, "Oh." Then he added in a calm voice intended to cushion the words he spoke, "His blood pressure has dropped to 50/20. We need to put a line straight into his artery in his neck or his groin so we can get medicine into him to bring up the blood pressure as quickly as possible." He explained the risks and I said, "Can you do the groin if that's less dangerous than the artery in his neck?" After checking with the doctor supervising the ER, he returned and said, "No, it has to be the neck. All of you must go outside while we do this." "He was humoring you, Mom. They were never going to do it in the groin," Aaron said.

Finally, they were ready to take Mark upstairs to the critical care unit. By this time Frida, Aaron's wife, who was seven months pregnant with our first grandchild, had joined us and brought us food, though we did not feel like eating. We all followed the gurney through the empty halls of Saint Luke's and across the glass bridge over 114th Street that Mark passed every day on his way to his office. When we all entered the CCU, the nurse looked at us with surprise but quickly understood how serious the situation was. She took charge and asked us to stay in the dark and dreary waiting room across the hall until they got him settled.

I started writing down the doctors' names, most of which were foreign, unfamiliar, and difficult to remember. I needed to understand who was who but, more important, this information gave me some sense of order, even if not of control.

When we returned to the CCU, we were not prepared for what we saw: tubes, electrodes, and wires connected Mark to monitors that registered a steady flow of numbers. Two young doctors watched the screens carefully and discussed what they saw in Spanish. I could not have known then that they would not take their eyes off those machines until dawn.

BRIDGE TO ELSEWHERE

In a few minutes the doctor who had accompanied us from the ER came in to talk with us. "May I speak with you alone?" he asked me directly, casting a glance at the rest of the family.

"Anything you will say to me you can say to all of us. We're a family and are in this together."

In a gentle Indian accent he continued, "Your husband is very, very sick. He is in septic shock, and his vital organs are in danger of shutting down. For the moment his heart and lungs seem OK, but his kidneys are showing signs of distress and we are worried about his liver. He is, however, receiving good care. You all should go home and get some sleep. There is nothing more you can do. Give us your phone number and we will call you if anything changes."

We asked some questions because we are all used to a world in which information gives power, comfort, and control. Finally, I summoned the courage to ask the question I had been dreading, "But he is going to be OK, isn't he?"

"Your husband is very, very sick," the doctor repeated. And then, with eyes cast down, he added, "We are doing everything we can." Only Kirsten understood what this really meant.

⣿⣿

Dinny's account of those hours left no doubt about how critical my condition had been. During the days that followed, we all came to understand what Kirsten already knew—the doctors did not think I would live. The mortality rate for septic shock is 40 to 75 percent, and my case was severe. The first night I realized it could go either way, but by morning thought I was out of the woods—I was not. It would take five days in the critical care unit, five more days in the hospital, and a month of intravenous antibiotics before my condition stabilized. Though I had been dreading turning sixty for a long time, there was no way I could have anticipated just how difficult that anniversary would be. I spent my birthday in the hospital with few distractions and more time to think than I wanted. While still in the CCU, a doctor I had never before seen delivered news that did not exactly fill me with holiday cheer—I would have to have a second biopsy in the near future. I was finally released a few days before Christmas and was able to return to the Berkshires for the holidays. As we gathered around the dinner table, Aaron offered a toast for the Christmas that might not have been. During the long, dark winter days that followed, I struggled to get back in shape, knowing I would likely have to go through it all over again in a few short months. As I feared, my respite proved to be brief. The following May, merely five months after my collapse, a second biopsy was positive, and I had to undergo surgery to remove the cancer that was destroying me from within. Persistent diabetes and the aftereffects of sepsis complicated my condition and made the outcome uncertain. With extraordinary medical care, as well as the support of family and friends, I survived, though the future, as always, remains uncertain.

These experiences have changed me in ways I am still struggling to understand. I have devoted my entire professional life to thinking about existential issues, but life has a way of putting ideas to the test. While the language of the writers I study, teach, and write about is abstract, I have always believed that the problems they explore are frightfully concrete. The challenge of teaching, writing, and, indeed, living is to join the abstract and the concrete in thinking about questions that truly matter. For more than thirty years, I have considered writing a book that combines philosophical and theological reflection with autobiographical narrative. But I repeatedly delayed this process because the moment never seemed quite right. Such a work, I realized, cannot be rushed because the experiences of life and death constitute the necessary research. After the past year I am persuaded that I have finally done enough fieldwork—writing is not only possible but now actually seems necessary.

Field Notes from Elsewhere is the journal from the trip of a lifetime. After such a journey nothing, absolutely nothing, remains the same—everything must be reconsidered and reevaluated. Family, friends, foes, colleagues, values, ideas, work, play, success, failure are no longer what they had previously seemed to be. Things never get back to normal because the axis of the world shifts, even if ever so slightly, and what passes for normal changes. Even when the diagnosis is good, full recovery remains an idle dream. The problem, as I had long suspected, is not to find a cure but to learn to live with the impossibility of cure. In the course of this unending journey, I discovered that Kierkegaard was right when he observed, "Death is a good dancing partner."

"Elsewhere" is not so much a place as a condition that renders whatever had seemed familiar utterly strange. This is not the first time I had been elsewhere, but never had I lingered so long and never was I so uncertain of returning. With no map for this unsettling territory, my journey was filled with surprises: secrets I never suspected, births and deaths of which I was unaware, relatives I never knew I had, diseases that overwhelmed me, cruelty that crushes, grief that paralyzes, pain that baffles, betrayals that chasten, monsters that terrify, ghosts that haunt, pleasures simple and forbidden, and, at the end of the night that has no end, the gift of hope from a granddaughter I might never have known.

The effect of having been elsewhere cannot be erased; the more I try to crowd these experiences out of my mind, the more insistently they intrude into my consciousness. What is left unsaid, I have learned, is as important as what is said, and the invisible is often as significant as the visible. The experiences discussed in this book leave little doubt that paradoxes and contradictions form the very stuff of our lives. Looking at life from elsewhere, you are led to confess that thinking can be difficult but life is more so. In a world obsessed with speed, celebrity, and excess, the life of thought often seems detached and even downright boring. But what could be more dramatic than unraveling a long-held family secret, passing an endless night at the bedside of a critically ill child, comforting a friend whose wife has lost her mind, lying awake listening to the howls of a grief-stricken father, telling your family you have cancer, taking responsibility for the suicide of a close friend, and even returning from the land of the dead?

Life is lived forward but understood backward. Looking back over the years, there appears to be a discernible trajectory to this story. And yet the way remains episodic rather than continuous; events do not always follow a consistent narrative line but twist and turn in premonitions and repetitions that create the intricate web that forms our lives. It is my hope that as you turn these pages, you will see aspects of your own life reflected in a story I once thought was merely my own.

P.M.

Origin

The beginning is not the same as the origin. When the beginning emerges, the origin recedes, leaving in its wake a past that becomes our future to form a circle that never closes. Though I believe I know when and where *Field Notes from Elsewhere* began, its origin lies buried in a childhood beyond memory that I never suspected until one lazy summer day in 1956, when I was ten years old. It was one of those days when the New Jersey heat and humidity made it too hot for my brother, Beryl, and me to play outside. We had finished lunch, and I was sitting on the couch in the living room. Bored but not tired, I picked up the family Bible, which had been on the step table

FAMILY BIBLE

with my mother's mementoes and knickknacks for as long as I could re-member, and distractedly turned its pages. Maps, photographs, drawings, and paintings rather than words attracted my attention: *The Cedars of Leb-anon, The River Jordan, Christ with the Fourth Commandment, Sermon on the Mount, Jesus Healing the Man with Dropsy, The Via Dolorosa, The Crucifixion, After the Resurrection—Jesus by the Lake, The Ascension.* Pictures made it all seem so real. But while lost in a world that claimed to be more than imagi-nary, I stumbled on something completely unexpected. Between the Old and the New Testament, I discovered a "family register" with four pages: "Parents' Names," "Children's Names," "Marriages," and "Deaths." On the first page the names of my mother and father were written in my mother's hand. On the second page I was startled to read the names of not two but *four* children: before my name my mother had written "Baby Girl Taylor," and between my name and my brother's name, "Brent Taylor." The mar-riage page was blank; on the page labeled "Deaths," she had written:

Baby Girl Taylor   Nov. 9, 1944
Brent Taylor   May 25, 1954

FAMILY SECRETS

As I struggled to absorb what I had read, my head started spinning. For a few minutes I sat quietly trying to regain my balance. Eventually, I went into the kitchen where my mother and father were finishing lunch, put the Bible open to the page with the names of four children on the table, and said: "What does *this* mean?" They glanced at the book and then stared at each other for what seemed like an eternity. I shall never forget the look in their eyes. They had known that this day would come but obviously were not yet prepared for it. Though they were both teachers—my father taught biology and physics, my mother American literature—in the deaths of their children they never found a lesson they could pass on to others. Attempting to avoid the question, my mother began to make up some kind of story. But my father quickly interrupted her: "No, it's time for him to know." He paused, took a deep breath, and turned his piercing brown eyes toward me. In a voice measured by the weight of his words, he said: "You had a sister and another brother. Your sister died at birth a year before you were born, and your brother, who was born almost two years after you, was very sick and was never able to come home."

I do not remember what else was said that afternoon or in the days that followed. But that moment remains seared in my memory in ways I still cannot comprehend. In the blink of an eye everything changed. It was as if I had been transported elsewhere and now looked back to discover that all that had been familiar had become strange.

OPFN BOOK

For the next six years, nothing more was said about my dead sister and brother—absolutely *nothing*. In the summer of 1963, our family drove from our home in New Jersey to California and back. Though billed as a vacation, it was more of an extended lesson in history, geography, and ecology. Teachers, it seems, can never stop teaching. On our way out we stopped in Kankakee, Illinois, to see the town where our parents had lived and worked during the war and where I would have been born had they not moved to New Jersey in the fall of 1945. After driving around the factory where my father had been a chemical engineer in a facility that produced explosives for the campaign in the Pacific, we stopped on the street where they had lived in a third-floor flat. We could not enter the house, but my mother described their small living room, bedroom, and kitchen in vivid detail. Even at the time I realized that she was speaking more to herself than to us.

I didn't know how desperately lonely she had been in Illinois until many years later, when, while looking for stamps in her desk, I discovered a diary she had kept during the year before my sister's birth/death. It was a small daybook with a light blue cover and pages bordered with soft green designs. For each day there was a biblical quotation. The vivid words and carefully wrought phrases were those of the literature teacher she had been and once again would become. Until I read these pages, I had not realized that when she described the flat while sitting in a car parked on a Kankakee street, she had failed to mention a second bedroom—the room she had prepared for their first child. The scene she depicted in the diary was bright with expectation: the crib, the curtains, the freshly painted walls, the quilt she had so lovingly crafted. I do not recall any diary entries after the death, but there might have been some. Before I had finished reading the diary, I heard my mother's footsteps coming up the stairs and quickly returned the book to its hiding place. She never knew I had read it.

As we were about to leave Kankakee, my father said: "There is one more place we are going to stop. We want to go to the cemetery where your sister is buried. We have not been back since we left Illinois; it's important for both of you to come with us."

The cemetery, which was on the edge of town, was unremarkable. After parking the car, my father reached for his wallet and pulled out a small, tattered card. Looking over his shoulder, I saw that it was a form from the cemetery with the grave location typed on it. I had never known that he always carried this card with him. The only marker on the grave was a small, flat stone with no inscription. As the four of us stood around the grave, nothing was said. We silently returned to the car and continued to drive west.

In the last years of their lives, my parents occasionally mentioned their daughter but never their son. It was several years after the cemetery visit before I discovered the reason for their reticence. Though they continued to resist talking about my brother, my father eventually explained reluctantly that my sister had died of strangulation when the umbilical cord became wrapped around her neck at birth. To their dying day my parents felt that her death was the result of the doctor's mistake. When my father explained that they had planned to give my sister his name—Noel—the paradoxes multiplied: father as dead sister, sister as dead father. Noel … No El. El, after all, is one of the names for the unnameable God. My sister, like God, remained unnamed. Why didn't they name her? Were they saving the name for her replacement? Or was there something more profound in their refusal to name what they could not understand? Was the death of the father/daughter/sister the death of God?

KANKAKEE MEMORIAL PARK

NAMELESS

The repressed, Freud has taught us, does not disappear but repeatedly returns to dislocate patterns that long seemed secure and disrupt the stories we tell ourselves as well as others to get through the night. On that summer day in 1956 the narrative of my life changed forever. In the twinkling of an eye, I glimpsed the abyss over which life is forever suspended. We come closest to the real, I believe, in moments that are profoundly unsettling. If you are patient enough to linger with loss and ponder the most troubling moments, you will discover lessons that make life richer even if much more complex.

It is important not to confuse beginning with origin. Origins are always obscure even when beginnings are not. While beginnings mark points in time, the origin is never present—nor is it absent. That from which I emerge approaches by withdrawing. As creation myths ancient and modern teach us, in the beginning— before the beginning—there is loss. The cosmic and the personal intersect in an ever-receding moment that can never be recovered. It often takes a lifetime to learn that birth is always traumatic. My birth as a thinker, teacher, and writer was impossible apart from the death of others as well as myself. It has slowly become apparent to me that in one way or another, everything I have written and taught over the years bears the trace of my nameless sister and unmentionable brother. The presence of their absence creates the void at the center of my being,

which makes me what I am and who I am not. The loss that has always occurred before I begin leaves an emptiness that can never be filled. Though
undeniably devastating, the lack that lingers from such a loss opens the
space of desire, which is the void from which the creativity that marks
every beginning eternally emerges. Paradoxically, the gift of death is the
gift of life.

THREE

A.M.

Elsewhere

I have been elsewhere. The distance is short, though its crossing takes a lifetime. Elsewhere is not far—it is near, ever proximate, never present. It is a place or placeless place that is strange because it is so familiar. Rather than beyond, elsewhere is between the places I ordinarily dwell or think I dwell. When journeying elsewhere, you do not leave the here and now; it is as though elsewhere were folded into the present in a way that disrupts

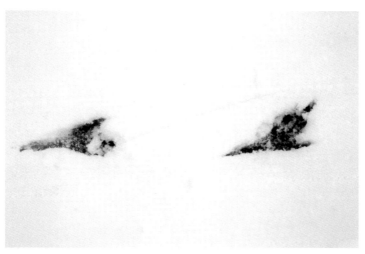

TRACKS LEADING NOWHERE

its presence. The everyday world does not disappear when you linger elsewhere—all you care about approaches from a distance that increases as it diminishes. Gradually, you begin to realize that nothing is merely it-self—everything, everybody, is always also something else, someone else, somehow else, somewhere else.

When you are elsewhere, vision, and, with it, awareness, doubles and, as you recognize this doubling, doubles yet again. Far from confusing, this doubling and doubling of doubling clarifies by disclosing an elsewhere that is always there by not being there—like a looking-glass world into which you can always slip but never leave. The mind is split, divided, torn not only between consciousness and the unconsciousness but also within consciousness itself. Two in one, one in two—neither separated nor uni-fied, neither many nor one. Just as the everyday does not disappear when you are elsewhere, so elsewhere does not vanish when you attempt to come back. Once you have been elsewhere, you can never come back be-cause elsewhere always returns with you.

P.M.

Silence

In a world where noise is incessant, silence is as rare as it is essential. When was the last time you actually heard silence? Even in the dead of night silence has become as elusive as darkness. The ticking of clocks, the hum of machines, the rumble of trucks, the honking of horns, the ringing of phones, the vibrating of pagers, the howling of coyotes create background noise that cannot be switched off. It would, however, be a mistake to op-pose noise to silence; nor should one assume that silence offers relief or promises renewal, for it is often dreadful.

Though rarely heard, silence echoes in many different ways. Sometimes noise can silence. I know a person who cannot sleep without a white noise machine beside her bed to silence the sounds of the city. More often, noise silences silence and thereby seems to bring a measure of relief from the emptiness silence portends. What makes silence both disturbing and alluring is that it gives you time to think, perhaps even to reflect. When reflection is serious, it is unsettling because it threatens to undo so much of what we have done. Eager to avoid the specter of silence, we allow the endless chatter of everyday life to distract us. When home alone, the TV is always on, not because people are watching and listening but because they cannot bear the silence that haunts the house. With silence threatening to follow them when they leave houses that are no longer homes, people plug into connections that don't connect. On the bus, in a subway or classroom, iPods plug ears with noise and everyone is wrapped in silence that brings no solitude.

Silence is not, of course, always noise; it can also interrupt noise in ways that give pause to words. Silence can be carefully calculated—words thoughtfully left unspoken because the time is not right, words cruelly withheld when they are sorely needed, words saved now so they can be spent later. Silence is often awkward and begs to be broken. The uttered word releases tension even—perhaps especially—if nothing is said. At other times silence is pregnant with a fullness no words can capture. In search of the plenitude this silence promises, monks, secular as well as sacred, flee to deserts near and far.

Though rarely heard, there is another silence that is neither noise nor its absence. This is the silence that has always fascinated me, though fascination harbors ambivalence. Without this silence, words can neither be spoken nor heard, and without words silence is inaudible. Silence paradoxically limns language as both its necessary condition and its impossibility. This silence is not just in the gaps and spaces that punctuate sentences but is rather the lack within words that renders them articulate. For those with ears to hear, all saying is unsaying and every word is also a not. There can no more be word without silence than silence without Word. The origin, then, is always duplicitous: In the beginning is the Word.... In the beginning is Silence. The quiet echo of this silence is profoundly unsettling—in it I hear the Not that I am. Though we may long to escape it, silence can never be silenced. When we forget or refuse to listen to silence, we no longer know who we are because we do not know what we are not.

FOUR

A.M.

Reflections

FAMILY HOMAGE TO KIERKEGAARD

"Such works are mirrors." So begins Kierkegaard's *Stages on Life's Way*, though every book he published implicitly bears this preface. In all his writings Kierkegaard holds up to the reader a looking-glass in which he or she can see the stages of his or her own life reflected. In this way the reflections of the writer are reflections of and by the reader. But exactly what are such reflections and why do they make readers reflect?

The first thing that must be said about reflections is that they take (and give) time, though not all do so in the same way. To reflect is to pause long enough to ponder, deliberate, even meditate. The person who is reflective is not hurried or hassled but is pensive, sometimes even contemplative.

She is patient enough to take time to gather her thoughts before speaking or writing, patient enough to wait until the moment is right. Previous eras valued this virtue as the source of wisdom that could stand the test of time; in our day reflection is mistaken for indecisiveness, which makes timely intervention impossible.

There are other reflections, often the most telling, that are untimely. They do not result from prolonged deliberation but occur in an instant so fleeting that it is barely present—like a face briefly glimpsed in a store window on a busy city street. Though such reflections are occasional, the insight they bring can be so surprising that it overwhelms.

Walking nourishes untimely reflection, especially when it is pointless, purposeless, errant. Reflections often occur to me when I walk but almost never when I run. I have always suspected that is why Thoreau deems walking holy: "Saunter … *Sainte Terre* … to the holy land … a Saunterer, a Holy Lander." When the saunterer is rapt in reflection, the Holy Land is not merely elsewhere but is also the city street or the mountain path where he roams as if without purpose. *Holzwege*: Paths that lead nowhere. During errant interludes thought is not of this world, where chatter drowns urgent ideas that threaten to seep through the familiar. Reflection interrupts the interruption of the endless play of reflections on all-consuming screens surrounding us and thereby creates the chance for a reader who takes time—if, indeed, time can be taken—to pause and read quietly, at least for a while. In these rare moments reflective works become mirrors in which we might see ourselves otherwise.

P.M.

Reticence

As I begin gathering my thoughts for this book, difficult questions become unavoidable. What should I say and what should I not say? What should I write and what should I not write? What should I show and what should I hide? About myself and about others? Should I tell my secrets? Do I have a right to tell the secrets of others? What if some things cannot be said? What if some secrets can never be revealed? What if Poe is right—we hide best by showing? What if Freud is right—we inevitably show what we most want to hide? What if every person harbors an interiority that cannot be fathomed? What if I am or the *I* is a pseudonym for something else, someone else, I do not know?

As questions proliferate, ethical dilemmas abound. I cannot understand myself apart from others, but I remain uncertain whether I have a right to expose them in telling a story that is not merely my own. If I do not know myself, then how can I ever fathom an other? And if the other is forever elusive, am I obligated to remain silent? Such questions give pause and that pause creates a lacuna that might better be left unfilled.

Not everything that can be said should be said. Reticence is a particularly important virtue, especially in a time when everything as well as everybody is overexposed. Obscenity, we have learned, is the loss of interiority that occurs when the private becomes public and the public invades the private. All too often people become complicit in the colonization of their own inwardness by soliciting the very publicity that inevitably undoes them. When this occurs, thoughtful reflection gives way to thoughtless spectacle: I am seen, therefore I am. What those who seek the spotlight rarely realize is that exposure decreases rather than increases interest in them. When there is nothing more to see or say, *People* moves on. As the churn rate accelerates, 15 minutes becomes 15 seconds, which in turn becomes 1.5 seconds.

Reticence is not the same as modesty. Modesty is not only a lack of pretentiousness but, more important, involves a moderation that respects decency and propriety. The modest person enjoys polite company. Reticence, by contrast, suggests a covert excess that might or might not be indecent and improper. Perhaps this is what makes reticence erotic. What is available, accessible, exposed does not seduce. Reticence arouses desire, by implying what is not there and suggesting what is not known. Hiding, not showing—concealing, not revealing, keeps desire in play. That is why neither obscenity nor pornography is erotic. Not the bride stripped bare but the woman whose garment leaves gaps is seductive. The spell of eros is broken when everything is exposed. The play of hide-and-seek is what makes reticence so fascinating.

Good writing, like good sex, requires reticence; in books, as in life, what is left unsaid is often more important than what is said. The instant of hesitation that reticence creates leads to expectations that should never be fulfilled. This is one of the many lessons Kierkegaard has taught me. Few writers seem to have been less reticent than Kierkegaard. In published works and private journals, which he was confident would be published one day, he relentlessly revealed his deepest thoughts and most private feelings until his life appears to be an open book. And yet he repeatedly takes away what he seems to give by warning his readers, "I have a secret I will never disclose." He called this secret "the thorn in my flesh." The obvious biblical allusion suggests that his secret has something to do with the sacred. Kierkegaard's writings echo this secret without ever breaking its silence. His refusal or perhaps inability to explain this essential point renders everything he writes doubtful and makes every analysis of him and his work incomplete. Though we will never know his secret or why he kept it, we know enough to realize that his reticence transforms every book he wrote into a *Diary of a Seducer*. His *Dagbog* (day book or diary), which is also a *Natbog* (night book), holds lessons for writers and nonwriters alike: the person who tells it all has nothing left to say; the writer whose reticence is excessive remains strangely fascinating.

FIVE

A.M.

Premonitions

I had always been suspicious of reports about premonitions until one night when I was seventeen. That was the summer that our family drove from our home in New Jersey to California and back. We spent the last night on the road with my father's brother near Gettysburg, Pennsylvania. Though our two cousins, Noel and Chuck, were older, my brother and I had fond memories of hunting with them on the nearby farm where my father and his siblings had grown up. We were eager to share stories from our trip with our cousins and were disappointed to discover that they were out for the evening. Tired from the long drive, we went to bed early. Around 4 A.M. a state trooper's pounding on the door woke us. I heard him say to my uncle: "I'm afraid I have some bad news. There has been an accident—you must come to the hospital immediately." As we sat in silence, waiting for further news, my mother was the first to speak. "I had the strangest experience during the night. I was awakened by what sounded like church bells. I looked at the clock and it was 2:10."

Several hours later my uncle returned with bad news about Noel and his wife. "Sharon is dead and I don't think Noel is going to make it. An eighteen-wheeler ran the stoplight at Cross Keys and hit their Volkswagen broadside. Sharon was crushed and Noel was thrown from the car. He's unconscious and bleeding internally. They aren't sure where the blood is coming from. The police say the accident occurred at 2:10." With cries of anguish surrounding us, I turned toward my mother. Our eyes met in a gaze filled with both recognition and incomprehension. I do not believe such things really happen, but I have no doubt about what I heard her say. I never spoke about that moment with her or anyone else and still do not know what to make of it.

Though I often thought about what had happened that night, the memory of it came rushing back twenty-five years later. As was our custom, Alan, who had been my editor for several years, and I had met for dinner the night before the annual conference of the American Academy of Religion began. In addition to catching up on personal news, we discussed our various projects. Always concerned about what was coming next, Alan pressed me for details about my new book. After describing at some length the book I had already started to write, I briefly mentioned a different kind of work that had begun to take shape in my mind. I had little more than a title: *Betrayal*. I have always liked single-word titles that carry double meanings. I was drawn to *betrayal* because it means not only to violate trust by delivering someone or something to the enemy but also to show or reveal what had been concealed—as when I betray a secret. I explained to Alan that I envisioned a text that would weave together theological and philosophical reflections with autobiographical narratives. That kind of work, I stressed, cannot be hurried, for its research is nothing less than life itself. Almost two decades later the work I described to Alan that evening has become the book you are reading. The morning after our conversation I checked for messages at the hotel desk and found a package from Alan waiting for me. I opened it and discovered an inscribed copy of Paul Auster's *The Invention of Solitude*.

REVISIONS

Though the title changed, *Betrayal* eventually proved to be another premonition of events I never anticipated. At the time I had not heard of Auster; I stuck the book in my bag to look at later.

The meetings of the American Academy of Religion always fall on the weekend before Thanksgiving. Weather and the holiday season make traveling at that time of year chancy. When I reached the airport, I discovered that a bad ice storm had led to the cancellation of all flights to Albany, the airport closest to my home in the Berkshires. Since we were planning to drive to my parents' home in Westfield, New Jersey, for Thanksgiving, I called Dinny to tell her that I was taking a flight to Newark and we could meet in Westfield the next day. On the plane I began reading *The Invention of Solitude*: "One day there is life. A man, for example, in the best of health, not even old, with no history of illness. Everything as it was, as it will always be. He goes from one day to the next, minding his own business, dreaming only of life that lies before him. And then, suddenly, it happens, there is death." I knew immediately why Alan had given me the book. He realized that I would see my own thoughts reflected in Auster's words. The similarities were uncanny: we were the same age, grew up a few miles apart in New Jersey, played high school baseball, perhaps against each other, and my parents even bought their appliances at Auster's, the store his uncle owned in my hometown and where Paul worked in the summers. More important but much less obvious, it was immediately clear to me that Auster and I are pursued by similar demons. Was all this nothing more than "the music of chance"?

MY MOTHER, WRITING

The next day, as I lay on the couch with Auster's book, my mother asked what I was reading. An erstwhile English teacher, she always wanted to know what books interested me and what I thought she should be reading. I responded: "You don't want to know." Nothing more was said until a few days later when she handed me the copy of *The Invention of Solitude* I had been reading and said: "You're right; I don't want to know." Three weeks later she was dead.

As she read Auster's words, did she have a premonition of her own death, just as she had unknowingly anticipated Sharon's death when she heard church bells chiming that August night? I will never know—nothing seals death more than the questions you cannot ask those who are gone.

P.M.

Postcards

Kerry was one of the most remarkable students I have ever taught, though it took a while for me to realize just how special she was. She was elusive, even evasive. It was not until I read her first paper that I began to understand that she saw things differently. Writing gave her cover to express what she could not say directly. Over the years she offered brief glimpses of the pain that deepened her thought and gave her uncanny awareness. Poverty, suffering, abuse—or so she told me.

One day Kerry gave me the results of some unusual research she had done for me. The well-known sculptor and earthworks artist Michael Heizer and I were working on a book about the nests of desert packrats. Living in the middle of the Nevada desert, Michael unexpectedly began to feel a strange affinity for packrats. He became convinced that the complex nests they created were sophisticated works of art and architecture. At first I thought he had been out in the desert sun too long or that all the acid he had done years ago had fried his brain. But as we roamed the desert for many days taking photographs of the nests, I began to see these lowly creatures and much else through Michael's eyes. As we talked, we decided to do a book together—he would take the photographs and design the layout, and I would write the essay. I titled the book *Deserting Architecture*, but unfortunately we never finished it. I asked Kerry to research packrat nests for me and was amazed by what she discovered. There are two kinds of nests, I learned; the first are built in caves and are called middens. They are the longest continuously inhabited dwellings in the western hemisphere. The rats mix their own excrement and urine to create something like cement. In the dry heat of the desert, the mixture crystallizes to form remarkably durable structures. We were determined to photograph the middens and, ignoring the serious threat of rattlesnakes, entered the caves. The loaded pistol Michael always carried was only somewhat reassuring. The second and more common type of nest is made from sticks, twigs, and debris. I knew that these constructions can be quite elaborate but did not realize how sophisticated the underground designs are. The rats build nests that have different rooms for different functions—storing food and eating, sleeping, disposing of waste, and burying the dead. In addition to this, the nests are built in such a way that the temperature remains constant at all times despite wild fluctuations between hot and cold on the desert floor. Lowly packrats know more about sustainable architecture than any of today's so-called green architects.

When Kerry came to my office to give me the materials she had gathered, she shoved a stack of papers into my hands, quickly turned, and ran away without saying a word. A few days later she returned to talk. "Sorry I was so abrupt yesterday," she said. "The rats freaked me out; they brought back too many bad memories. I grew up on a small farm in New Hampshire and my dad was pretty rough with me. We never had much money and we raised rabbits for food. I had to tend them and came to hate those damn rodents. I guess it was because I could not separate the rabbits from all the bad stuff my father did to me." I knew enough not to ask more.

The better I got to know Kerry, the more uneasy she made me. Often I had the sense that she was watching even though I did not know where she was. After she graduated, she stayed in town and worked in the local bookstore, where, in pre-Amazon days, I bought my books. On occasion I would call to order a book and she would respond, "Mark, you don't need that book—you already have it." I have no idea how she knew but she was always right

Eventually, she broke her tie with her alma mater and moved to Indiana. We lost touch until she unexpectedly called me one day. She had heard that I was going through a rough stretch and wanted to know how I was doing. I had developed diabetes and was having trouble coping with it. At first I was hesitant to talk about personal matters with a former student. As our conversations continued, however, I discovered that the distance separating us created a closeness that allowed us to discuss what we otherwise would have avoided. In the months that followed, she called often and we talked at length about many things. Late one night she confessed to me that one of the reasons she was so concerned about me was that she too had been diagnosed with an autoimmune disease—lupus—and so appreciated what I was up against. During subsequent calls we shared our thoughts about the physical and psychological difficulties of dealing with chronic disease.

For several months she had been telling me that she was preparing a tape to send me. Rarely willing to express her deepest thoughts directly, Kerry often borrowed the words of others to say what she was thinking. She sampled songs by her favorite artists to create a new work that was more hers than theirs. I was disappointed but not surprised when the tape never arrived.

Just as suddenly as the calls had started, they stopped for no apparent reason. I was puzzled but once again not surprised. Then one day a couple of months later, I received a call from Tom, another former student, who was one of Kerry's closest friends. With trembling voice he told me that Kerry had committed suicide the previous night. She had locked herself in the garage and started the engine of the car. Her body, however, was not found in the car but was on the back steps near the door to the house. There was no note to answer the countless questions she left. How long had she planned it? Had this been what she was saying by not saying it during our long phone calls? At the last moment had she concluded that the most important decision of her life was a terrible mistake?

A month later a small group of friends gathered to spread Kerry's ashes beneath a majestic white birch on a hill overlooking Williamstown. Even the damp gloom of a cold March day could not diminish the wintry beauty of the mountains. The vista seemed to have been fashioned after a Constable painting. I knew this place well because I had run down the hill every summer day for years. We gathered in a small circle, offered reflections, and read from Kerry's favorite works. I spoke about the uncanny prescience that radiated from her darting eyes. I wondered but did not ask what she had seen that she had finally found unbearable. When we had finished, we scattered her ashes and smashed the pottery urn in which they had been held. I have never been able to return to that place or to run down that hill again.

Before her friends left, we shared our memories of Kerry over dinner. When Debbie, her companion during the last year, told me about the depth of Kerry's depression, I asked whether she thought it was the result of the lupus. I was shocked when she replied, "Kerry didn't have lupus. She was in the best health of her life." I had no idea how to respond. At that moment everything I thought I had known about Kerry became uncertain. Had she lied to me about the illness we seemed to share? If she had lied about something so important, had she ever told me the truth? Was our whole relationship based on lies? Perhaps she did not know or could not admit what she was hiding. Perhaps she could tell the truth only by lying.

About six months after our dinner conversation, I was startled when an envelope with my name and address in Kerry's handwriting arrived in the mail. Inside was an audio tape with a note from Debbie: "Here is a copy of the tape Kerry said she would send you before she died. I found the mailer in her house addressed to you." It was a remarkable collection of tunes by many of her favorite artists and mine: Bob Dylan; Bruce Springsteen; Peter, Paul, and Mary; Lucinda Williams; Emmy Lou Harris; and others. The voices were not Kerry's but the words were hers, and her unsent message was

POSTCARD FROM BEYOND THE GRAVE

painfully clear in retrospect: "Orphan Girl," "500 Miles Away from Home," "More Than One Way Home," "Not My Way Home," "Black Tunnel Looking Down the Path," "When Morning Comes Around," "Tryin' to Get to Heaven." I have played the tape countless times and the longer I listen, the more questions I have. If she had sent the tape before she died, would I have heard her despair? Has she finally found her way back to the home she never had? Has she made it to heaven?

I knew Kerry's whole life had been a struggle to return to the home she never had, and it pained me to admit that I had not helped her. As I listened to the postcard she sent me from beyond the grave, I could not avoid asking myself whether the lessons I had taught her had contributed to her death. Was she ready for the books I asked her to read? Is anyone ever prepared to face the questions some writers ask? Perhaps Kerry had ventured into the night beyond night and had tried but been unable to return. I attempted to picture her limp body lying at the threshold of her home but could not bear the image.

SIX

A.M.

MY FIRST HOME

My earliest memory is of bringing my brother, Beryl, home for the first time, when I was three and a half years old. I sat holding him in my arms, squeezed between my mother and father In our 1945 maroon Chrysler with hideous Scottish plaid seats. I remember his pink face with peeling skin, as if he had been out in the sun too long. While my father drove, my mother hummed a tune from a hymn I had heard but whose words I did not know. There is no way I could have imagined the relief and joy they must have felt that day. After losing a daughter and having a son who would never be healthy and was doomed to an early death, their anxiety in the months leading up to the birth must have been overwhelming. I do not recall arriving home or much that happened in the days that followed, but I do remember that three weeks later my brother disappeared and a week after that my mother vanished. I eventually learned that my brother had developed a severe abdominal condition, which then was fatal in 75 percent of the cases, and had to be rushed to New York City for emergency surgery. A few days after my brother's operation, doctors discovered a nine-pound tumor on my mother's kidney. She had emergency surgery in the same New York City hospital where my brother was recovering. The tumor was not malignant, but the surgeon had to make an incision halfway around her body to remove it. Because she was unable to care for my brother, he did not come home again for six months. While teaching, coaching, caring for my mother, and visiting Beryl, my father continued to make weekly trips from New Jersey to Long Island to visit my other brother (about whom I then knew nothing), whose condition would never improve. Though neither Beryl nor I can recall much from that year, traces from those dark days are buried beyond memory. In ways that are impossible to calculate those obscure experiences have shaped everything both of us have done and, perhaps more than anything else, have made us who we are.

As the years have passed, homecoming, I have discovered, is a complicated process. Home is less a place than a state of mind. When you feel at home, things seem settled, which does not necessarily mean secure. The lingering lack at the center of our being renders all security and every certainty little more than an idle dream. I have long suspected that the struggle to find home leads some people to become obsessed with genealogy. I had known that Beryl was intrigued by family history but did not realize just how deep his interest ran until he approached his late fifties. He was determined to trace both sides of our parents' families back to the European villages they had left behind. Our parents had told us some of the story, but the deeper my brother dug, the more gaps he uncovered and surprises he discovered. Some were inconsequential—simple oversights or trivial mistakes; others were more important and involved the kind of revelation that can transform your sense of who you are by disclosing what unknown others had been.

GRANDMA AND GRANDPA TAYLOR ON A SUNDAY DRIVE WITH FRIENDS,
DEVIL'S DEN, GETTYSBURG BATTLEFIELD, 1912

Two of these discoveries proved to be particularly significant. We always had been told that our heritage was thoroughly Protestant—Calvinist (Scotch Irish), Anabaptist (Swiss), and Lutheran (German). On my father's side of the family, anti-Catholicism ran so deep that one of his brothers banned his only daughter from returning home for more than twenty-five years because she had married a Catholic. I was therefore surprised to discover that Catholic blood flowed in my veins. In the dusty basement of a Pennsylvania courthouse, my brother found files that revealed that my maternal grandparents came from Catholic rather that Protestant Ireland. They brought their religion with them to America but, when confronted by the anti-Catholicism raging in the coalfields, decided it would be prudent to practice Methodism. It remains unclear whether they ever converted to Protestantism because one of my great-grandmother's sisters refused to be buried in the Protestant cemetery and insisted on being buried in the nearby Catholic graveyard. Though I had studied religion most of my adult life, I had been mistaken about my own religious identity.

The second surprise was considerably darker and much more troubling. I had long suspected that Beryl's fascination with genealogy was related to demons that had entered both our lives during the first six months of his life. Having been sent into exile a few days after he came home for the first time, it seemed as if his entire life had become a search for the home he had lost as a newborn. Perhaps by filling in every blank and closing every gap in our family line he could rejoin the umbilical cord that would finally bring him home. But in the tangled lines of the family story he was tracing, he discovered a void that threatened to consume him. One day he received in the mail an envelope from someone he had never met. When he opened it, he found a copy of an article that had been on the front page of the newspaper in the town where our mother was born, raised, and now is buried. It was dated April 6, 1921, and bore the headline "Williamstown Man Hanged Self":

> John Raudenbush, aged 77, a lifelong resident of Williamstown, hanged himself on Monday afternoon at about five o'clock. The deceased, who had been in ill health for several yrs, suffering with an incurable disease was well known in the town and was an active member of the Lutheran church. On Monday afternoon, one of the family saw him entering the chicken house, and thinking it strange when he did not come out right away, went to investigate and found him hanging from one of the rafters. Help was summoned and he was taken down and carried into the house where it was found that life was not extinct, but that he was dying of a broken neck. Dr. Bobb was summoned and did all possible but the end was inevitable.

This tragedy had never been mentioned to my brother or me. Williamstown is a small coal-mining town, and my mother was ten years old at the time of her grandfather's death. There is no way she and her sister could not have known about the suicide, yet neither they nor our grandparents ever told us what had happened. Not until my brother uncovered this se-

TAYLOR FAMILY

cret did I realize that no one had ever said anything to us about any of our great-grandparents. All I know about them are their names, and my children do not even know that.

The house where my great grandfather took his life is two blocks from where my mother grew up. When Beryl and I were young, Grandmother's sister, Kate, and her husband, Tom, lived in the house where my great-grandfather had committed suicide. What I most remember about the house was its mustard color—rare in a town of white houses surrounded by coal-black hills—a marvelous wraparound porch with swings and rockers and, above all, the chicken house. Since I had often gathered eggs for my aunt, when Uncle Tom asked me one day if I wanted to go to the chicken house with him, I did not hesitate to tag along. I did not realize that he was not going for eggs but was planning to kill and clean a chicken for dinner. While he got his hatchet, he told me to catch the biggest hen I could find. When I brought him the chicken, he instructed me to hold down her wings while he grabbed her head and put on the chopping block. He raised his hatchet and quickly cut off the chicken's head. When blood splattered over my arms and shirt, I was so startled that I let go of the hen. Only then did I learn that the expression "running around like a chicken with its head cut off" is more than a figure of speech. As I read the newspaper article about John Raudenbush's hanging in the chicken house, I relived the slaughter as if it were happening right before my eyes.

For several weeks Beryl was preoccupied with his discovery of the suicide and would frequently call to discuss it. He kept repeating that he could not believe that no one had ever told us about it and, as so many times before, expressed his frustration that no one was alive who could answer his urgent questions. The more he talked about the hanging, the more apprehensive I became about his obsession. I had heard all this before, and my concern grew out of yet another family secret. There was another suicide by hanging, in my father's family. My father and his brother had been the youngest in a family of eight and were extremely close growing up. In later years life took them in different directions and they drifted apart. Nonetheless, a close bond remained, even if it did not always bridge the distance separating them. One day my father received a phone call from his sister-in-law, who told him that his brother had hanged himself. He too had had health problems and had been suffering from depression. My father was shattered by the news and, like my brother, became obsessed with the suicide. My mother had sometimes intimated that my father had gone through periods of severe depression but had never been specific. By the time our uncle took his life, my brother and I were old enough to be aware of what was going on. I still remember my father compulsively repeating that he simply could not believe what his brother had done. Though he tried to convince himself that this tragedy had been caused by medical problems, he never really believed that was the whole story. Until his dying day my father remained tormented by questions he too had no one to ask. I worried that this family history harbored a dark fate. My brother, Beryl, is named for my father's brother who hanged himself. Names are never innocent and sometimes can be fatal.

Over many years my brother made countless trips to Pennsylvania to talk to people, follow clues, and search cemeteries for names that time had erased. When he returned from his trips, he was eager to share what he had learned and immediately called me with his latest report. Just after my sixtieth birthday, and facing issues of my own, I decided to accompany Beryl the next time he went to Pennsylvania so he could share his discoveries and I could learn more about myself. He is three years younger than I but was already dreading age. I knew no one else should go with us; we left his home in rural New Jersey on an unseasonably warm January day. As the New Jersey Turnpike turned into the Pennsylvania Turnpike, we left behind city and suburbs and were surrounded by fields and mountains. Fog obscured vision, leaving little to see and time to talk. As our conversation circled and recircled what had been left unsaid for far too long, we both knew more than genealogy was at stake. Grave matters, indeed.

We began with my mother's side of the family—the Coopers and Raudenbushes in Williamstown and proceeded to Taylors and Shenks in what is now Amish country. Children wearing white bonnets and dressed in black, just as my grandmother had done her whole life, still walk along country roads to one-room Mennonite schoolhouses. My brother showed me the land where Henry Shenk first settled almost two and a half centuries ago. The house where our paternal grandmother, Emma, was born

COOPER FAMILY

in 1869, as well as the houses and farms where her four brothers lived and worked are still standing. At the edge of this farmland is a Brethren church and a small cemetery. My brother had been here many times before and had identified almost every grave. As he opened the gate, he said to me, "You are related to every person in this graveyard." He then proceeded to show me, first, the tombstone of Henry Shenk, who is our great-great-great-great-great-grandfather and then the grave markers of every other great-grandparent. Our grandmother was the first to be buried elsewhere. He dug out his charts of the family tree and explained all the links between us and those surrounding us. As he told our story, I remembered reading this line somewhere: "It is the men without roots who are the real poor of this century." Standing with my brother in that small cemetery, looking out across the field, where we could glimpse cattle grazing in the fog and mist, I felt very rich indeed. My brother broke the silence when he said, "This might sound weird, but even though I didn't know this place existed until a few months ago, when I come here and look at those rolling fields, I feel like I'm home." Then I realized why we had come to this place together. In that special moment we both knew but left unsaid that we had finally completed the trip home that had been so cruelly interrupted more than half a century earlier.

GHOSTS

P.M.

Afterlife

Once it happens you know it will happen again. I was not prepared for the impact of the first anniversary of my collapse. It began as a visceral uneasiness and over several weeks gradually came into sharper focus. At first I thought it was the usual problem of November. When the golden light of October gives way to the cloudy gloom of approaching winter, melancholy inevitably turns into something darker that is difficult to name but whose effects are unmistakable. Lethargy deepens until it threatens to paralyze the soul. I began to suspect that this fall was different when the looming darkness was not dispelled by the crystalline light of the azure sky on those rare days when the trees on the mountaintop have been painted white with a brush whose strokes no lens can capture. Instead of lifting, the somber mood only deepened as autumnal gloom continued to settle.

Slowly, very slowly, I began to feel that I was not really living in the present but was dwelling not only on but also in the past; more precisely, I was living the present by reliving the past of a year ago as if I had then known the future. I did not fully realize what was happening until our family gathered for Thanksgiving. In addition to the usual festivities, we traditionally trim our fourteen-foot Christmas tree the Saturday after Thanksgiving. I always enjoy the moment we turn on the gaudy tree lights because the cold gray of November suddenly seems to melt into the warm glow of December. Such light, or its memory, often helps to get me through winter nights that seem endless.

But this time the joy of the moment was disrupted—the present was torn between a past that insistently returned and a future that relentlessly intruded. My awareness was split—it doubled and then doubled again. What obsessed me was not simply how close I had come to not being here for this precious moment but, more important, what I did not realize was approaching the last time we staged this annual family ritual. Unable to settle in the present, I was compelled to relive every moment of the past with the awareness of the collapse that had occurred a few days later. As I did so, the present was transformed—everything looked different, sounded different, tasted different, even smelled different. I was distracted by an echo I could not quite hear yet was unable to ignore. I was, of course, more preoccupied with the future than the past. The greatest difference between now and then is knowing what it means to be elsewhere. "The cradle," Nabokov writes, "rocks above an abyss, and common sensc tells us that our existence is but a brief crack of light between two eternities of darkness. Although the two are identical twins, man, as a rule, views the prenatal abyss with more calm than the one he is heading for (at some forty-five hundred heartbeats an hour)." Where I once was, I once again shall be.

When the anniversary of the collapse arrived, I was driven—the word is not strong enough but I know none better—to return to the scenes where it occurred: the room at Columbia where I taught my last class, the number 1 train that I rode back to the apartment where I drifted into the delirium, the lobby where I waited for help. After revisiting these now uncanny places, I retraced the route the ambulance took from my apartment to the hospital emergency room. I had to do all this in solitude—absolute solitude. Repetition compulsion indeed, but it was not precisely beyond the pleasure principle. For some reason reliving the traumatic experience of my death was strangely pleasurable. The pleasure, it seems, was not that I survived but that I died. I was not weary of life and had many reasons to live. Nonetheless, death exercised a mysterious attraction that baffled me. Lingering on the threshold of death, I became detached from all I hold dear. Looking back at myself from this uncanny place that is no longer the land of the living, the weight of the world lifted, and the significance of what once had seemed overwhelmingly important simply evaporated. At first this experience was terrifying, but gradually it became liberating. When the unavoidable approaches, I discovered there is nothing left to say but "Amen—so be it."

I have never believed in the afterlife yet somehow now find myself having returned from the dead. The only way I can describe this posthumous existence is as ghostly. Nothing is simply itself—everything, everyone, is doubled by a shadow that never fades. Far from oppressive, this shadow casts life in an entirely new light. Having returned from the dead, I can no longer live as I once did. I now understand what Kierkegaard meant when he described the knight of faith as making a double movement. First, there is the movement of infinite resignation in which you let go of everything that once possessed you; only then do you become free to reappropriate what you have given up by receiving life as a gift from an other you can never comprehend.

SEVEN

A.M.

Stealth

BUCK ON STONE HILL

November 26, 2006. Every morning for the past two weeks, a buck, a doe, and two fawns have greeted me outside my study window. Apples and pears have fallen from the trees, and deer always return this time of year to eat them. It is rare, however, to see a buck; usually, there are only doe and their fawns. Buck are much more wary and thus elusive. This buck is young—perhaps two or three years old—and seems calmer than most. In the predawn light we have been staring at each other, and after a few days he has begun to recognize me; after checking each other out, he now returns to the apples and I defer the morning's work to watch him and his partner. Though I do not know their language very well, it is clear to me that they always talk over morning breakfast—furtive glances, anxious wiggles of the ears, knowing nods, playful flicks of the tail. The two of them often seem to move as one, like a couple married for many years.

I come from a family of deer hunters. By the time I was old enough to carry a gun, we had given up deer for grouse, pheasants, and rabbits. As deer hunting stopped, however, the tales about it got longer and taller. My grandfather was a great hunter but an even better storyteller. He shot many deer in his lifetime but never the right one in the right season—in buck season he shot doe and in doe season he shot buck. He insisted this was not intentional but was just the way things worked out. One of my fondest childhood memories is crawling into bed with my grandfather before anyone else woke up and listening to his stories about how he eluded state police and game wardens. When he shot a deer out of season, he would hide it under a pile of leaves deep in the forest and return after dark to retrieve it. Years later I lost my way and learned the hard way just how skilled you have to be to find your way in the woods at night. He understood the woods better than anyone I have ever known and always found his deer. Though he insisted the police never caught him, my father was not so sure.

I hunted with my grandfather only once, but he had passed on his knowledge of the woods to his sons. As my father and I hunted for grouse in the mountains, he taught me how to read the texts deer write as they roam the forest—the trees where they had rubbed the velvet from their rack, the leaves where they slept, the twigs they had nibbled, the paths they followed. From the slightest footprints my father knew whether it was a buck or doe, how big the deer was, how many deer there had been, and how long ago they had used the trail. Though I never hunted deer, I remember these lessons well, and while hiking the mountains, I always read the signs they leave. I regret to say that I have not passed on to my son and daughter the lessons my grandfather and father taught me.

As I watch the buck, doe, and fawns quietly eating apples and pears, all these memories come rushing back. My neighbor is a gifted hunter who prides himself on getting a buck every year—for serious hunters doe don't count. The reason he is so successful is because, from late summer until

GRANDPA TAYLOR, HUNTING

hunting season begins, he conducts thorough research by diligently stalking deer on the hill where I live. He reads the texts deer write as carefully as I study complicated philosophical works. My neighbor knows all their hiding places, every trail they follow, and even the special habits of individual deer. Though I have never seen him in the woods, I am sure he is watching the deer on my land.

Tomorrow is the first day of deer season. The family of deer will return for breakfast, and the buck and I will greet each other once again. We have begun to understand each other, but neither of us speaks the other's language well enough yet for me to warn him about what is coming. I know that when the buck, doe, and fawn leave my garden and bound across the field tomorrow, my neighbor will be waiting for them and I will hear his shot.

MY FATHER'S TEENAGE DIARY (1922)

P.M.

Sacrifice

In our family there was no clear line between religion and hunting. From the time I was big enough to keep up, I accompanied my father, his brothers, and my cousins on hunting trips. We usually hunted small game—mostly pheasants and rabbits on the farm where my father grew up, which one of his sisters and her husband still worked. We would hunt in the morning, break at noon for unforgettable farm dinners, and continue hunting until dark. My grandfather was a legendary shot who hunted well into his eighties. He always used dogs—hounds, not bird dogs, because, he explained, "Hounds can track pheasants, but bird dogs can't point rabbits."

I hunted with my grandfather only once and what I remember most was his gun. Throughout most of his life he had used a muzzle-loader whose barrel he had shot paper-thin. In the final years he hunted, my grandfather carried a single-barreled twelve-gauge shotgun. This seemed strange to me because every other hunter I knew used a double-barreled or a pump shotgun. When I asked my father why Grandpa used a single-barreled gun, he replied, "He never needs a second shot." I soon learned that my father was right.

In the evenings after the hunt, the stakes of this family ritual became clear. I always had to help my father clean the game we shot. It was a bloody affair but blood, I discovered, was what bound my father and his family to the land where they were born. My father had to return to the land each fall to renew the bond and teach his sons a lesson words could not convey. Far from idle diversion, hunting was a ritual sacrifice in which blood was the stuff of a communion I still struggle to fathom.

In 1922, when my father was fifteen, he kept a diary about his life on the farm. As I now read these fading pages, it is impossible to comprehend the distance separating his childhood from our time. He tells of rising before dawn to tend the livestock, walking three miles to a one-room schoolhouse, and then returning to labor behind a horse-drawn plow until long after dark. Though the entire diary is fascinating, an entry in which my father interrupts the record of his daily routine to comment on something troubling him remains most memorable. After tending cattle, hogs, and chickens for years, "they became friends—almost part of the family." It is very difficult, he reports, to see them slaughtered and to know that they soon will be on the dinner table. With a resignation remarkable for one so young, he concludes, "I guess that's the way it has to be."

Many years later—I forget exactly how long—the ritual slaughter was reenacted on the farm of one of my father's sisters. We were visiting with other family members to celebrate the new year and to help with the slaughter of a steer. Having been insulated from such rituals by cellophane and supermarkets, I had no idea what to expect. As the patriarch of the clan, my grandfather had the honor of killing the steer. While others held the animal's head by the horns, he approached the victim with a pistol and shot him behind his left ear. This stunned the steer and allowed his heart to keep pumping blood for a few minutes before he died. As soon as the steer dropped, others wrapped a chain around his back feet and hoisted him into the air. They then slit the jugular vein to let the blood drain from

THE TAYLOR HOMESTEAD NEAR GETTYSBURG

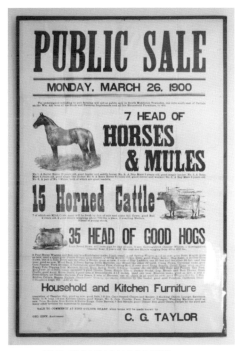

TAYLOR FARM SALE POSTER, 1900

COVERED BRIDGE NEAR TAYLOR HOMESTEAD

the body. The rest of the afternoon was devoted to butchering the carcass. Not even cleaning game had prepared me for the blood involved in this part of the ritual. A favorite family story repeated as long as I can remember was about Grandpa's brother, who suffered from anemia. Whenever a steer was slaughtered, he would catch the blood in a glass and drink it to restore his own diminished supply.

Having dispatched the steer, my grandfather retreated to the house, where he visited with family and gave advice about dealing with the carcass when asked to do so. Around midafternoon he got up from his chair but stumbled slightly. When others caught him and helped him to sit down again, he was confused and his speech was slurred. The local doctor was summoned and said that my grandfather had suffered a stroke and should be taken to the hospital immediately. In the weeks that followed, his condition improved; he eventually recovered all his physical capacities, but his short-term memory was impaired for the rest of his life. He was never again able to hunt. I have always been puzzled by the timing of the stroke. Was it a coincidence that it occurred right after he shot the steer? Was the stroke that condemned him to living death an act of retribution—divine or otherwise? Does blood sacrifice involve a restricted rather than a general economy? Are those who eat the flesh of the victim condemned by the sin of the father?

EIGHT

A.M.

Killing

My father taught me to kill. We began with insects and proceeded to birds and eventually to animals. The first thing I remember killing deliberately was a small white cabbage butterfly. One day when I was seven, my father came home from school with a butterfly net and announced, "We're going to start a butterfly collection." Not until then did I realize that he had been developing his lesson plan for a long time. A couple of years earlier, we had planted a butterfly bush in our backyard. Each summer many dif-

GROUSE HUNTING IN PENNSYLVANIA MOUNTAINS

ferent species of butterflies were drawn to the fragrance of its lovely lavender flowers. My father began by showing me how to hold the net poised for the strike and demonstrated how to approach the bush furtively and pounce on my unsuspecting victim with a quick efficiency that left no time for flight. Before my instruction in the proper technique of capturing and killing my prey, I had spent long hours watching these powdery creatures lighting and dancing on the bush's blossoms and thus knew many of their habits.

Once I had mastered the art of capture, my father showed me how to remove the butterflies from the net by carefully pinching their wings together and then how to place them in a killing jar that contained a piece of cotton dampened with chloroform, where their spasms eventually gave way to a lethargy that slipped imperceptibly into death. The subtle scent of butterfly wings lingered on my fingers long after the pungent smell of poison had dissipated. When the specimen was dead, I removed it from the jar and let it dry before mounting it on a bed of cotton in a glass-covered display case. After practicing on common and rather uninteresting cabbage butterflies, I progressed to the more impressive species whose colors

MONARCH BUTTERFLY ON MILKWEED, STONE HILL

remain in my mind's eye—brown, blue, purple, chartreuse—but whose names have long faded. I do remember the bright yellow of swallowtails reflecting the July sun and the autumnal amber of monarchs gathering for their August migration southward. As I examined these remarkable creatures under glass, I was startled by their stunning designs, delicate colors, and disturbing fragility. One day my father brought home a microscope so I could examine more closely the specimens I had collected. When I gazed through the lens for the first time, I was immersed in an invisible beauty I had never imagined. My most memorable catch was a stunning lime-green Luna moth. As my collection grew, my father would explain the distinctive characteristics of each species, just as he had done with the pressed flowers he had gathered over many years. One day I asked him, "Why are there so many flowers and butterflies and what good are they?" For many years I would not understand the non-Darwinian answer this biology teacher gave: "What they are good for doesn't matter. What matters is their beauty and the pleasure it brings."

I was not prepared for the next step in my father's pedagogy. When I turned ten, the lessons became more serious. Without setting aside my

MY FATHER'S FLOWER AND LEAF PRESS

butterfly net, I took up a gun. The first shot I ever fired was from a .22-pump rifle with a highly polished mahogany stock and a scope. Every time we would go to Pennsylvania—after all, you can't learn to shoot in suburban New Jersey—my father would take me out for target practice. I started with boxes, jars, and cans and eventually moved to paper targets. When I had improved sufficiently, my father declared it was graduation time—I was going to move up to the shotgun and go live. He said there was a pigeon shoot the next day and he had signed me up. While I had watched these strange events on the bare baseball diamond across the valley from the back window in my grandparents' kitchen for as long as I could remember, I had never actually attended a pigeon shoot.

People in Pennsylvania have a different relation to pigeons—and to much else—than the average city dweller. Far from regarding these commonplace birds as an annoying nuisance or even flying rats, the sons and grandsons of miners respect pigeons and raise them for sport. Driving through these depressed and depressing towns today, you still see many pigeon cages on roofs and in back alleys. Most of these pens are for homing pigeons, which are raised to race. Pigeon breeders are every bit as savvy about genetics as horse breeders, and stud fees for champion homing pigeons can run as high as several thousand dollars. Birds that do not make the cut for racing are used in pigeon shoots.

The ritual of the pigeon shoot brings the community together in a festive atmosphere that resembles nothing so much as a carnival. Even today on Sunday afternoons in summer, people defy picket lines of animal rights protesters to gather with friends and family for picnics in open fields where the contests are held. Trapshooting with clay pigeons is a pale imitation of the bloody original. The rules of the game are simple: A pigeon with a bell attached to its leg is put in a small wooden trap with a long cord attached to it and placed in the middle of a circle with a diameter of twenty-five yards. A person with a gun stands near the trap and, when ready, shouts, "Pull!" Someone outside the circle jerks the cord, which opens the trap, releasing the pigeon. The bell makes the bird fly erratically and thus the shot becomes much more difficult. The object is to kill the pigeon before

FAMILY GUNS

it gets beyond the circle. Participants agree on the number of birds before the contest begins, and the person who kills the most birds wins. Stars of the sport kill as many as 150 birds without a miss.

I did not participate in the contest, but my father had arranged for me to shoot at ten birds. I had never before used a shotgun and was anxious about how bad the kick of my father's double-barreled 12-gauge would be. After I had watched for about an hour, it was my turn. Standing at the center of the circle with others watching, I shouted, "Pull!" As the bird darted from the trap, I shot almost immediately. When I missed the first five times, my father called "time out" and came to talk to me: "You are jerking the gun and shooting too fast. Slow down. Start with the bead pointing down, and when the bird comes into view, slowly draw the barrel upward. When the bead is on the bird, squeeze the trigger gently. Remember, you have to lead the bird just a bit." Easier said than done when it all has to take place in a split second. On the next try everything happened just as my father had

MY FIRST HUNTING LICENSE

described it. I raised the barrel slowly and steadily, drew the bead on the bird, and gently squeezed the trigger. Much to my surprise, the pigeon instantly dropped one yard short of the line. I vividly remember but cannot adequately describe the feeling that overcame me at that moment—pride, accomplishment, of course, but there was something else that I can only describe as ecstasy. It was as if I were no longer standing in place but were somehow outside myself, looking down from elsewhere. The spell that had been cast lifted as quickly as it had settled. I missed the next two birds, killed number nine, and missed number ten. Two for ten—not a very good average, but I knew I had crossed a line that could never be erased.

When I had finished shooting, I went over to see the two birds I had killed. Picking up the first one and holding it in my hands, I remembered something my father had once told me. "Pigeons," he had explained, "are really doves." As I looked at the pigeon, the bright afternoon light turned its feathers iridescent; its body was soft and warm and its eyes wide open, staring at nothing. Only then did I realize that this bird, which I never before would have given a second glance and most people disdain as a pest, was, like the luminescent Luna moth under glass, stunningly beautiful. I felt my father's hand on my shoulder and heard his quiet words, "You did a good job. Put the bird on the pile with the others. It's time to go home." Without telling my father, I plucked a tail feather from the pigeon before throwing it on the pile of birds that had been shot that day. This feather is tucked inside my first hunting license, which still hangs on my bookshelf.

P.M.

Elemental

What we most long for is elemental. Earth, Air, Fire, Water. The elemental is the original, the first principle, the ground of whatever is and whatever is not. It is the underlying substance without which nothing can be. As such, the elemental is that from which everything emerges and to which all eventually returns. Is the elemental singular or plural, one or many, or, perhaps, their interplay? How might the elemental be figured, even if it cannot be thought?

For reasons buried in the distant recesses of my mind, I have always imagined the elemental to be earth. Matter, *mater,* matrix is where life and death stage their infinite dance. Examine earth carefully and you will discover decay teeming with life. One of my greatest pleasures is turning soil and preparing it for new growth. Last summer I became preoccupied with what remained of a former pond I had seen from the window of my study in the barn. The pond had been dry– or so I thought—for years, and the woods had almost completely overtaken it. Having become obsessed with reclaiming the land, I decided to cut the trees and clear the dense tangle of bushes and vines. The forest did not give up its gains easily, and I found myself once again engaged in a prolonged border struggle. When the trees

LEDGE, STONE HILL

and bushes were finally gone, I realized I would have to bring in heavy machinery to remove the stumps or my victory would be short-lived. As the last dump truck pulled away, I thought my work was done but soon discovered that the land was not finished with me.

The longer I pondered what I had uncovered, the more I felt the earth wanted something else from me, though it gave no clues about what it might be. Once again I took up shovel, pick, and rake and began the long process of cultivation. As days turned into weeks, Dinny started describing the work as my summer project—I insisted it was not a project. I had no plan and, indeed, could not really figure out why I could not stop sifting and shifting earth. I never actually heard voices but had no doubt that I was being drawn by someone or something I could not hear.

After nearly a month I gradually saw what had previously been invisible. I uncovered outcroppings of ledge that had never been exposed. There is a reason, after all, that they call this Stone Hill. I also began to discern figures and shapes in the earth that I had never imagined. Where the pond had been, the earth forms a beautiful symmetrical bowl that gradually folds into the slope of the hill. Far from immobile, the land is always moving to rhythms we ignore at our own peril. One day an artist friend stopped by to see what I was doing. When I explained that I still wasn't sure what this was all about, he said, "Seems obvious to me. You're creating an earthwork like your friend Heizer." I had never thought of it that way but immediately disagreed. "No, it's nothing like what he's doing. Michael is imposing his will on the land; the earth is imposing its will on me."

One afternoon in early August, while sitting on the slope of the erstwhile pond, my eye fell upon a large rock at the edge of the clearing. I had seen this rock countless times but now it looked different. It was richly colored limestone that time had shaped and etched in ways no human sculptor could match. In that instant I realized what the earth wanted me to do. I would create a rock garden similar to those I had admired in Kyoto temples years before. In subsequent weeks I drew up plans, selected the rocks, and laid out their arrangement. I decided make the outcropping of ledge the anchor and to place the other rocks around it. The centerpiece would be the sculpted rock. I used a fine gray gravel for the garden bed and surrounded it with thick grass. Over the next several weeks the gravel settled and the dusty earth was covered with a verdant carpet. At one end the exposed rock carried messages from the underworld, and at the other end rocks floated weightlessly on a surface that runs deep. There is an undeniable symmetry to it all, but it is not my creation.

When I am writing and my thinking meets a hurdle, I lift my eyes above the computer screen to contemplate the garden. If I am patient, the impasse fades and words once again flow freely. The garden, I am discovering, changes with the light as well as the seasons. Yesterday we had the first snowfall of the season, and the garden was transformed. The pond I thought was dry has a stream running through it, which creates patterns in the snow worthy of Jackson Pollock. As dusk began to fall, I glimpsed a slight movement from the corner of my eye. When I looked out, the huge

ROCK GARDEN

owl I often hear on moonlit nights was gazing intently at me. I froze so I would not scare him. After a few minutes the owl began a strange hopping movement. Looking more closely, I saw a red squirrel dangling in his claws. I sat transfixed for more than half an hour while the owl dragged the squirrel across the snow-covered rock garden and disappeared into the woods. The next morning I trudged through the snow to follow the owl's path. In the middle of the garden there were not only tracks but also a thin trail of blood that appeared to be a line written by an unknowable author.... Earth.... Blood.... What could be more elemental?

NINE

A.M.

Abandonment

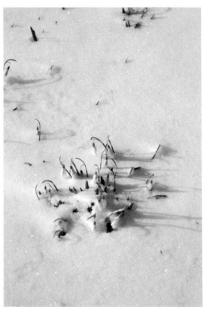

SNOWDROPS

Before the beginning, there is abandonment. I am, we are, abandoned, not once but again and again and again. Being comes to pass as abandonment; to be, therefore, is to have been abandoned. Nothing abandons, yet there is abandonment; abandonment occurs as having taken place without ever taking (a) place. Always already past, abandonment remains shrouded in oblivion. I have no memory of the primal event that allows me to be, and, more important, to become, what I might yet be or not be.

Since abandonment happens before the beginning, I am forever after — after the past that never was but eternally returns as the future that never arrives. I am therefore simultaneously after before and before after. I am abandoned *to* time, which is always abandoning me. I never have time—it has me. The abandonment *to* time, the abandonment *of* time, keeps everything in motion by keeping all in play. Though profoundly disturbing, this infinite restlessness is not merely the labor of the negative.

Abandonment transforms the world into a desert where what once was called God approaches by withdrawing. In the wake of this retreat, I am, we are, always after God. In the desert elsewhere is near without ever becoming present. Since abandonment is originary, it involves no loss; it is, after all, always after all, impossible to lose what you never possess. Abandonment therefore does not lead to dispossession, dereliction, destitution. Rather, it creates the fullness of emptiness that gives by taking what I never have. Far from the land of exile, the desert is the placeless place of an erring that never ends. To err is to wander with no expectation of return or arrival. Abandonment holds open the space of desire where the promise of satisfaction is the mask of death. Can't get no satisfaction—don't even want it. Always giving by taking, abandonment is the gift of life that is the gift of death and the gift of death that is the gift of life.

At the end of the day, I am always abandoned. Beginning and end mirror each other without closing the circle: nothing abandons, yet there is abandonment. Abandonment is a radical passivity that is also an activity. Having always been abandoned, I inevitably abandon others, even those to whom I am closest. Though I cannot do otherwise, I feel guilty for abandoning my students, friends, and family. This guilt cannot be forgiven—it is original and makes me what I am. My lingering hope, fragile though it is, is that I might pass on to them the gift of abandonment that has been given to me.

P.M.

Mortality

Life is a tale of leavings, not all of which end well. Paging through one of my notebooks recently, I stumbled on the following entry:

July 10, 1992

A certain melancholy accompanies departures—especially when leaving alone for a foreign country. Often the sense of loss is stronger than the anticipation of gain. I suppose part of it is the solitude and the recognition of the isolation that lies ahead.

But there is something else at work, for such departures often have as their last stop a visit with my father. I know he enjoys the visits, and yet I also realize that he dreads the partings. When you are eighty-four, you have suffered too many losses for leave-taking to be casual. I know how much my visits mean to him and yet they are difficult for me. It is depressing—terribly depressing—to watch him struggle with age. He will never get over my mother's death and seems convinced that his life ended with hers. With little to look forward to, there is nothing I can say to comfort him. He gets frustrated by the betrayal of his body. As I look at him, he is growing smaller, not just thinner but smaller—as if his body were slowly disappearing. Every death sentence ends with the contraction into a point. His shoulders are becoming rounded and his gait is steady but not as quick as it once was.

Even more depressing than watching my father struggle with age is anticipating myself in his place. His days are long, his nights longer still. There is never enough conversation to fill the emptiness. In the midst of this silence, I feel guilty for not spending more time with him. But time seems too precious to spend sitting in New Jersey doing nothing. And yet, when I reverse the situation and think of what Aaron's and Kirsten's visits mean to me, I have a sense of how important my trips are to him. Perhaps idleness and silent conversations are not a waste of time, but the most valuable way to spend it.

Confronting—or at least acknowledging—such thoughts as I depart deepens the sense of loss and dislocation. I realize more and more that all departures are glimpses of the unavoidable departure toward which we are inexorably moving.

After visiting with my father, I left for a colloquium devoted to the writings of Jacques Derrida in the village of Cerisy, four hours outside Paris. In the decade I had known him, Derrida had gone from a little-known French philosopher to one of the most famous and controversial intellectuals of his generation. While critics relentlessly attacked him for irresponsible nihilism, I considered his thinking profound and knew his personal and political commitments ran deep. Though his American detractors regarded Derrida as the quintessential Left Bank intellectual, he was an Algerian Jew who remained an outsider wherever he went. What few people realized until the later years of his life was that Derrida's religious identity lies at the heart of all his work. His enthusiastic followers can, however, be a bit much. Being confined to a country chateau for ten days with seventy-five academics who are obsessed with deconstruction is some people's idea of heaven and other people's idea of hell. I was somewhere in between—four or five days would have been quite enough. It was, nonetheless, a productive time spent reconnecting with old friends and colleagues and meeting new people whose work I had long been reading.

After the colloquium ended, I had only one afternoon in Paris and decided to spend it with Arlette Jabès, whom I had known for years. Her husband, Edmond, had been a distinguished poet, who fled Egypt during the Suez Crisis and spent the rest of his life on the Left Bank. His powerful poetry is an extended meditation on the silence and apparent absence of God after the Holocaust. I will always be grateful for the exceptional hospitality he and Arlette extended to me over the years. Our conversations invariably were long and as deep as my French would allow. Edmond taught me many lessons about what it means to pursue a life of thinking and writing. It was also through Edmond and Arlette that I first met Paul Auster, whose work is also greatly indebted to Edmond.

After Edmond died, Arlette was frightfully lonely; they had been unusually close yet had managed to allow each other enough space to breathe. I was sensitive to Arlette's plight because I had seen what loneliness had done to my father after my mother's death. My time with Arlette that afternoon was reminiscent of my visits with my father. Our conversation circled around death and the impossibility yet necessity of going on. Much of the time we did not speak but simply sat surrounded by the silence about which Edmond had written so eloquently.

My father and Arlette had met once. In an effort to lift his spirits after my mother died, I had taken him with me on a trip to Paris two years earlier. Though he had been to Europe several times, he had never visited Paris. I took special pleasure in showing him many of my favorite Parisian haunts, and he seemed delighted to follow me around the city. A lifelong photographer, he snapped pictures wherever we went. He savored the food, and the long years he had refused to drink any alcohol seemed to pique his taste for good French wine. He enjoyed nothing more than sitting in a café sipping wine and watching the world pass by. Never in a hurry because he had nowhere left to go, sometimes he forgot himself and even smiled.

The pleasure of our trip was interrupted by a frightening reminder of the very death we were attempting to evade. Two nights before we were scheduled to leave, my father woke me in the middle of the night; he was in an agitated state and told me that he thought he was having a heart attack. Though in his eighties, he was in the best of health and had no history of ill ness. As I frantically searched the Paris telephone book for the names and phone numbers of hospitals and cardiologists, he decided the palpitations were subsiding and wanted to wait until morning before doing anything. When dawn arrived, he insisted everything seemed to be fine and said he did not need to see a doctor. I was not convinced but, with nowhere to turn, agreed to give up the search for help. The condition never returned, and we never again discussed what had happened that night.

Later that day I told my father about Edmond and Arlette and explained that I wanted to visit her before we left Paris. He said he would like to accompany me. After the episode the night before, I was worried about the exertion, but he assured me he would be fine. Though their life experiences were worlds apart, age and the death of a loved one drew Arlette and my father close together. As they talked late into the afternoon, it seemed as if they had known each other for a long time. For a moment I fantasized that if they were not separated by an ocean they might have gotten together. In

THE LAST PICTURE OF MY FATHER AND ME

the years after he would ask me from time to time how Arlette was doing, and I could always hear not only concern but also affection in his voice.

When I returned to the States after my trip to Cerisy, I again spent a couple of days with my father. With fond memories of our stay in Paris, he was eager to hear all about my trip. He asked about Arlette, and when I reported that she was still struggling with her loss, he responded: "She will never get over it; some wounds never heal." Two weeks later, when a friend called to tell me that Arlette had died, my father felt he had lost a rare friend.

With the passing of years leave-taking becomes more and more difficult. For reasons I did not understand at the time, it was especially hard for me to leave my father that August. But the first hints of color were in the leaves, a new semester was beckoning, and there was work I thought had to be done. As I waved to him standing alone in the driveway, it would be the last time I would see my father alive.

After hearing of Arlette's death, I wrote a note to Paul to tell him about it. While I was reading the note he sent in response to the news, I received another phone call announcing death. The familiar voice of a long-time family friend said, "Mark, your father just died. We don't know what caused his death." With my mind spinning, words from Paul's book, the ones that my mother returned to me a few weeks before she died, came rushing back but did not fill the void I felt.

> One day there is life.... And then, suddenly, it happens there is death. A man lets out a little sigh, he slumps down in his chair, and it is death. The suddenness of it leaves no room for thought, gives the mind no chance to seek out a word that might comfort it. We are left with nothing but death, the irreducible fact of our own mortality. Death after a long illness we can accept with resignation. Even accidental death we can ascribe to fate. But for a man to die of no apparent cause, for a man to die simply because he is a man, brings us so close to the invisible boundary between life and death that we no longer know which side we are on. Life becomes death, and it is as if this death has owned this life all along. Death without warning. Which is to say: life stops. And it can stop at any moment.

My father was 84 so his death should not have surprised me. But Taylors don't die so young—his father died at 92, one of his sisters at 99, and a brother at 104. Even when expected, death's arrival comes as a surprise and, when unexpected, it brings an astonishment that transforms the question with which Aristotle claims philosophy begins. Rather than asking, "Why is there something rather than nothing?" I was driven to ask, "Why is there nothing rather than someone?"

TEN

A.M.

Displacement

REFLECTIONS ON ART

I split my life between city and country—New York and the Berkshires. My friends in the city cannot understand why I have stayed in the country for thirty-five years, and my friends in the country have no idea why after so long I would want to live in the city.

My apartment in the city is on the thirteenth floor of a building at the corner of Broadway and 103rd Street. I have an unobstructed view due north to the Cathedral of Saint John the Divine and beyond to Morningside Heights and Harlem. To the left new high-rises with expensive condos are going up, and to the right just one block away are huge housing projects. The street is always alive and, for a person who for more than three decades has not been able to go to town to pick up the paper without bumping into someone he would rather not talk to, the anonymity of the crowd is liberating. In New York I become something of a Parisian flâneur, roaming the streets for hours without ever meeting anyone I know. As I walk, I am fascinated by store windows—especially Barneys and Bergdorf, where displays are often more artful than the work for sale in downtown galleries. Sometimes when my gaze is momentarily arrested and I look at rather than through the window, it seems as if my identity virtually dissolves before my eyes. The play of reflection becomes infinite—windows reflect windows to create a city of glass where homeless nomads roam. Looking for myself in a mirror that does not return my gaze, I recall the words of a writer I know: "By wandering aimlessly, all places became equal, and it no longer mattered where he was. On his best walks, he was able to feel that he was nowhere."

There are, of course, important differences between New York City in the twenty-first century and Paris in the nineteenth century. Though steel and glass remain, the arcades have become digital, and the commodities virtual. In the city place is transformed into the space of anonymous flows. When technologies shift first from steel and steam to electricity and then to information networks, currents are redirected and the rate of change speeds up. Mobility, fluidity, and speed intersect to effect repeated displacements in which everything becomes ephemeral and nothing remains stable or solid. In this world faster is always better and speed becomes an end in itself. For those circulating in these currents, there is never time to pause and ask, "Faster and faster but for the sake of what?"

As acceleration accelerates, perpetual displacement becomes a mark of what once was called authenticity. To be is to be on the move, and to settle down and stay put is to slip off the grid and disappear from the radar screen. Eventually, things reach the tipping point and more becomes different. Speed renders life ever more transient and thus increasingly ephemeral—everything solid melts into ether(nets). The proliferation of media, information, and telematic technologies in infinitely complex networks creates the new domain of cyberspace, where realities that are the "substance" of our lives appear to vaporize and everything becomes virtual. In this placeless place so-called real time is no longer temporal yet not quite eternal. Glimpsing my face in Windows on terminal screens, I realize that I am no place, perhaps even nowhere.

When real time interrupts "real time," the flow stops just long enough for me to realize that the time has come for me to return to the country. What my friends in the city do not realize is that living in the country is perhaps the most radical thing I do. In a world where speed is sacred, slowing down is revolutionary.

P.M.

Place

Place matters. What you think is, in large measure, a function of where you think. Having spent almost my entire professional life in one place, I know all too well both the delight and the horror place can breed. If to be is to be on the move, then how can one possibly stay in one place so long? Movement, however, is complex, and all too often people mistake motion for movement. Many of the people whose minds are most mobile move least, and some of those who are least mobile move most. Kant never left Königsberg; Kierkegaard left Denmark but once; Hegel spent his whole life in what is now Germany; Emily Dickinson rarely left her house in Amherst.

I read and write in a converted barn perched on a hillside facing due west, overlooking the Taconic Range. These hills are haunted by the ghosts of some of the writers I most admire. Behind me is Mount Greylock, which Melville saw through his window at Arrowhead, while he sat at his desk writing *Moby-Dick*; less than twenty miles down the road is Hawthorne's red cottage at the edge of Tanglewood, and nearby is The Mount, where Edith Wharton lived and wrote. Sometimes when I work late into the night, I hear the voices of these ghosts as they pass through the woods at the edge of the field.

WINTER ON STONE HILL

The southern end of the Taconic Range is marked by Monument Mountain, where, on the sweltering Sunday afternoon of August 5, 1850, Oliver Wendell Holmes, Nathaniel Hawthorne, Herman Melville, and others gathered for a picnic. They climbed the 1,642-foot peak to drink champagne and read William Cullen Bryant's poem "Monument Mountain," which recounts the Indian legend of a Machian maiden who, in despair because she could not marry her cousin whom she deeply loved, jumped from the cliffs to her death. I have long suspected that was the afternoon Melville conceived what would become the greatest American novel ever written.

For some reason I cannot write in the city. I read and take many notes, but nothing happens until I am back in the barn, which, admittedly, is better suited to the nineteenth than the twenty-first century. As I gaze at the mountains, especially in the early morning light, thoughts begin to flow and soon are rushing through me as fast as I can write them down. Much of what I have thought and written about the tangled interrelation of the nineteenth and twenty-first centuries would have been impossible with-

PLAQUE MARKING POE'S PLACE

out the tensions created by my retreat to this place. Vision becomes more acute as distance increases—I cannot see the city until I am far away. From my perch in the mountains I am free to insist that displacement does necessarily lead to authenticity, any more than being settled inevitably alienates. When you slow down and take time to reflect, you realize that speed is as often destructive as it is creative. Serious thinking can never be hurried.

Winters in the country are long, dark, and cold and everything slows to a crawl. As the sun heads south, the mountains close in and the valley becomes narrower and narrower. A night always arrives when I wake up with trouble breathing and know it's time to go back to the city. While roaming the streets around my apartment the other day, I discovered a plaque on a building at the nearby corner of Broadway and 84th Street.

As I read this plaque, I remembered that two blocks to the west Paul Auster staged the baffling meeting of his characters Quinn and Stillman.

The afternoon was well advanced: the light like the gauze on the bricks and leaves, the shadows lengthening. Once again Stillman retreated to Riverside Park, this time to the edge of it, coming to rest on a knobby outcrop at 84th

Street known as Mount Tom. On the same spot in the summers of 1843 and 1844 Edgar Allan Poe had spent many long hours gazing out at the Hudson. Quinn knew this because he had made it his business to know such things. As it turned out, he had often sat there himself.

Often when I am searching for a bit of the country in the city, I walk in Riverside Park and on occasion sit where Poe, Quinn, and Stillman once sat on Mount Tom. But I know nothing about the house where Poe lived and do not know whether he wrote anything else during this period. A few blocks farther downtown, Melville lived the last forty years of his life in silence and anonymity. After he moved to the city, America's great author stopped writing. What would have happened if Melville had left the city and returned to the country?

ELEVEN

A.M.

Creativity

"God and the imagination," the poet Wallace Stevens avers, "are one." To appreciate this rich insight we must expand our notion of the imagination and transform our understanding of God. Wherever form emerges from formlessness or pattern appears in the midst of confusion, the imagination is at work. The imagination is not only within us but is also in the world around us. Theologians have had it wrong for centuries—God is not the Creator, creativity is God. Rather than a person, God is the infinite process in and through which everything arises and passes away. The good news is that creativity is embodied, even incarnate, whenever and wherever the new erupts. Never limited to the human imagination, creativity is at work in the entire cosmos—from the lowest to the highest, from the inanimate to the animate. Human creativity is always surrounded by a creativity infinitely greater than itself.

If God is creativity, the world is a work of art—the poem is always a poem within a poem and the painting a figure of figures. Since the world is a work of art, the mind can see itself in nature and nature becomes aware of itself in the mind. Divine and human, mind and world: two but one, one but two. Far from unreal, the imagination is the real in the process of formation. Once again, Stevens makes the point: "The real and unreal are two in one."

In moments when others think I drift furthest from reality, I believe I come closest to it. The end of the poem I am always writing is nothing other than the infinite poem itself. Whether I write the poem or the poem writes me remains uncertain. What I do know is that critics who insist that creativity ends with modernity are wrong. Indeed, if there is no creativity, there is no life. Though the moment of creativity emerges with a suddenness that surprises, it appears after a long preparatory process. The structure and operation of this process are the same regardless of the medium in which they occur. The Word is incarnate in molecules that form the very stuff of life. Life began in something like a primal soup. For life to emerge there must be a sufficient density and diversity of molecules and sufficient time for the soup to simmer. There is no recipe, program, or design—life is a self-organizing process that begins by chance. Given enough time, molecules eventually bump into each other and form bonds that then begin the long evolutionary process that eventually leads to minds capable of understanding how they have emerged.

From Word to molecules and back to words: I honestly do not know where the books I write come from. I begin by reading broadly and deeply until ideas gradually accumulate. Like the primal soup in which life emerges, the mix swirling in my mind becomes dense and diverse and, when left to simmer, slowly reaches the boiling point. As the temperature rises, ideas collide and combine to create noisy insights as well as noise that sometimes is insightful. Though seemingly arbitrary, associations are not totally free and interactions not completely random. Chance and constraint are braided in such a way that each becomes the condition of the other. The more I read and write, the faster I read and write. Writing generates positive feedback loops in which the speed of creation accelerates. As diverse ideas circulate like colliding molecules, the mental stew approaches the tipping point and I suddenly *see* the book. The work does not take shape slowly but appears as a whole in an instant. It is as if some switch were thrown, releasing an uncontrollable rush of words; I am unable to write fast enough to record the flow of thoughts. When writing in such a heightened state of

MY PYRAMID SCULPTURE

awareness, I cannot for some reason compose on the computer but must write with a pencil—always number two. The last thing I do each night before retiring is sharpen my pencils for the next day. Though seemingly inconsequential, this private ritual carries echoes of ancient rites that end the day by summoning a new dawn. There is something about the direct contact of mind, hand, and paper that completes the circuit of thought. I suppose that is why such works are called manuscripts (*manu scriptus,* written by hand). As my hand struggles to keep up with my mind, I am often driven to the edge of chaos, where I am sometimes abandoned. In such moments, I do not really compose but, rather, lose my composure and settle into a state of agitated restlessness.

Though metaphorical, the invocation of inspiration and the muses is actually an accurate description of the creative process. The muses are, of course, one of the many guises of God. When creativity stirs, I do not write but an Other writes through me. I—the I—become(s) the vehicle for a Word that is not my own. In the moment of creativity, I am not (an) I—my name is but another pseudonym of an Other I can never know. If this creativity, which is never precisely my own, is of a piece with the creativity that is the origin of life itself, then "my" activity is but a moment in an infinite creative process. When the creator God becomes divine creativity, "my" words become the Word. Blasphemy is the only credible creed: I am God incarnate! Madness? To be sure, but divine madness.

P.M.

Thinking

MY FATHER'S BASEBALL CAP

If you are a writer or a thinker, the danger is running out of ideas before you run out of time. When ideas take flight, days once devoted to reading, research, and reflection must be filled with ever more crafty strategies of diversion and distraction. Committees were invented to occupy those who have nothing left to think.

My problem has always been the opposite— running out of time before I run out of ideas. The older I get, the more urgent the issue becomes. One day you wake up and realize that you have more books in your head than time left to write them. I must confess that I do not always welcome ideas because there are times when my head literally aches with the buzz they create. I am not in control of this mysterious process and thus am not sure whether I should take responsibility for it. Thinking is as much a gift as a choice, perhaps more. It has rhythms of its own—arriving and departing when and where it will. You cannot flick a switch to make ideas circulate— nor can you flick a switch to turn them off.

As long as I can remember, ideas had never ceased to flow—even when I wished they would leave me in peace. I was therefore surprised and somewhat dismayed when, in the days after surgery, ideas suddenly ceased. I had known it would be weeks before I was strong enough to write again but assumed I would be able to read, so I gathered books before I left for the city—mostly fiction: Poe, Melville, Beckett, Solzhenitsyn, Updike, Auster, Powers, Danielewski, all friends both old and new. I began, perhaps predictably, with Solzhenitsyn's *Cancer Ward*. Though the conditions he describes in the dark and dingy hospitals of Soviet Russia were vastly different from those in which I found myself, my experience resembled that of the patients in the novel more than I ever could have imagined. I particularly remember his vivid account of the endless nights endured by a woman suffering through the final stages of ovarian cancer. Sex and death are never far apart but never more so than in the cancer ward. It is not just the malignancy eating away ovaries and testicles or spreading from breasts and prostate to blood and bone. It is something far more pernicious and much more deadly. Cancer gnaws away at the spirit until the last traces of vitality drain away like cloudy fluids in a disposable bag.

My reading during those difficult days and nights was different than it had ever been. Though the book could not have been more timely, Solzhenitsyn's finely crafted prose did not engage me. My mind drifted and I was easily distracted. More puzzling, words that usually would have taken me elsewhere fell dead on the page. Solzhenitsyn's thoughts spurred none of my own. For the first time in my life, what I had long dreaded, yet sometimes secretly desired, seemed to be occurring. Thoughts had stopped flowing and I could not turn on the switch to start them again. What most surprised me, however, was not that my thinking was blocked but that my response was pleasure rather than panic. The lack of thoughts and impossibility of thinking came as a welcome relief. Rather than pressing harder like a baseball batter in a slump, I simply let go and drifted into a lassitude from which I did not want to be roused. A sense of detachment settled over me that still has not lifted completely.

TWELVE

A.M.

E/Mergence

E/mergence is the space-time of the aleatory. In this interval the music of chance plays without end. This score opens a wound that is as creative as it is destructive. E/mergence takes place without taking place before the beginning; it is an event that is neither planned nor programmed. It occurs without why and thus surprises, sometimes even astonishes. The interval in which e/mergence erupts gives pause, and this pause is the beginning as well as the end of reflection. Always a "matter" of chance, the event of e/mergence is without reason, which is not to say it is irrational. The pause of e/mergence gives thought "its" matter without becoming "its" substance. In the wake of e/mergence, thought is always afterthought because thinking is inevitably after a before it forever seeks.

The before that thinking is after is, however, a strange before. No one, no thing, ex/ists before e/mergence. This no thing is not precisely nothing, nor, of course, is it either something or someone. E/mergence happens at the margin between being/nonbeing, is/is not, presence/absence, difference/indifference. It is the vibration or oscillation of the strings from which the fabric of the cosmos is woven. Because the threads of this text can never be pulled together, life, in the final analysis, cannot be figured. Instead of spelling defeat, the impossibility of figuring e/mergence marks the limit of endless thinking. Thinking, in the proper sense of the word, articulates differences that make a difference. The slash of e/mergence outlines the alteration between difference and indifference. All that is and is not hovers along this boundary. To think this limit, which is, of course (the) impossible, is to figure the arising and passing away that does not arise and pass away.

P.M.

Emptiness

Emptiness, mystics ancient and modern as well as eastern and western tell us, is a lack that is a fullness, a void that is a plenitude. The well-known Christian mystic Meister Eckhart goes so far as to insist that emptiness is nothing less than our point of contact with God. "You must know that to be empty of all created things is to be full of God, and to be full of created things is to be empty of God." For those who believe God is the transcendent Creator of the world, these words are meaningless, if not downright blasphemous. But what if God is not the creator *beyond* the world but is creative activity *within* the world? To find this lack that is a fullness, we must look within, where, much to our surprise, God lurks by hiding.

When I turn inward, I discover a void at the center of my being that can never be filled. It is difficult, perhaps even impossible, to know what to say about this void. No specific trait, no particular action, can articulate such inwardness. However characterized, it remains something else, something more, something other. Like the God of negative theology or the *sunyata* the Buddha taught, all I can say about this emptiness is that it is not this and not that.

To glimpse this vanishing point, try a thought experiment: Sit quietly and attempt to list every specific trait that makes you what you are. Take as much time as necessary, for the list will be long, and such reflection cannot be rushed. Say to yourself, "I am a, b, c. . . . " When you think you have finished, ask yourself, "Does the sum of these characteristics exhaustively define me?" I suspect not. Now reverse the experiment. Start with the list you compiled and subtract everything you identified—a, b, c—and then ask, "What is left over? What am I without these traits?" If you think long enough, you will discover that nothing is closer to what you believe yourself to be than this sheer sense of I-ness, which resists every determination. This *I* that remains forever unnameable, is the no/thing that makes me what I am. If I try to express this *I*, all I can do is echo the words of a God that once seemed distant: "I am that I am."

As the primal indeterminacy from which everything determinate repeatedly emerges, emptiness is the creative origin that begins anew in every word and deed. Just as creative activity cannot be reduced to creative product, so the *I* cannot be exhausted by any specific deed. If the *I* is always beyond as well as within any specific activity, then I am never more myself than when I am empty. And yet at precisely this point, my *I* becomes something other than simply itself. The *I* is; I am a moment in a creative process that both includes and infinitely surpasses me. Emptiness dwells within me as that which is never my own but without which *I* cannot be. It overwhelms me in a "cloud of unknowing" that undoes me. Far from defeat, this undoing makes all that *I* do infinitely valuable. Emptiness gives by taking—gives nothing by taking everything deemed my own. Never bringing the rest that comes with doing nothing, emptiness leaves me infinitely restless. Always running on empty, I must repeatedly become what I can never be. Emptiness is the *nihilo* out of which creation eternally emerges and with which (the) *I* finally merge(s).

THIRTEEN

A.M.

Walls

GRANDFATHER'S AX

As I hike the Berkshire Mountains, I often stumble on stone walls that the forest has overtaken. Many of these walls are long and their patterns intricate. When I occasionally find the foundations of nearby houses and barns, I pause and try to imagine the lives of the people who once farmed this land. The length of the walls is an abiding testimony to how grudgingly New England earth yields to shovels and plows. Sometimes there is a small family graveyard near the remaining traces of the homestead. Hidden deep in the woods, the lichen-covered tombstones etched with fading names are the only memory of those who built these walls.

When we built the house that was our first home, I cleared the wooded lot and did the landscaping. Though I had never used a chainsaw, I managed to fell the trees and cut them up into firewood the weekend before classes started. Since I had designed the gardens to include trees, I left clusters standing in carefully planned patterns. When the house was finished and spring finally arrived, I realized I needed help creating what I had imagined. A friend suggested I call John, who worked for a local nurseryman but also freelanced on the side. When we met, it quickly became clear that John was no ordinary landscaper—he had the mind of an artist—earth, rocks, flowers, and shrubs were his chosen media. I described my plans and asked if he would be interested in helping me. He was intrigued and responded cautiously, pointing out what he thought was good and what was bad in my design. Most of his ideas actually strengthened the overall plan. The longer we talked, the more I noticed something slightly troubling about John—in his long, frizzy hair, darting eyes, and frenzied speech punctuated by long silences, I detected hints of what seemed to border on madness.

During the weeks and months that followed, we worked together for many long hours, moving earth, contouring land, and laying out gardens. Until we could figure out what to do with the countless rocks we dug up, we collected them in a big pile. Slowly, very slowly, I gained John's trust and he began to talk; it was then that I discovered my suspicion was not misguided. He and his brother, he hesitantly told me, had grown up in a small farmhouse at the end of a wooded lane. His father had died when they were young, and his mother, who worked as a housekeeper for wealthy townspeople, had raised them. Shortly after John's father died, his mother's brother, who was troubled and could not hold down a steady job, came to live with them. One day, when John was five and his brother seven, their uncle retreated into his bedroom beside the living room on the first floor and never again came out. Though the boys were not allowed to enter the room, they could not avoid hearing his moaning, crying, and screaming as well as their mother whispering futile words of comfort to their uncle. Throughout their entire childhood, they never invited friends to come to their house to play. Imagine—just try to imagine—growing up in a house where play as well as so much else was forbidden. While he never said so directly, I soon realized that John feared his uncle's fate would become his own. Once he did try to break free but failed. An extremely good student, John was admitted to one of the country's best colleges, located in the Midwest. He traveled west alone on a train but returned after only one semester to live with his mother and uncle. For almost three decades he never left town again.

The longer I worked with John, the more I came to appreciate his intelligence, sensitivity, and creativity. He had an impeccable sense of design: he placed rocks with the eye of a sculptor and selected the hues and shades of shrubs and flowers with the care of an artist choosing just the right paint from his palette. His aesthetic was not flashy but was always subtle and understated. We never used a bright flower when a muted hue would do, never planted an ornate shrub when natural grasses or plants could be found in nearby fields. I knew quite a bit about gardening, but John's quiet lessons taught me things I had never imagined.

One day when our work was about half done, John's brother, whom I had never met, appeared at our front door to deliver the news that John could no longer work with me. When I pressed for an explanation, he said that John was going through a rough time. He recounted the story of their uncle, and I did not let on that I already knew about the situation. After more than thirty years, John's brother continued, the family had finally decided it was time to move their uncle from his room to a state facility about seventy-five miles away. Though John agreed with the decision and acknowledged they should have done it years earlier, he was still having trouble coming to terms with the change. He seemed paralyzed and was unable to work at home or elsewhere. Gazing at the mountain of dirt still to be moved, I, rather disingenuously, insisted that work was precisely what he needed most. His brother agreed to talk to him again.

A week later John showed up driving a front-end loader and started moving the earth to contour what would become the lawn. When he had finished, he rang the bell and simply said, "I'm sorry, things were just closing in." Knowing enough not to ask more, I turned the conversation to a discussion of the remaining work to be done. The biggest decision involved

UNFINISHED WALL

what to do about the pile of rocks. I suggested that we terrace the lawn and use the rocks to form a retaining wall along the serpentine row of trees I had left standing. John agreed, and the next day we began building the wall. By this time we knew each other's rhythms, and I had learned when to talk and when to remain silent. It was hard work that left me refreshingly tired every night. I came to appreciate more than ever just how much labor went into those walls I happened upon in the woods. John and I were making good progress and were about half done, when one day he disappeared again. This time his brother did not stop by and I did not call. I waited a few days and then decided to continue building the wall by myself; it was hard work and took me about a month to complete the job. For reasons I cannot comprehend, I always had the feeling John was watching me, even though I never saw him during that time. The afternoon I finished the wall, I felt great satisfaction; with John's help the landscaping had, indeed, become a work of art.

While we were eating dinner that evening, the doorbell rang. It was John: "I see you finished the wall. Looks good. Sorry I disappeared on you; I just couldn't go on because I don't know what's on the other end of that wall." "Nor do I," I responded. Though neither of us said so, John and I knew we learned something important that spring and summer. Walls, we discovered, don't always have to separate but sometimes can also connect. Working with me enabled John to tear down some of the walls that had held him hostage far too long. We both also knew that the forest where each of us roamed alone would one day overtake the wall we had built together.

From time to time I see John around town, mowing and gardening, but we have not talked often since that summer evening many years ago. Looking back, it seems as if our relationship that summer carries hints of a slightly illicit affair—as if John had confided things he would rather have kept secret. He still lives with his mother, and I don't know whether he has ever left town again.

P.M.

Garden

If the world is a work of art, then gardening, like writing, is always a poem within a poem. My gardens, I confess, are as important to me as my books. Indeed, I would go so far as to say that gardening is the form of writing that keeps me grounded. I do some of my best thinking while gardening. Each garden has its own vocabulary, grammar, and style. Trees, shrubs, and bushes frame the work; plants and flowers—some annuals, others perennials—provide the words; placement and arrangement create the style. I never read books about gardening or study the work of others. Though it has changed over the years, my style has always been improvisational, sometimes almost free. Like many of my most creative thoughts, I do not know where the designs for my gardens come from. Nor can I explain why one shrub or plant is right and another is wrong. The proper plant is le mot juste that completes the thought I did not realize I had.

My education in gardening began when I was very young. Raised on a Pennsylvania farm in the first decades of the twentieth century, my father eventually became a biology teacher in a suburban New Jersey high school.

MY FATHER'S PLANT CONTAINER

But he never lost his love of the earth and was determined to pass on to me the lessons his father had taught him. I must confess I was not always a willing student. While our friends played, my brother and I cut lawns and worked in gardens. To this day the smell of freshly cut grass remains one of the sweetest fragrances I know. My father taught us how to turn the soil, plant the seeds, weed, hoe, and rake all summer long. We tended two kinds of gardens: utilitarian and nonutilitarian. In the former we grew fruit and vegetables—peas, beans, onions, beets, carrots, turnips, potatoes, cucumbers, squash, corn, and strawberries. We had no machines to help us but did everything by hand. When we harvested our crops, my mother froze and canned what we had grown. Even as a child, I realized that the point was not simply to save money, though that was always an issue. Rather, the garden was the classroom where my father could teach only by showing and I could learn only by doing.

When he was a young man, my father somehow made his way from the small Pennsylvania coal-mining town, where he started his teaching career, to Duke University, where he earned a master's degree in botany. Until the day he died, he knew the Latin names of any plant he found. As we hunted the Pennsylvania mountains and hiked the Carolina hills, he would recite the scientific names of the trees and plants we saw. My granddaughter's middle name is Linnea, which can be traced to the great Swedish botanist Linnaeus. Though I have never asked her parents, I suspect this was a quiet act of homage because her father was one of the best students his grandfather ever taught.

The years of college and graduate school left me little time and no opportunity for gardening. When we moved to the Berkshires, however, I discovered my father's lessons returning. It was the early '70s and the nearby Vermont mountains were filled with hippies, and the back-to-the-land movement was all the rage. For almost a decade we had a vegetable garden and repeated the rituals I had been taught as a child. I planted and tended, Dinny canned and froze. But gardening in New England is not the same as gardening in the Garden State. Spring starts late and summer ends early. Most of the summer we had nothing from the garden and then, for three weeks in August, we had more beans, zucchini, and tomatoes than the whole neighborhood could eat. Though I knew it was crazy to work so much for so little, I persisted until I was able to admit that I was gardening out of a sense of guilt rather than because I enjoyed it. It seems silly now, but telling my father that I had given up the vegetable garden was one of the hardest things I had done.

ONE OF MY FLOWER GARDENS

I did not, however, stop gardening completely, though my designs were no longer utilitarian. When we built a house, I did all the landscaping—I designed the gardens, moved earth and rocks, built the long stone wall, selected and planted all the shrubs and flowers. Ten years later, when we moved to the mountain hillside where we still live, I began all over again. With more land to work with, my designs became not only bigger but also more subtle and complex. I learned to listen to the land, following its undulating lines and repeating its flowing rhythms. Rather than removing rocks and reshaping hills, I found it more effective to leave things the way they were. When I finally realized that less is, indeed, more, I began to understand that the earth is already a work of art.

Gardening, like writing, is endless and, many insist, useless. In both cases pointlessness seems to be precisely the point; activity does not have to be productive to be creative. Hoe as pen, pen as hoe: Cultivation is where nature and culture meet. Nature, like art, is purposeless or, more precisely, it has no purpose other than itself.

Though gardening is endless, I realize my gardens will end because weeds eventually will overwhelm them. Here, as elsewhere, defeat is victory. Once many years ago I enlisted my daughter's help in conducting my annual assault on the dandelions I thought ruined my lawn. An unwilling worker like her father had been, she asked me one day, "Daddy, why don't we like the pretty yellow flowers in the grass but do like them in the garden?" I had no answer so I told her she could quit. What I never admitted to her was that because of her question, I gave up my battle against dandelions. Weeds are weeds because they don't fit our grid, but there are always other grids and sometimes there are no grids at all. Weeds, as much as flowers, are expressions of nature's infinite exuberance. Gardens create the space for the unceasing border struggle between the woods and field, order and chaos, the settled and the unsettling. Looking back on the lesson I began in my father's garden, I realize that my life is a brief episode in an infinite creative process that began long before I arrived and will continue long after I am gone.

FOURTEEN

A.M.

Painting

DRAWING LESSONS

What I most remember are not the colors but the smells—the linseed oil with which I mixed my paints and the turpentine with which I cleaned my brushes. From the age of nine until I was twelve, I spent every Tuesday afternoon from 3:30 to 5:30 taking painting lessons from an elderly widow, Lillian Owen, who lived two doors up the street from us. She also gave my brother violin lessons. As a small token of our appreciation, we spent Saturday evenings during the summer watching the *Perry Mason* TV show with her while sipping ice cream sodas that she made for us. Mrs. Owen was an accomplished woman who, had she been born two generations later, would have had a significant artistic career. My mother was an amateur artist and took adult education classes whenever Mrs. Owen taught them. When my mother reported that I often amused myself by drawing and coloring, Mrs. Owen offered to give me drawing and painting lessons.

She was a demanding teacher who began with the basics of drawing and gradually worked her way up to canvas and oils. I started by learning the principle of perspective and how to draw simple objects. Mrs. Owen bought me drawing books and gave me homework each week. She would begin each session by criticizing my drawings and showing me how to improve them. One afternoon about six months after we had started, she presented me with a gift and said, "Now I know you are serious and I want you to have this." It was a wooden case lined with metal dividers for paints and brushes and a well-worn palette she had used for many years. "It is time," she added, "to graduate to paints." For the next two and a half years, every Tuesday afternoon she guided my hand as I struggled to translate vision to paint. In good weather we painted outside and in bad weather inside. I painted mostly landscapes and still lifes, which, she explained when I was only nine years old, is in French *la nature morte*. She showed me how to create compositions of fruit and flowers—always an odd number of objects, never even; height: the vase should be one-third the height of the flowers, never more or less. As I learned how to mix paints, I was intrigued by the palette and the rich consistency of the paints oozing from their tubes as much as by the canvas.

Once again we returned to basics and I relearned how to draw in preparation for painting—rather than detailed figures fashioned with sharp pencils, rough outlines sketched with charcoal. When you use oils, the work emerges by mixing and remixing paints on the canvas. The most valuable lesson she taught me was the least obvious at the time: how to see light. Her method was always indirect; she never explained in words but always demonstrated with paint. What I most remember is how she changed a shade ever so slightly to cast a shadow that revealed light in a way I had never before seen. This is when I began to suspect just how many secrets shades harbor. By making what had been invisible visible, she re-created the contours of my world in ways I would not understand for many years.

With time the results improved and, by the end, my paintings were rather decent for a kid. I still have many of the paintings, and a few of them even hang in a hallway in our home. By the time I was twelve, adolescence

GRANDPA COOPER'S SKETCHBOOK

arrived and sports were beckoning. I set aside painting though never really let it go completely; from time to time I have taken up my brushes again but never long enough to develop whatever talent I might have.

Somewhere in these early experiences lie the roots of my lifelong fascination with the visual arts. It took many years for me to begin writing about art, and, when I did, I felt like I was returning to territory that was very familiar. In the early 1990s I was commissioned to write an essay on Michael Heizer's imposing earthwork *Double Negative.* In preparation for this task, I spent a week with Michael and his wife, Mary Shannon, who is a gifted painter. Over the years I have returned several times and during these visits have had some of my most memorable conversations about art and much else. Michael and Mary live in the middle of the Nevada desert, farther from civilization than I had ever been. Their art is inseparable from this place. As I roamed the desert, sometimes with Michael, often alone in solitude, I once again began to see light. Desert light is unlike any other I had ever seen. Its crisp clarity gives an edge to vision that allows subtle hues usually overlooked to emerge more vividly than gaudy colors visible in more temperate zones. On long walks that led nowhere, what most intrigued me was the subtle interplay of earth and sky. It was not so much the shadows that the clouds cast on the land as the remarkable desert colors—reds, browns, ambers, umbers, and lavenders—above all, lavenders—reflected in the sky.

While Michael works with earth on a massive scale, Mary works with paint on a scale that seems more manageable. I was intrigued by her work and, before leaving, purchased a painting that now greets people when they enter the front door of our house. It is largish (a sixty-inch square) and abstract, indeed, almost ethereal. I was first drawn to the work by its colors—light blues and multiple shades of white that suggest clouds playing on a hot summer afternoon. In the middle of the canvas is an apparition that reminds me of the specter that appears in the closing lines of Poe's *Diary of Arthur Gordon Pym*:

> The darkness had materially increased, relieved only by the glare of the water thrown back from the white before us. Many gigantic and pallidly white birds flew continuously now from beyond the veil, and their scream was the eternal *Tekeli-li!* as they retreated from our vision. Hereupon Nu-Nu stirred in the bottom of the boat; but upon touching him, we found his spirit departed. And now we rushed into the embraces of the cataract, where a chasm threw itself open to receive us. But there arose in our pathway a shrouded human figure, very far larger in proportions than any dweller among men. And the hue of the skin of the figure was of the perfect whiteness of snow.

Almost capturing what we cannot grasp, Mary's painting fulfills the two criteria I use in judging works of art: the work must take me elsewhere, and it must never appear the same and thus remain inexhaustible. Frank Stella was wrong when he declared, "What you see is what you see." In the only art that matters, what you see is not what you see; to the contrary, what you do not see is what you see. Since the visible and the invisible are inseparable, figuring and disfiguring are woven together in such a way that you begin to apprehend, which is not to say comprehend, something else—something that is not exactly there or is there by not being there. This invisible that is present in its absence is what keeps you coming back for more. As I pondered Mary's painting day after day and year after year, I gradually began to notice, peeking through layers of paint, rich earthen hues I had seen in the desert sky. I knew then in a way I had not before that the boundary between

CHILDHOOD ART

earth and sky is the origin of the work of art where gods dwell and beauty is truth.

Fifteen years after I had hung Mary's painting, I realized that I had seen the colors of her desert sky years earlier. One day while contemplating Mary's painting, it suddenly transported me to another work I have long admired. It is an invaluable painting by Renoir in which I sometimes glimpse beauty. It depicts a young girl wearing a large red hat sitting in what appears to be a garden. The flesh of her cheeks glows with the colors of fresh apples and pears that only Renoir can paint. It is not her face, however, that I find beautiful; it is the background that dimly fades, figuring nothing. I have never see this shade of color anywhere else, and I cannot find the words to express it. Nor can I paint it, though I have tried; photographs and reproductions do not capture what makes it special. It is a mixture, no, not quite a mixture, of blues, reds, pinks, ambers, and yellows that glows but illuminates nothing. Perhaps in this mysterious lavender—if that is what it is—powerlessness finally overwhelms power.

How with this rage can beauty hold a plea,
Whose action is no stronger than a flower?

This shade never leaves me and often comes to mind when I least expect it. If there is a heaven, this is its hue.

P.M.

Play

Sometimes we come closest to the gods in moments of play. When play is genuine, time is suspended, and we are lifted into an eternal Now, where passing away seems to pass away. The value of play, like fine art, is intrinsic. We might say of play what Heidegger says of a rose, that it is "without why." Always purposeless, the beauty of play is that it is not utilitarian; it is valuable because it is impractical. As Nietzsche teaches in his *Gay Science*, play, which is beyond good and evil, reveals the wisdom of unworldly folly and the folly of worldly wisdom.

In our sports-obsessed world, true play is rare. Ever eager to make a profit, crafty investors turn play into serious business. Customer recruitment begins when players are very young: children barely old enough to walk punch away on cell phones that carry video games; Nike runs sports camps to hook seventh-graders on expensive shoes; kids not yet in their teens compete for countless hours in massive multiuser online games, where they learn skills better suited for the trading floor than the playing field. When nothing escapes the logic of the market, losses become incalculable. These distortions of play have serious consequences—a society that has forgotten how to play has lost its way.

I have long thought the historic phases of economic development can be charted by the games people play: agrarian society loved baseball; industrial society, football; network society, basketball. It is not only the grass that makes baseball a field of dreams but also the leisurely pace of the game—nobody ever seems to be in a hurry. The long warm-ups, breaks between innings, walks to the mound, jumping in and out of the batter's box seem designed to slow everything down. Baseball is not governed by the clock and often seems to go on forever.

And then there is the spitting—what *is* it about baseball and spitting? In no other sports do athletes spit like baseball players. They spit on the ground, in their hands, on their bats, in their gloves, and, when they can get away with it, on the ball. It seems to be a ritual vestige of an earlier era when times were rough edges and had not yet been smoothed.

Football is all about strategy and timing, and as such it is the ideal game for the military-industrial complex. Metaphors of war dominate discussions of football, and violence is intrinsic to the game. More important, football is rigidly hierarchical—the command structure is strictly top-down. Plays are first diagrammed by coaches acting like generals and then executed by troops with the latest high-tech body armor heading into battle against a hostile enemy. Carefully staged rituals make the point obvious: fighter jets flying low in tight formation over stadiums, military paratroopers landing on fields, color guards carrying the flag, and high-soaring falcons released while fans belt out the national anthem. Warriors one and all.

Basketball is improvisational and spontaneously emergent rather than programmed and deliberately plotted. Like jazz, basketball is played best when it flows freely. Though some plays are planned, most are riffs that cannot be anticipated. The structure of the game is lateral rather than vertical, distributed and not hierarchical. Basketball does not conform to the logic of the industrial grid (iron) but follows the alternative logic of information networks. Though the court is circumscribed, the game is decentralized and the action is free-wheeling. If football players following commands recall movements on a chessboard, basketball players bumping into each other as they constantly adapt to the continuously changing flows surrounding them resemble packets darting across worldwide webs.

I enjoy no sport more than North Carolina basketball—not Red Sox–Yankees baseball, not Williams-Amherst football, but Carolina-Duke basketball. Several years ago I taught at UNC and had the good fortune to get to know Dean Smith, who is one of the most impressive people I have met.

CAROLINA VS. DUKE

What drew us together was my love of Tarheel basketball and his love of Kierkegaard. Dean reads theology and philosophy—Karl Barth, Paul Tillich, Rheinhold Niebuhr, and, above all others, Søren Kierkegaard—as seriously as I follow the team he coached for so many years. I guess it makes sense for the greatest coach in the history of college basketball to like the philosopher whose name is synonymous with "the leap of faith."

During my stay in Chapel Hill, we met regularly and our conversations drifted back and forth between basketball and religion. It quickly became apparent that basketball is a religion for both of us, but our faiths are different. Our contrasting faiths, we discovered, reflect alternative understandings of Kierkegaard.

Throughout his demanding writings, Kierkegaard identifies three stages through which each person must pass as he or she progresses from immaturity to maturity: aesthetic, ethical, and religious. At the aesthetic stage life is controlled by desire and people are immersed in sensuous immediacy. In a manner reminiscent of the Garden of Eden, the life of pleasure lies in the present. Without awareness of, or concern about, the future, there is no worry about tomorrow—the now is all that matters. The most obvious example of this stage on life's way is the infant, who is a creature of immediate desire and has not yet developed a broader sense of self and self-restraint. Aesthetic life, however, is not limited to infancy but can also be found among people who seem to be mature individuals. Adults remain infantile when their lives are governed by nothing more than the pleasure principle.

At the ethical stage people realize that life is about more than the pursuit of pleasure. They become aware of their freedom and their responsibility for their own lives. No longer completely controlled by desire, they learn to follow moral principles handed down by parents, pastors, and professors. For the ethical person life is a serious business and the stakes are very high. It is our responsibility to make the world a better place by following the principles and rules established by a moral god.

While never leaving behind the pleasures of the senses or rejecting the dictates of morality, religion is, according to Kierkegaard, beyond good and evil. In a manner reminiscent of aesthetic existence, religion involves an experience of eternity within time. At the decisive moment the eternal God enters history to redeem the believing individual by releasing him from the travails of time. This instant is the eternal Now in which time is suspended, death is overcome, and thus passing away passes away.

As Dean and I discussed these tangled issues at considerable length, we gradually began to realize that for him, religion and basketball are ethical, while for me they are aesthetic. Though a fierce competitor who never wants to lose, Dean believes that the value of the game is not intrinsic but lies in the lessons it holds for life after basketball. Always practicing what he preaches, he has devoted his life to defending the civil rights of others and promoting social justice for all. The game is never simply about itself but is always about life's larger lessons.

Dean was the first to integrate the Atlantic Coast Conference, and, when local restaurants would not serve his players, he accompanied them and refused to leave until they did. Several years ago my daughter, Kirsten, broke family ranks and went to Duke Law School. When she was writing an article about the death penalty, she called Dean and he gave her an interview about his opposition to it. What greater coup than publishing an interview with Dean Smith in the Duke newspaper! While the final score is important, for Dean Smith the game is really won off the court.

I do not, of course, deny the pedagogical value of sports. Throughout my youth I played baseball (first base), football (offensive guard and defensive tackle—times were different then!), and basketball (center). I have no doubt that I never would have written so many books without the discipline I learned on the field and court. But what makes a game a game is not simply the way it prepares us for the future but the way it locates us in the present. We play games for those rare moments when time stands still: the perfect contact of ball and bat, perfect angle for a clean tackle, perfect touch on a last-minute jump shot. In that instant players do not resolutely move toward the future by following the rules of the game; to the contrary, floating freely as if released from gravity, they live as fully as possible in the present. In this moment I no longer play but something else, something other, plays through me.

I know only three other experiences that come close to this moment: losing oneself in sexual bliss, immersing oneself in a work of art, or standing outside oneself in a moment of religious ecstasy. I suspect an experience like this is what Saint Paul had in mind when he wrote, "I live; yet not I, but Christ lives in me" (Galatians 2:20). As the very sense of self melts away, time and eternity actually become one. Though this instant inevitably passes, the memory of it creates the hope it might return once again.

Whenever I watch Carolina play, I always recall the lessons I learned from my conversations with Dean. My friend John and I get together to watch *the* game: my house when the Tarheels are at home, his house when the Blue Devils are at home. John is the former president of Williams College and past chairman of the Duke board of trustees, and at eighty-three he has lost none of his zest, either for the game or for life, if indeed the two can be distinguished. When the Heels have a bad night, I know my first e-mail in the morning will be from John, rubbing it in. When Duke falters, I always return the favor.

As professors of religion, we both know that any living religion needs its rituals so we have devised our own. We don our fool's caps and costumes—he wears his Duke hat and sweatshirt and I wear my Carolina hat and T-shirt. While eating popcorn and drinking soda, we leave behind the gravity of the moral problems facing our world and abandon ourselves to the "exuberant, floating, dancing, mocking, childless and blissful art" of basketball.

What I know, but John has yet to learn, is that the color of heaven is not Duke blue—it's Carolina blue.

FIFTEEN

A.M.

Perhaps

Perhaps you will have noticed that *perhaps* is one of the most important words in my vocabulary. I repeat it often, though perhaps not often enough. The issue is not just linguistic; it is philosophical, theological, perhaps even metaphysical. *Perhaps*: per (by) + chance (hap). It is not, however, by chance that I use this odd word so much. My design is deliberate, quite calculated—calculated, in fact, to suggest what I cannot exactly calculate.

Perhaps: Possibility with uncertainty, suspicion or doubt.
                    Something that may or may not happen (or exist).
                    A mere possibility.
                    A possible impossibility.
                    An impossible possibility.
                    Qualifying a word or a phrase, usually with ellipsis points....

… *Perhaps* … gives pause, interrupts, makes one hesitate even if only for an instant. The interval of … creates space and gives time for reflection that raises doubts without answering questions. "Perhaps." "Did she really mean it?" "Perhaps." "Did he really do it?" "Perhaps." "Did she really say that?" "Perhaps." "Is that really possible?" "Perhaps." "Isn't that really impossible?" "Perhaps."

In an age obsessed with certainty, we rarely hear the word *perhaps* anymore. Those who believe they are in power take *perhaps* to be a sign of weakness, perhaps unmanliness. They tout strength, not weakness; the unconditional, not the conditional; the unqualified, not the qualified. When *perhaps* insinuates itself into a conversation, a plan, or a program, everything goes off the rails. As long as *perhaps* is whispered, no one can be sure about anything or anybody. That is why its utterance is forbidden. It is, however, precisely because it is forbidden that *perhaps* must be spoken today more than ever. Though seemingly an inconsequential, perhaps even unnecessary, word wherever it occurs, *perhaps* is one of the most powerful words I know. In the presence of certainty and power, no other word is so disarming.

"Perhaps."

"What do you mean, 'Perhaps'"?

"Perhaps, just perhaps."

Precisely when it is least appreciated, *perhaps* must be repeated again and again and again....

P.M.

Numbers

For Pythagoras numbers were the substance of things seen and unseen—pure forms that transcend space and time yet nonetheless constitute the program on which the world runs. For those who know the code, nothing remains mysterious. If analysis is careful and calculation precise, numbers explain everything. This ancient faith still has many followers but I have always been skeptical. What if numbers do not tell the whole story? What if things are not so precise? Is life actually quantifiable? Is it numbers all the way down or all the way in? Can everything be measured? Everyone calculated? Every code broken? Every program debugged? What if nothing really and truly is incalculable?

In the beginning number or In the beginning word? I have always bet on word, Dinny has always bet on number. Perhaps my wager was the result of my inability to figure numbers. When faced with numbers to calculate, my synapses simply do not fire. This problem is not new and surely has not gotten better with age. In high school there were three subjects I never understood—algebra, trigonometry, and physics. I knew enough to avoid calculus. Unfortunately, Dinny and I had my father for physics, who, as a result of what seemed to me to be a misguided sense of fairness, refused to help me. Fortunately, Dinny was already there to bail me out. When I couldn't balance the equations or solve the problems, she invariably could. I do not know whether my father ever knew how much of my work was actually hers. My difficulty was more than a matter of ability, or so I liked to tell myself. It was metaphysical—all these numbers and calculations did not add up because they seem hopelessly abstract and totally removed from real life.

But all that changed in the critical care unit. During the interminable first night, no one spoke to me in a language I could understand. It wasn't just the Spanish of the two young doctors who never left my bedside, but even more baffling were the numbers—all kinds of numbers. I had no idea what they meant or even what they measured. When morning arrived nothing changed; new doctors, same language—numbers, numbers, and more numbers until my head was spinning. This was Dinny's domain, not mine, but she was not there to help me decipher the figures. Numbers I had never heard of the day before suddenly became a matter of life and death. While most of what the doctors said to me was incomprehensible, I understood enough to know that my condition was still critical. Dinny finally arrived to bail me out yet again. For the next four days she recorded numbers and plotted my ups and downs on graphs that charted my chances of survival.

As the days wore on, the numbers added up or, more precisely, did not add up. Numbers, countless numbers: 120/80 (blood pressure), 80–120

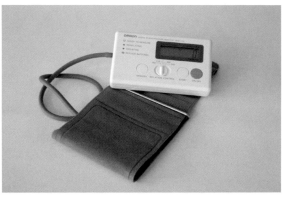

PRESSURE

(glucose), below 7 (glycohemoglobin), below 200 milligrams per deciliter (HDL cholesterol), below 100 (LDL cholesterol), 8,000–12,000 (white cell count), 12 million (red cell count), below 7 (Gleason score), below 3.5 grams per deciliter (albumin), 136–144 milliequivalents per liter (sodium), and finally a number Dinny and I had never heard of—creatinine. Creatinine, we learned, is a metabolic by-product maintained in the blood that provides a measure for kidney functions. The normal creatinine level is between 0.6 and 1.2 milligrams for every deciliter of blood. My reading was above 4, which signals serious distress or even organ failure. By the fourth day my kidneys still were not functioning. The doctors no longer thought I would die, but the creatinine level refused to move below 4.0, which, when the test is physical rather than mental, is a failing grade. My diabetes complicated my condition, and the doctors were very concerned about risking further damage to my kidneys. They reluctantly decided to start dialysis. Before attaching me to the machine I had dreaded ever since being diagnosed with diabetes, they did one more blood test. Much to their surprise, my creatinine level unexpectedly had dropped to 3.8, which was still dangerously high but was at least heading in the right direction. Over the next few days, this mysterious number continued to drop, and my kidneys gradually began to function again, but it took two months for my creatinine level to return to normal. The final blood test for this condition showed that my kidneys had sustained no permanent damage. Only then did Dinny put her graph away.

Though I had always resisted the conclusion, I had to admit that Pythagoras might be right—perhaps it is numbers all the way down and all the way in. How many more numbers that take life's measure remain unknown to me? What will it take for me to discover them? At critical moments life turns on a point as small as a decimal. In the CCU metaphysics takes a backseat—I joined Dinny and bet on numbers. I have no doubt that this is one time my father would not have minded Dinny's helping me with my homework.

SIXTEEN

A.M.

Pleasure

PURITAN GHOSTS

Pleasure is never satisfying because it always leaves one wanting. Satisfaction overcomes lack and restores balance by fulfilling expectations. Though rarely admitted, the sense of completion that satisfaction brings harbors death even if life continues. Those who are satisfied are the living dead roaming, which is not to say erring, in our midst. Fulfillment, it seems, is a perfect equilibrium and as such is entropy in which differences become indifferent. As the circle closes, Omega and Alpha finally become One—completion brings the loss of difference.

Pleasure, or its prospect, by contrast, is never fulfilling—it unsettles, disrupts, and throws off balance. Instead of realizing our expectations, the prospect of pleasure disturbs by interrupting our plans and suspending projects. Neither satisfying nor dissatisfying, pleasure creates blissful dis-ease that leaves everything incomplete. Always approaching when least ex-pected, pleasure surprises, often overwhelms; it is given rather than sought. Whatever, whoever, gives pleasure inevitably teases—pleasure's giving is a taking, its draw a withdrawal. Freud had it wrong: pleasure increases rather than decreases tension. When opposites meet but are not united, tensions approach the breaking point by keeping irreconcilable differences in play. The greater the difference, the more the tension, and the more the tension, the more the pleasure. That which is rent cannot be whole. Rather than the moment of release, pleasure is the instant just before it, when differences are united in the strife that divides them. Maximizing instead of minimiz-ing tension, pleasure is inseparable from pain; indeed, the tears of pain are the joy of pleasure. Herein lies the inexpressible pleasure of crucifixion without resurrection: time and eternity, hate and love, violence and peace, death and life joined but not united in one exquisite instant.

Pleasure is always excessive—enough is never enough. In the moment of pleasure, the only word that can be uttered is *more, more, more*. Far from echoing a void to be filled, this *more* resounds with the emptiness of life overflowing. Equilibrium must be infinitely deferred for life to continue. In the incalculable calculus of pleasure, things are always out of balance, slightly off key, and life is richest far from equilibrium. When life is want-ing, pleasure is endless. The pleasure zone is the boundary, margin, limit beyond which I cannot go and without which life, which is never my own, is impossible.

P.M.

Money

For Protestants sex is a problem but money is a bigger problem. Ac-cording to the gospel by which I was raised, those who save are saved and those who spend are damned. In this vision of life money is always filthy lucre, which, as Luther never tired of preaching, is the work of the devil. The faithful do not labor so they can spend but work so they can save. In the austere lines of the faces of my puritanical ancestors, I read the gospel of redemption: saving saves. Nothing is further from this Protestant principle than the gospel of easy wealth and prosperity preached in today's high-tech megachurches and promoted in the bully pulpits of our hectoring politicians and theological economists.

In the house where I grew up, we never talked about sex but always talked about money. This was, in part, because there often was not enough of it. Money was scarce and for many years medical bills were exorbitant. In addition to this there was, of course, my parents' ever-present memory of the Depression. Having lived through the uncertainties of that period, they and their generation never could believe the future was secure. One lesson they learned was that no matter how tough the times, borrowing is never an option. My mother and father had been taught by their parents that debt is sin in more than a metaphorical sense. I cannot count the times my mother drilled into me the principle upon which her father insisted the economy of salvation rests. Since she taught literature, it was fitting that her catechism was Shakespearean rather than biblical.

> Never a borrower nor a lender be;
> For loan oft loses both itself and friend,
> And borrowing dulls the edge of husbandry.

Through all their difficulties my parents never had a single nickel of debt; indeed, they didn't even take out a mortgage to buy the only house they ever owned. Although he was earning a paltry $3,000 a year and had two sons at home, one son institutionalized, and his wife in the hospital for long stays, my father somehow managed to pay for our house in cash.

Just as sex is never simply about sex, so money is never simply about money. The underlying or overriding issue in both cases is pleasure. What my parents seemed to fear more than anything else was pleasure and the excesses it often brings. There is, admittedly, something promiscuous about money that arouses suspicions even among those devoted to it. Especially when it is ungrounded and becomes nothing more than bits of light flickering on terminal screens connected on worldwide webs, money always threatens to reproduce so fast that it loses its value. When family discussions turned to the perils of spending, as they often did, it was hard for me not to sense the presence of my grandmother's ghost. She wore only black dresses and her Mennonite bonnet her whole life and forbade dancing, drinking, and cards in her home—all forms of pleasure were banned. She had eight children but sex, I suspect, was more a duty than a pleasure. Though she died young, she obviously had enough time to teach her son well—indeed, all too well.

I have searched the most distant corners of my memory, and it is difficult for me to conjure a single image of my parents enjoying a pleasurable moment. After their deaths I did, however, find a small photograph that might have captured a rare moment of pleasure. They were young and did not yet know the difficult hand life soon would deal them. They are standing under an outdoor shower at the beach in their bathing suits; my father wears a broad smile and my mother actually seems to be giggling.

HAPPY TIMES

Long after it was unnecessary, my parents insisted on saving as much as possible. In later years they continued to believe they could not afford what they clearly could. More than a way of life, not spending had become a justification of the lives they had chosen to lead. My brother and I often encouraged them to enjoy the rewards they surely had earned, insisting that they had more than paid their dues. But it was to no avail—they would not or could not enjoy themselves. As the years wore on and old patterns persisted, I began to see something else at work in their resistance to changing their habits. It was not so much that they rejected pleasure but, having denied themselves so long, they had actually come to take pleasure in their refusal of it. Of course, they never could admit this to themselves without calling into question their most basic beliefs. Up until the end of their lives, my mother and father were unable to see in their saving the very pleasure they condemned in others' spending and so could never embrace what they had so long found unacceptable. One of the lessons I have drawn from the lives that my parents lived is no doubt the opposite of what they were intending. When saving becomes excessive, it no longer saves, and the refusal of pleasure can warp the very soul it is designed to redeem.

But, then, one night when the waiter brings the check and it is considerably more than I expected, the specter of guilt once again raises its head. Against my will I find myself asking, "What would Mom say about this?"

SEVENTEEN

A.M.

Vocation

VISITING KIRCHE WURZBRUNNEN, ROTHENBACH, SWITZERLAND,
THE CHURCH WHERE MY NINTH GREAT-GRANDFATHER AND -GRANDMOTHER
WERE BAPTIZED IN 1598 AND 1602, RESPECTIVELY

Is it possible to believe in vocation if you do not believe in one who calls? I have never considered my work a job or even a career; indeed, I'm not sure I really regard it as work. Rather, teaching and writing are vocations and that means they are callings. It is no accident that many of the oldest and most prestigious universities and colleges in this country were founded by New England Protestants and initially were led by pastors. The commitment to the Word runs deep even in those who do not know or even vehemently reject their own heritage.

If, however, teaching and writing are vocations, who calls and what is calling? Though I was raised a Protestant, when others hear voices, I hear silence. I don't believe you can ever be sure that what you hear is the voice of God. For Protestants, God is always a *Deus absconditus,* who shows himself by hiding. Even when Luther could do no other, he, no more than Kierkegaard's Abraham, could be sure the voice he was hearing was that of God rather than Satan.

But what if neither God nor Satan were calling? In the absence of God, it is always possible that what sounds like a call from beyond is actually the echo of an inner void that can never be filled. If there is a vocation without one who calls, then perhaps silence is the Word that must be spoken. The responsibility of the teacher and writer who hears by not hearing is to sow seeds of doubt wherever there is certainty, to find fault in every foundation deemed firm, to weave insecurity into the very fabric of security. The vocation of the person called by the silence of the Word is not to expose the impossibility of faith but to show the inescapability of faith for those who believe it impossible.

P.M.

Teaching

Teaching is serious business and should never be taken lightly. Over the years I have discovered that the most difficult question I face as a teacher is how far into the night beyond night to take my students. It is easy, all too easy, to lure with meditations on dread, despair, and death adolescents who are struggling with questions of their identity. They are vulnerable at this age, and that vulnerability poses both a danger as well as an opportunity. I never fully appreciated the threat posed by the materials I teach until one of my students committed suicide. There have since been others.

Though I had pondered the responsibility of teaching over the years, the question emerged with unavoidable urgency during an undergraduate seminar I taught in the spring of 1988. The title of the course was "Noth-

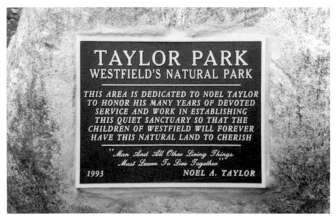

PLAQUE AT THE PARK HONORING MY FATHER, WESTFIELD, N.J.

ing" and the authors we read included Nietzsche, Poe, Melville, Kafka, Heidegger, Mishima, Sartre, Beckett, and Blanchot. Though all the writers proved challenging to the students, it was a particularly bleak account of a dinner conversation in Sartre's *Nausea* that prompted the question that had been lurking just beneath the surface all semester.

> "I was just thinking," I tell him, laughing, "that here we sit, all of us, eating and drinking to preserve our precious existence and really there is nothing, nothing, absolutely no reason for existing."

I began the discussion by placing Sartre's remark in a tradition extending from Kierkegaard through Heidegger to Camus. When I mentioned Camus, a student raised his hand and asked, "Isn't Camus the guy who killed himself in a car wreck?"

"Yes," I answered, "but that's not the only response to the human dilemma as existentialists see it. Rather than making life unbearable, the absence of a given meaning for our lives gives us the opportunity to create our own meanings. Far from the most radical act of freedom, suicide is a flight from the very freedom that makes us human."

Though Jake was silent, I knew he was not satisfied, and eventually he intervened. He knew all too well that many writers that I teach never came back from elsewhere.

"That's too easy," Jake insisted. "The real question is about hope. If Sartre is right, how can we hope? And if we cannot hope, why go on?"

In that moment time stood still—the issue I had been avoiding for so many years suddenly was on the table. Should I tell the students what they wanted, perhaps needed, to hear or should I tell them what I really thought? A lifetime of reading, writing, and teaching flashed through my mind in that instant. Having learned my lessons all too well, I once again avoided the unavoidable by ducking the question. Rather than telling them what I really thought, I proceeded to explain how the writers we were reading would have responded to the question. Scholars, after all, are not supposed to think for themselves but are trained to analyze and report what others have already thought. Jake was generous enough not to press his question. But he knew that I had not answered his query, and, when our eyes met, I knew that he knew that I knew I had failed his test.

I suspect Jake has long since forgotten his question but I have not. Indeed, I ponder its far-reaching implications every semester. The joy of teaching the young is watching them come alive as they encounter questions and ideas they never before imagined; the frustration of teaching the young is that they have not lived long enough to be able to understand many of the most important lessons I would like to share with them.

This is the abiding dilemma of teaching: On the one hand, do I have the right to deprive young people of hope by telling them of the suffering and uncertainty awaiting them? On the other hand, if I am not honest with them about what lies ahead, will they think I betrayed them when they inevitably encounter what we spend most of our lives trying to avoid? Does the journey to the end of night prepare young people to cope when darkness surrounds them or does it draw them into a bottomless abyss? After forty years of teaching, I still do not know the answers to these questions.

EIGHTEEN

A.M.

Last

HAUNTING GRAVE RUBBINGS OF MY GHOSTS

Though always singular, the last time is endlessly repeated. Sometimes you know, often you don't—the last chance, the last class, the last book, the last dance, the last laugh, the last time you make love, the last time you see your daughter or son, the last supper. The last lesson my mother taught me—not once but twice—was the importance of the last time.

When the phone rings in the middle of the night, it's never good news. The trembling voice on the other end of the line was my father's, telling me that my mother had suffered a massive cerebral hemorrhage and was on life support. This was not the first time I had received such a call; seventeen years earlier I was in Copenhagen writing my dissertation, when my father had called with the same message. That time she survived, this time she would not—her brain, the doctor explained, "had exploded."

I arrived the next day and met my father and brother at the same hospital where she had undergone brain surgery nearly two decades earlier. As we stood around her bed, the silence was broken by the rhythmic pulsation of the respirator. Late in the afternoon we met with the neurologist and he repeated his assessment: she could be kept alive indefinitely but there was absolutely no chance of recovery. The decision was clear though no easier for that reason. Her surprising—indeed, seemingly miraculous—survival after the first stroke made the decision all the more difficult this time. If then, why not now? Dad was a scientist and knew it was impossible, though it took time to persuade his heart to let go. Finally, we made the decision we knew we could not avoid and returned to the ICU to say good-bye for the last time. Before leaving, I leaned over and kissed her on the cheek—her body was warm, her face damp with perspiration. Four hours later the phone once again rang in the middle of the night; it was the doctor informing us that my mother had died at 2:10 A.M. The timing was uncanny: premonitions of premonitions.

The last time I saw my mother, she was lying in the casket wearing the clothes we had chosen for her. She looked remarkably serene. A few years earlier my father's closest friend had asked him to take photographs of his wife while she was in the coffin. Though appalled, Dad could not decline the request. As he stood beside his wife for the last time, he recalled taking those pictures. Since my parents had decided they did not want public funerals, we had a brief ceremony for the immediate family before driving 140 miles to the Pennsylvania cemetery where she would be buried. When others left, I lingered for a private moment with her. Once again I leaned over and kissed her cheek for the last time. Her body was no longer warm and moist but was now hard and cold—stone hard, stone cold. One moment there is life, the next moment there is death. What vanishes in that instant?

Ever the teacher, in death my mother had a final lesson for me: every moment is the last moment or, in terms I would later read elsewhere, the last time returns eternally. This awareness need not weigh us down, though it often does; rather, it can lift us up by helping us to realize the infinite value of what is always passing away.

P.M.

Burial

In our family cremation was never an option. "Proper" burial was an obligatory ritual whose script remained constant from generation to generation: evening reception and viewing with open casket, morning service at a funeral "home" or "parlor," procession to the cemetery, brief words delivered by a minister at graveside, lowering of the casket into the ground, and, finally, tossing a handful of earth on top of the highly polished coffin. After the service family and friends gathered at the home of the deceased for a light lunch—no alcohol allowed.

GRANDPA COOPER'S JEWELRY STORE, WILLIAMSTOWN, PA.

The first burial I remember was that of my maternal grandfather, whose name I bear. There had been other funerals that probably had a greater impact on me but of which I was unaware when they occurred—a sister before I was born and a brother when I was eight. I remember every detail of Mark Cooper's funeral in the small erstwhile coal-mining town of Williamstown, Pennsylvania, as if it were yesterday—the faces of his wife and daughters; the words of condolence offered by friends; commemoratives with name, birth and death dates, and biblical verse left like calling cards for eternity; the excessively sweet smell of the lilies; the order of the service; the Lutheran hymns; the dampness of the earth; the dirt on my hands after sending him my final missive; the Pennsylvania Dutch spread my grandmother somehow managed to prepare. As more deaths followed, the familiarity of the ritual brought a sense of continuity and even a semblance of comfort.

All this changed, however, with the unexpected death of my mother. My father was devastated; his grief so incapacitated him that my brother and I had to assume responsibility for, as they euphemistically say, making all "the arrangements." Unlike so many couples, my parents had discussed death and knew each other's final wishes. Rather than be buried in the town where they had lived, raised my brother and me, and buried their son, whose casket they could not bear

COOPER GRAVESITE

to leave open, they decided to return to the town where they had met and be buried in the ground where I first saw an open grave. As we worked out the details with the minister and funeral director, the ritual that had seemed reassuring became brutally disturbing. The funeral director posed intolerable questions with a scripted sympathy designed to disguise financial interests: What kind of vault? The better the company, the more concrete, the thicker the walls, and the firmer the seal. What kind of casket—metal or wood? If metal, what color and gauge? If wood, what kind and what finish?

Whether metal or wood, what color for the satin lining? Unlike the vaults, the coffins were displayed like freezers lined up in an appliance store at the local mall. And for everything the price list was carefully calibrated to gauge guilt. How can you cut corners when it's for eternity? All this was bad enough but the funeral director's final words were the most shattering: "First thing tomorrow morning, please drop off the clothes and jewelry you want me to dress her in for burial." How can you possibly decide what clothes your mother wants to wear for eternity?

Though unnerved by my mother's burial, we followed the same ritual when my father died four years later. The experience was less traumatic only because we knew the drill. Matching vaults, matching caskets, only the color of the satin is different. Knowing beforehand that we would have to choose my father's burial clothes made the request to deliver them less shocking. Left to ourselves to make decisions, we honored his wishes but made some modifications: only family, open casket; Reformed, not Lutheran, service; Twenty-third Psalm; Lord's Prayer; no hymns. The drive to Williamstown seemed longer than ever.

Years later I was writing an essay for a collection of photographs of the graves of figures I dubbed my ghosts. As my work approached completion, I concluded that I could not finish the book without coming clean about what will happen to my body after I die. As I pondered this final decision, I realized that old customs die hard. Cremation was no more an option for me than it had been for my parents and grandparents. I will not, however, return to the Williamstown of my ancestors but will remain forever in the Williamstown where I have lived, worked, and raised our family.

I will be buried at the edge of the cemetery that lies on the edge of town in the shadow of Mount Greylock. The plot is close to a stand of white pine that line a gentle bend in the nearby Green River. I have always believed that the edge is the only place where it is worth living and will not give up that conviction in death. Though I believe death is final and there is nothing beyond the grave, along the edge nothing remains fixed. The only hope I harbor is that the noise of the river will keep me awake so I can wander with my ghosts and perhaps haunt others as they have haunted me. I have not told Dinny, Kirsten, and Aaron what clothes I would like to wear for eternity. That decision will be theirs.

MY GRAVE MARKER

NINETEEN

A.M.

Solitude

LOOKOUT

Solitude is what everyone has in common and as such is what consti-
tutes our essential humanity. Whereas isolation separates and individual-
izes, solitude relates and universalizes. Far from suppressing singularity,
the essentiality and universality of solitude cultivate the singular as their
necessary condition. While singularity makes us unique and thus irreplaceable, it is not the source of our identity because the singular can never
be identified as such. It is utterly idiomatic and therefore is inevitably lost
in translation. Since the untranslatable cannot be communicated, what I
hold in common with others is the incommunicability of a singularity that
is never precisely my own.

The difficulty of bearing the demands of singularity leads to the ten-
dency to seek distractions in specious forms of universality in which all

are one, even if one is not all. The so-called community that arises from such universality is a distinctively modern disease carried by the technologies of mass media and the mass movements they facilitate. Every form of universality or essentiality that represses the differences that make a person what he or she is should be resolutely resisted. This is not to imply that individuals are windowless monads with nothing in common. The choice is not between a unity that represses differences and oppositions that fragment commonality. Solitude points to a third alternative that some describe as the middle way.

Even when eagerly desired, solitude can be neither willed or chosen; it arrives as an unexpected event—perhaps even gift—for which no preparation is adequate. Solitude usually occurs in liminal situations when experience is most intense. These moments can be times of overwhelming joy or devastating grief. Essential solitude emerges not only when we are alone but also when we are with others who sometimes are very close to us. What characterizes all such experiences is the awareness that they cannot be shared. Solitude therefore involves a profound paradox: we are most apart when we are most together and most together when we are most apart. Far from exclusive opposites, universality and singularity are inseparable: singularity is inescapably universal, and universality can be only in and through multiple singulars that it relates without uniting. Drawing together by holding apart and holding apart by drawing together, solitude reveals a community without communion that can endure the trials of tine.

P.M.

Loneliness

In the end it was loneliness that killed my father. When he closed the door as I drove away, the only house that had ever been his home became a crypt from which he could not escape. No matter how wide he opened the windows, there was not enough light for him to see or enough air for him to breathe. You don't have to be interred to be buried alive.

When his home became a tomb, he would go outside. Day after day he would walk mile after mile—three, four, five, sometimes seven miles. His body, unlike mine, had not betrayed him. He once told me that he never thought about getting old until he turned eighty! Up to the day he died, his stamina was extraordinary. He cut his own grass, cultivated his own garden, and gave the flowers and vegetables he grew to friends. Twenty years later I received a note from a woman telling me that she still made pies from the rhubarb he transplanted from his garden to hers. In winter he cleared the snow not only from his sidewalk and driveway but from the sidewalks and driveways of all his neighbors, many of whom were less than half his age. All these activities were, however, diversions and, at the end of the day, when night once again closed in, they failed to divert.

What he missed most were the small things—a late-afternoon glass of wine in the backyard, sitting in the kitchen while my mother prepared dinner, quiet talk over morning coffee. The wisdom of philosophers notwithstanding, at a certain point in life idle chatter comes closer to reality than anything else. In her absence empty hours were impossible to fill. Visits from friends and phone calls from family brought momentary relief but, when they were over, the void returned and with it my guilt. In his time of greatest need, I could not be there. His sincere understanding of the personal and professional obligations I faced offered no consolation and only deepened my guilt.

LIKE SON   LIKE FATHER

When the end came, he was alone. A neighbor whom my father regularly greeted on his walks missed him for several days. When the neighbor entered the house, he found Dad on the floor. I do not know how long he had been dead—my brother and I refused to authorize an autopsy. Regardless of what the coroner would have written on the death certificate, I knew the cause of death: loneliness.

The curse of old age is loneliness. Even when others are near, loneliness is inescapable. When I now think about him, I realize that my father's past is my future—and the future of every person I hold dear.

TWENTY

A.M.

Things

GRANDMA COOPER'S STEREOSCOPE

Things never seem stranger than when cleaning out the possessions of the dead. For the living, things are not mere things but are animated by the lives lived through them. Animists are not completely mistaken: things *are* the extension of the person, even the embodiment of spirit. We know each other by the things we value and possess. Though we appear to own things, they really own us.

While things were never very important to my parents, as they grew older, they became obsessed with a few special things: my mother's antiques, figurines, and pitcher collection; my father's cameras, photography equipment, and hunting rifles, shotguns, even his father's muzzle loader. And, of course, their books—above all, their books. During our visits in the years before their deaths, my mother often felt compelled to lecture my brother and me: "Now when we die, don't throw out this stuff—it's valuable." Tired of her badgering and eager to keep her occupied, we bought her a book that listed current market prices of glassware so she could catalogue the value of her collections. It was to have been a Christmas gift but she died five days before she would have opened it. Her point, of course, was never the things or the money but her dread of oblivion. What she feared was not the loss of her things but the loss of the memory of her life.

When Beryl and I were cleaning out the house after they both had died, we discovered that our mother had tucked slips of paper in many of the pitchers and cruets with notes explaining when and where she had acquired them and what they meant to her. We did not sell them or give them away—how could we with her warnings still haunting us? Their things, however, were not for us what they had been for them. So we wrapped the glass and china in newspaper and packed them away. When the life that enlivens them is gone, things are just things. While stuffing boxes with their things, I said to my brother, "Some day after you die, your sons will clear out your garage and will find these boxes of glassware. They will wonder where it all came from and why you had kept all of it." With neither reason nor space to keep what is no longer valuable or useful, they will dispose of their grandparents' most precious things.

KIERKEGAARD BOOKS

HEGEL BOOKS

The things that matter most to me are my books—nearly twenty thousand the last time I checked but I stopped counting years ago. People always ask me if I've read all the books I own and the honest answer is yes. Long ago I decided that if a book isn't worth reading, it's not worth keeping. Once I've read a book, I cannot get rid of it, even when I know I'll never open it again. The course of my life can be read in the books that line my shelves—I have become what they are. No one else—not even those closest to me—understands the story, and I know that when I die, my library, and with it my self, will be scattered beyond recollection.

P.M.

Ghosts

I realize that a person with two doctorates is not supposed to believe in ghosts, but I do. Though we are reluctant to say it, honesty compels us to admit that we are all haunted. The dead are not gone but remain present as absent, and their absence disturbs our presence. There is, I believe, no afterlife other than this haunting. But haunting is always double, for we are like ghosts to our ghosts. Having been elsewhere, I now suspect that the dead fear the living as much as the living fear the dead. Ghosts make us what we are by never allowing us to be ourselves, and in return we give them the only voice they have.

The longer I have been working on this book, the less certain I have become about who is writing it. Never merely representing what the writer already knows, the narrative transforms the author into a person he never before has been. Though events are always episodic and the script necessarily incomplete, there is no self apart from the stories we tell ourselves as well as others. Stories without facts are possible; facts without stories are not.

As the chapters accumulate, however, my doubt grows because I am no longer sure these stories are really my own. I have begun to suspect that words I thought were mine are really the words of others. I know it sounds crazy, but the only way I can describe what is happening is that spirits seem to be speaking through me. It is almost as if my words are resurrecting the dead. I do not know whether these shades were lurking at the edge of the world before I put pencil to paper or whether words I mistakenly thought were my own awoke them from their slumber. While words have become suspect, I have no doubt that these spirits are real and shadow me everywhere I go. Gazing through the scrims on which my world is screened, I glimpse fleeting faces of ghosts—some I recognize, many I do not.

For many years I have done grave rubbings of those I call my ghosts: Kierkegaard, Hegel, Marx, Melville, Poe, Sartre, Dickinson, and Stevens. These tracings are hanging in my living room, apartment, office, and study. I also collect relics of the dead. Nearly two decades ago I visited Hegel's grave in Berlin for the first time. He is buried between his wife and Fichte and a few rows away from Brecht and Bonhoeffer. When I saw that Hegel's grave is covered with ivy, I could not resist digging up a clump and smuggling it into the United States. It is still growing in my living room in Williamstown. From time to time I give a close friend a clipping with instructions on how to cultivate it and dire warnings of the consequences of letting it die. Since then I have added ivy from Melville's grave in the Bronx to my collection. It is sitting beside me on the desk where I am composing these words. There is something about material traces that draws me closer to my ghosts. I figure there must be molecules of Hegel and Melville in there somewhere.

Several years ago a former student, Christian Lammerts, and I published *Grave Matters,* which is a book of 150 original photographs of the gravesites of those I regard as the greatest modern philosophers, theologians, writers, artists, architects, and composers. At each gravesite we dug up some dirt and put it into film canisters. Once again I smuggled illicit material back into the country. The book aroused considerable interest and I was invited to do an art exhibition at the Massachusetts Museum of Contemporary Art. I had never done anything like that before and had to figure out what would most effectively complement the photographs. I finally decided to create a sculpture using the dirt we had collected. The work that resulted was surprisingly effective and now hangs in my barn.

Not all my ghosts, of course, are famous. On the bookshelf next to the sculpture of the remains of the 150 modern greats, as well as about twenty others who did not make the cut, there is a small container of dirt from the

GRAVE MATTERS

country Anabaptist church in Rothenbach, Switzerland, where my ninth great-grandfather and -grandmother were christened in 1598 and 1602, respectively.

These spirits do not talk to each other, nor do they speak directly to me even as they clamor to speak through me. Though their movements are lethargic, their actions are insistent. The ghosts I harbor seem to have been waiting many years for someone to lend them voice and now want to be heard. I did not ask them to appear and cannot make them disappear. As I have learned to listen to words I cannot silence, I am discovering that spirits always haunt the interstices of memory, allowing us to say what we say and preventing us from revealing what they want to conceal. If we are ever to understand ourselves, we must be willing to believe in spirits at least for a while. There is wisdom in the songs of shamans if we are patient enough to listen and free enough to dance.

The longer I listen to the clamor of my ghosts, the more I suspect that the silence of one overwhelms the noise of all the others. In ways I will never fathom, everything I have written is a testimony to my dead sister. Indeed, I doubt I ever would have become a writer or a teacher were it not for the constant presence of her absence. She leaves me no rest and for this I would like to thank her. But I cannot, and so all I can do is hope that the words I write might serve as the inscription on the tombstone she does not have.

TWENTY-ONE

A.M.

Levity

GRANDPA COOPER IN DRAG

The miracle: almost having after having had not. The indifference to in-difference harbors duplicity. In a world where nothing matters, nothing is ever what it seems. Having is having-not and not-having is, perhaps, the only way of having. Nothing seems more grave than indifference; indeed, the burden of "Nothing matters" can plunge one into a fathomless abyss of despair. After all, what weight could be greater than the weight of noth-ing? Yet "nothing matters" is light—terribly light. The recognition of the insubstantiality of it all can prepare the way for overcoming gravity. In this new physics, which is no longer a metaphysics, equations must be rewrit-ten and calculations refigured:

Gravity = Everything matters
Levity = Nothing matters

With the loss of gravity, nothing remains serious. When nothing weighs us down, we lose our moorings and are left to float freely. The levity that allows levitation is not measured by our distance from the ground but by the way we walk the earth. Paradoxically, the loss of gravity allows us to remain earthbound.

The lightness of touch signals—albeit indirectly—a serious grasp of nothing. To walk the earth with indifference, we must hold on by letting go. If we are not to sink under the weight of responsibility for making a difference, our holding must be a releasing. Having is a miracle because our having is always a having-not. When we have by having-not, we are able to hold on by letting go. If levity is what allows us to remain earthbound, then nothing is more serious than the lack of gravity. Far from insignificant, levity is nothing more and nothing less than the bearable lightness of being not.

P.M.

Grief

I never understood grief before the nights I spent with my father after my mother's death. Like everyone else, I had encountered and experienced the sadness and dismay that come with loss. I discovered, however, that such sadness is not really grief. Though there had been premonitions, my mother's death five days before Christmas and eight days before the party we had planned to celebrate their fiftieth wedding anniversary was nonetheless unexpected. Invitations had already been sent, and everyone was looking forward to a festive gathering of family and friends. But life or, rather, death intervened. Instead of last-minute shopping and wrapping presents, we spent Christmas Eve driving back from the small Pennsylvania town where we had buried my mother beside her father and mother. The next morning my father insisted that we proceed with the Christmas morning ritual by having the kids open their presents. Perhaps because his name was Noel, Christmas had always been a special holiday for him. It had been my mother's custom to accompany each gift with a short note about its significance. In recent years she had started supplementing traditional gifts with mementos that had been particularly meaningful to her. This year her notes took on added importance because they were the last things she ever wrote.

A haunted house is no place for children at Christmastime. We were, however, torn between our responsibility to our son and daughter and our obligation to their grandfather. Their presence brought him momentary relief from his crushing grief. Eventually, they had to leave to return to school, and my father and I were left alone. The silence was deafening but neither of us knew how to fill it. Her absence absolutely overpowered our presence. We both realized but could not say that her death was the end of his life. You just don't start over when you are eighty, and things never get back to normal when you lose the person who has been closest to you for more than fifty years. During the next week a steady stream of friends stopped by to offer their condolences. Since my father could not or would not speak, I was left to fill the void. Many of these people I did not know and others I had not seen for many years, so conversation was often strained. Though intended to comfort, their words left me angry: "This will pass." "Things will get better with time." "You must go on with your life—she would have wanted it that way." What life? Didn't they realize that she *was* his life? Didn't they know some wounds must be left open? Forgetting is the final insult hurled at the life that is no longer.

Days were difficult, nights impossible. With his grandchildren gone, constraints were lifted and the full fury of his grief erupted. Shortly after midnight on the first night we were alone, I awoke to the sound of a wailing I never before had heard. Coming from a depth hard to fathom, it was loud enough to fill the whole house. I could hear him thrashing in bed but was unable to decipher his occasional words. My first impulse was to rush to reassure him but on further reflection decided he needed to be alone. His moaning and screaming continued till dawn.

The next morning, nothing was said about the previous night. After all, what was there to say? We both knew that words cannot express the inexpressible; in the face of such grief, words of comfort become trivial. We tried to fill days with distractions—chores around the house, shopping, and long walks. He was not ready to get rid of her things but did want to go through them with me. He mumbled more to himself than to me: "Who would like this?" "Is this worth saving?" "Whom would she want to have that?" Night after night the wailing returned and still nothing was said—or perhaps what had to be said was said by saying nothing.

The day finally came when I had to leave. He insisted he was OK; I knew he was not. If his grief had been out of control when I had been there, what would happen when I was not? But I had no choice—family and work were calling. He cooked his specialty for breakfast—eggs, smoked sausage, and scrapple from his Pennsylvania Dutch homeland. We chatted idly about the upcoming semester and what I would be teaching. I told him I was doing a new course entitled "Nothing" that had the largest enrollment of any I had ever taught; he did not respond. As the time for my departure approached, I packed the car with many of my mother's things that he wanted me to have. Though it was a cold, gray January morning, he stood near the front door in shirtsleeves waving as I drove away. Nothing I have ever done was harder than leaving him alone that day.

TWENTY-TWO

A.M.

Humor

THELMA LOUISE AND MARK COOPER
STROLLING ON THE BOARDWALK,
WILDWOOD, N.J.

The most reliable index of a person's perceptiveness, I have long believed, is his or her sense of humor. In medieval physiology *humor* referred to one of the four bodily fluids (blood, phlegm, choler, and black bile) believed to determine a person's temperament. Gradually, it came to be associated with a particular disposition characterized by levity and playfulness. Far from the frivolous recognition of foolishness, this disposition grows out of a sophisticated awareness of life's contradictions, incongruities, incommensurabilities, even absurdity. Though I had written about humor, I did not really understand it before lingering in that night beyond night from which no one expected me to return. In that darkness I realized that if humor is not affirmed in the face of the most profound suffering and adversity, it is trivial.

Before that night I had never been sure why Kierkegaard, often dubbed "the melancholy Dane," always called himself a humorist. Insisting that humor is the form of awareness that most closely approximates faith, he once went so far as to claim that "Christianity is the most humorous view of life in world-history." The humorist accepts the limitations of human finitude and recognizes the folly of trying to overcome them. While irony reflects the sense of pride that accompanies the feeling of superiority, humor expresses a sense of humility that comes from a feeling of equality. The ironist's wink signals a higher awareness that comes when one knows a secret others do not. The humorist's laugh shows that he knows there is no secret, or knows that the most important secrets cannot be told, which amounts to the same thing. The ironist thinks he gets the joke; the humorist realizes the joke is always on him. While irony divides, humor unites; high becomes low, but low does not become high. Humor levels in a way that discloses our common humanity, which the social ranks of everyday life repress. The humorist realizes that we are all in this together and there is no exit.

Humor should not be confused with comedy. It is commonplace to understand Christianity as a divine comedy in which everything works out in the end and at least those who are chosen live happily ever after. Life, of course, never follows this script(ure)—endings are never happy precisely because they are endings. Humor makes it possible to accept the impossibility of happy endings and to insist on the folly of thinking it should be otherwise.

Humor brings release that is closer to Luther's grace than Freud's reduction of tension. The greatest levity is found in moments of the most profound gravity. Then, and only then, can we confess that the wisdom of the world is folly. Not until we let go of the conviction that things should be otherwise are we free to go on in the face of the inevitable failure of our struggles to make a difference. When life's darkest moments cast a shadow over all that had seemed important, the faithful response is to burst into uncontrollable laughter.

P.M.

Monsters

It is a mistake to assume that monsters are either from the distant past or are nothing more than idle fantasies of overheated imaginations; to the contrary, they actually dwell in our midst. We create fairy tales, science fiction, video games, hospitals, asylums, gulags, and prisons to protect us from monstrous realities in our midst whose presence we are not strong enough to bear. What makes monsters so threatening is not their difference from us but their similarity to us. The distance we establish between ourselves and those we deem monstrous testifies to a proximity we can never avoid. Though we struggle to deny it, monsters remain our close relatives. What, then, might it mean to have a brother who is a monster?

Brent was my parents' third child, born between Beryl and me. It was obvious from the moment of his birth that he was not normal; he suffered an acute case of Down syndrome and was severely deformed. In the years before amniocentesis and genetic screening, my parents had no reason to expect any problems during the pregnancy. But things went badly awry. My mother had been anesthetized for the birth for several hours so she had no idea what had happened. My father, who was not allowed in the delivery room, waited alone. I do not know where I was or who stayed with me. When the doctor emerged to greet my father, it was not the first time the news had been bad. Since Dad was a biology teacher, the doctor did not need to explain the details of Brent's condition or offer any prognosis. My father immediately understood all too well the implications of the devastating news. Offering what he thought were words of consolation, the doctor said, "We're doing all we can to save your son." My father responded, "Why?" My parents' regular pediatrician was not on call that night, and in later years they were haunted by his words: "If I had been there that night, you would not have had to bear this terrible burden all these years."

The following morning the doctor explained to my father that Brent's condition was so bad that he would never be able to go home and would need professional care as long as he lived. There was absolutely no chance he would ever approach normality and nothing could be done about it. At that time there were no state institutions equipped to deal with such children, so the doctor recommended that my father try to make arrangements for Brent at a Catholic home on Long Island. The first thing the next morning, my father left to investigate the facility. Though he had serious reservations about the home, he had no choice but to admit Brent as soon as possible. The following day Dad transferred my brother to the home, where he remained for four years, when he was finally placed in a state hospital, where he remained until his death at the age of seven. He never developed any cognitive functions and weighed only twenty-three pounds at the time of his death. In addition to the mental anguish this ordeal caused, the medical expenses placed a significant burden on our family. My father was making only $2,500 at the time and faced additional pressures as a result of the complicated health problems my mother and Beryl developed. When my father asked whether it was prudent to spare no expense to prolong Brent's suffering and the turmoil it created for the family, the priest in charge of the home threatened to take him to court.

Difficult though it is to believe, my mother never saw Brent. In the days after the delivery, doctors concluded she was neither physically nor psychologically prepared for the trauma that seeing him would cause. Over the years my father visited Brent regularly but always alone. At the time of Brent's funeral, my mother declined a final chance to see and perhaps kiss her son and insisted that the casket remain closed. I sometimes find myself wondering what clothes she chose for his burial. I knew nothing about my brother until two years after his death. And yet I must have sensed something was wrong, for life could hardly have been normal in such circumstances.

It is virtually impossible to comprehend such deformity. Imagine having a son you could never bear to look at. Did she love him? Hate him? Resent him? She must have tried to picture him, how could she not? What did she see or fear she would see? When I try to imagine Brent, and I cannot avoid doing so, my mind's eye is blank—I see nothing, absolutely nothing.

In the eyes of society, and perhaps his parents, this child was a monster who had to be kept apart. He was, nonetheless, my brother—my own flesh and blood. If Brent was a monster, so am I—a gene here, a chromosome there, and he is I and I am he. What is so disturbing about monsters is not the outward threat they pose, but what they show us about ourselves. Gazing at the other, I see myself. If we are honest, we must admit that we can never be sure who is and is not a monster. After all, sometimes the greatest monsters are not people who are so terrifyingly abnormal but who are so frightfully normal.

Though he was buried in the town where I was raised, I never visited Brent's grave until both my parents had died. Over the years my brother and I had mentioned him occasionally but never discussed what had happened or what his life and death had meant for us. After my father died, we spent several days cleaning out the only house where we had lived while growing up. It was a bittersweet time overshadowed by our loss but enriched by sharing memories and reliving a childhood now irrevocably past.

BRENT'S GRAVE

Sitting in the attic in the midst of carefully sorted piles of stuff, I turned to my brother and said: "You know, there's one more thing we have to do before we leave." He looked at me with a stare I remember having seen only once before, and without hesitating he said, "I know."

"Yeah, what?"

"We have to visit Brent's grave."

"That's right. But how did you know?"

"I don't know, just knew that's what you were going to say."

"Have you ever been there?"

"Yeah, when I was in high school, I went to the cemetery and found it."

"I've never been there. I thought about going several times but never did. I don't know why."

"Probably never will."

I have never been able to comprehend that conversation. After a lifetime of not talking about it—or of talking about it by not talking about it—how did we both know in the same instant that it was time to break the silence?

TWENTY-THREE

A.M.

"**Did** all this really happen?"

"What do you mean?"

"Did everything you write about really happen or have you made some of this stuff up?"

"Well, yes, I guess so—and, no, I don't think so."

"What do you mean you guess so, you don't think so?"

"Well, I don't think I made anything up, but I guess it depends on what the meaning of *happen* is."

"Don't mess with me. You know exactly what I mean."

"To the best of my recollection, everything happened as I've described it."

"'To the best of your recollection'—that's what they say on TV and in court when they know they're not telling the truth and want to cover their asses."

"No, that's not what I meant. It's just that sometimes my memory is fuzzy and things are obscure. You know, in some cases obscurity can clarify and so the only way to be clear is to remain obscure."

"Whatever. If you're trying to tell it like it is, why all the stories?"

"Because stories are the way we remember."

"Yeah, but are the stories we remember the way it really happened at the time?"

"Not always."

"Then did everything really happen or have you made some of this stuff up?"

"My memory of it really happened. That's the thing; that's *really* the thing."

"Not your memory of it—did *it* really happen?"

"I guess that depends on what the meaning of *it* is."

"And what about all these little stories? Do they fit together? Is there a story of stories?"

"I'm not sure."

"What do you mean, you're not sure?"

"I mean I'm just not sure."

"Are you sure?"

"What do you mean, am I sure?"

"Are you sure you are not sure?"

"Sure."

P.M.

Dishonesty

"Let me see if I understand your point correctly. On the one hand, honesty makes hope impossible and, on the other hand, there is an honest hope that is rendered possible by uncertainty. Is that right?"

"Presque, mon ami, presque."

"And much of what you say turns on the question of the child. But I am unsure about the eyes of children and the demand they make for hope. It might not be hope but just reassurance they need. It also seems to me that children themselves are part of the decision. What does it mean to bring children into a world that one sees as hopeless?"

"I am not sure. For anyone who honestly surveys the twentieth century and looks well into the twenty-first century, it would seem difficult, if not impossible, to be hopeful. And yet people hope. Is this because they don't think seriously or do think seriously but are dishonest about what history continues to reveal? I suspect it is neither. Hope seems to be a gift of youth, but here, as elsewhere, gifts can be poisons that lead to actions whose consequences are incalculable.

"In all honesty, I was not thinking about world historical events when we decided to have children. A couple of years ago, when Aaron and Frida were trying to decide when—not whether—to have children, we had a conversation about our decision to have Aaron. As we explained our decision or lack of decision, Frida was baffled: 'So, wait, let me try to understand this. You were five years younger than we are, still a graduate student making $2,500 a year, had no prospect for a job, the world was falling apart with a war nobody wanted, and still you decided to have a kid? Right? What *were* you thinking?' I had not realized until that moment that we were not really thinking about any of that but nonetheless did decide to bring a child into the world at a moment that was admittedly very dark. Does that mean that we had faith or were hopeful   these might, after all, be two ways of saying the same thing—that things would work out? No, that would be putting too grand a spin on it. We just were not thinking. Was that irresponsible? Perhaps, but, then, perhaps it is only by *not* thinking that anyone is able to take the leap of faith that having a child requires."

"Yes, but is that fair to the child? Once children are in the world, it is impossible not to give them hope (and, more generally, a large number of other things as well). But is that hope honest? Was it honest to bring them into the world *as* sites of hope themselves?"

"Is it fair to the child to give him or her life rather than not give it? The answer to that question seems self-evident. And, yes, I think it was an honest decision because I truly did not realize at the time just how hopeless things actually are. If hope is the gift as well as the *Gift* of youth, hopelessness is the gift as well as the *Gift* of age. Experience, after all, teaches us slowly just how fragile life is. The relevant question for you to pose is: 'If you knew then what you know now, would you have decided to have children?' It is, of course, an impossible question because once having come to know your children, how could you ever imagine not giving them life? And, yes, you are absolutely correct that once having made the decision to have a child, you have an obligation not only to give her or him hope but to be hopeful with the child because you cannot really give what you do not have."

"OK. I understand your point, but I remain puzzled by the way you think uncertainty and hope collapse into each other. What, after all, can we really hope for?"

"Hopelessness is a luxury we cannot afford—we can, no, we are obliged, to hope. What I hope for my children and now also my granddaughter is that they always will be able to hope. Is it dishonest for me to hope for them what seems impossible for me? I am not sure. Perhaps the only hope that is honest is the hope that simultaneously affirms both its impossibility and its necessity."

TWENTY-FOUR

A.M.

Inheritance

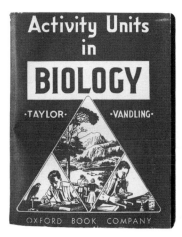

MY FATHER'S BIOLOGY BOOK

As a teacher and a writer, I believe the most valuable inheritance I can pass on to my children is immaterial rather than material. I will never be able to leave them great wealth, but I can give them the gift of knowing how to read and write well. This inheritance, however, involves far more than completing a few legal and financial transactions, no matter how complex they might be.

Having come to this realization when my children were still young, I decided to begin gifting our kids their inheritance in annual increments as soon as they left elementary school. From the summer after they finished sixth grade through the summer before they left for college, I made both write a three-page essay every week. It could be on any subject they chose, and the only requirement was that the essay had to be discursive, that is to say, they had to formulate a thesis, develop an argument, defend it, and draw a conclusion. I encouraged but did not require them to write on current events or what they were reading at the time. When the essay was finished, I corrected it, went over it with them, and they rewrote it. Initially, there were protests but they soon realized this was not negotiable. Having had my father as my physics teacher in high school, I knew all too well the perils of trying to teach your own kids. Aaron and Kirsten were not the only ones who learned from this long process—I discovered how difficult it is to teach writing, even when your students are very smart. There were many arguments and lots of tears. Sometimes we got through the week only with motherly help and mediation. Dinny was as committed to the project as I was and, when I reached the end of my rope, she took over, and with the patience I sorely lack invariably was able to get them to do what I could not.

Kirsten had a natural talent for writing and learned quickly. While I have saved many of the essays Kirsten and Aaron wrote, one in particular stands out in my memory. Kirsten was about fifteen when she entitled her weekly assignment "Realizations."

Sometimes you don't realize the importance of things until much later. It's easy to stay only in the present and do everything for the moment and yourself rather than thinking ahead and of others. If you're lucky, someone's there to remind you of this. If not, maybe you make a mistake. But it's hard to know at the time what is the right thing to do.

I found myself in this predicament, although at the time I didn't realize it, several years ago. It was a warm weekend in July, and I was tempted with an offer to go to a lake with a friend. It seemed like an ideal way to escape from my routine and enjoy myself. Unfortunately, my dad told me that the weekend I was asked to go was the same weekend we were going to visit my grandparents. Don't get me wrong, I loved visiting them, but at the time a weekend with my friend sounded much more appealing. So, being a kid, I argued, cried, fought, and finally pouted in a struggle to get my way. My dad tried to explain to me the importance of the rare visits and that someday they wouldn't be there for me to see anymore. Remaining selfish, I gave one last attempt before reluctantly agreeing to go. It was a fun weekend, but I had a hard time getting out of my mind what I could have been doing. That weekend was the last time I ever saw my grandmother.

The other day I was buying something to eat when I saw an older man sitting by himself, with a sad expression on his face. My heart went out to him and I immediately thought of this man like a grandfather, with his own grandkids. I began thinking back to that hot week in July. I realized how glad I was that I had gone. The weekend at the lake would have been fun, but there would be other weekends. I couldn't see my grandparents every day. I had been thinking only of myself. Fortunately, my dad was there to help me do the "right" thing. I guess it took me this long to realize that sometimes giving up a little for yourself can give a lot to someone else and, in the end, a lot back to you. I think that I'll write a letter to my grandfather now, and hopefully the man with the sad face will get a letter from his grandchildren to put a smile on his face.

Aaron inherited his mother's analytic ability and quantitative skills and initially found writing more of a challenge. Over the years, however, he made remarkable progress, and when he left for Dartmouth he flat out knew how to write. During his first semester the English course he took was writing intensive, and the initial assignment was to write a paper on Joseph Conrad's *The Secret Sharer*. When his essay was returned, his teacher had written a note asking to see him after class. She acknowledged the unusual strength of his paper but questioned whether he had actually written it. He assured her that it was his work and proceeded to explain how he had spent his summer vacation for the past seven years. When he reported that he was not sure whether she was incredulous or impressed, I was angry but restrained myself from intervening. A few years after he graduated, I was surprised when I received a letter from his professor in that course. She had read an article in the newspaper about what I was doing with technology in the classroom. She figured I must be Aaron's father and wrote to tell me how impressive she found his work and the story of his writing

MY MOTHER'S LITERATURE ANTHOLOGY

lessons. She apologized for having questioned Aaron and reported that she still used his paper in her classes as an example of the kind of writing she expects from her students.

During the years I was working with our children, I often thought about my own upbringing. In my childhood home reading was a religion. Every summer my brother and I would join the book club at our local library and would read at least twenty books. It was so much a part of our lives that it seemed completely natural. It was not until many years later that I realized how unusual it actually was. As I pondered the reasons I place such a high value on reading and writing, I began to realize that religion is at the heart of the issue.

Though I was raised in the Calvinist tradition, formal religion was never a big part of my life growing up. Informal or, perhaps more accurately, implicit religion, however, was important in our home. For my parents the classroom was the church, the lecture the sermon, and books the holy scripture. I had inherited this belief from them and now was passing it on to my children. They also received this tradition from their mother, who is a direct descendent of Roger Williams. Dissent, it seems, lies deep in their bones as well as my own. It has taken many years and more books read and written than I would like to count to realize just how Protestant I am. My paternal grandfather's name was, after all, Calvin. In both the Lutheran and the Reformed traditions that are my heritage, the Word of God, mediated orally through the sermon and in writing through the Bible, is the center of religious practice. Since the written word is so important, Protestantism has promoted literacy since its earliest days. Even before formal education began, children learned to read at home and in Sunday school so they could study biblical stories. I am heir to this tradition, and though I do not believe in scripture the way my Protestant ancestors did, I do believe that much of what we know about reality, however it is understood, is mediated by the word. Beyond all the practical reasons for teaching Aaron and Kirsten how to read and write well, the real inheritance I want to leave them is knowledge of the true value of the word. If they know this, I am confident their lives will be rich even when their bank accounts run low.

P.M.

Withholding

Parenting and teaching, which are, of course, inseparable, have taught me how hard it is to know what it means to give and what it means not to give. As long as there have been families, parents have wanted the lives of their children to be better than their own. Everyone has heard and most have likely said it countless times: "I don't want my kids to have to go through what I had to go through; I want them to have what I never had." Most parents are not merely willing but are actually eager to deprive themselves in order to provide for their children. Some parents take pleasure in giving, others feel guilt if they don't give. But is such giving really giving? If I receive pleasure or avoid guilt from giving, then do I give for the sake of my children or for my own sake? Though deeds often are declared disinterested and selfless, the one who gives often gets more from his gift than the one who receives. Even well-intentioned gifts come with explicit or implicit strings attached. The refrain is all too familiar: "After all we've done for you, how could you possibly—?" If given with the expectation of return, the gift cancels itself in a circle of self-interest whose aim is often to control others while appearing to do the opposite. When obligatory gratitude is the only tie that binds, it's time to cut the cord. But the play of give-and-take is never simple, and even if it were possible to give disinterestedly, a gift might not really be a gift.

I had known the couple for several years; they were fine people and well-meaning parents. They had two daughters, who were the center of their lives. They loved them dearly and gave them everything—the best clothes, the best summer camps, the best schools, the best clubs. The older daughter was sensitive as well as intelligent—more Upper West Side than Upper East Side, where she had grown up. There were problems in high school—the usual: drugs, tattoos, sex—but things had remained manageable. From time to time her father expressed concern to me, and I tried to reassure him that she would get through it. I had seen this pattern many times in my students and truly believed things eventually would work out. Predictably, she was admitted to one of the best colleges in the country, her father's alma mater. During her first semester everything fell apart. Caught in a swirl of drugs, alcohol, and sex, she failed every course. Even though my friend had kept me informed about her tailspin, I was not prepared when he called shortly before the Christmas holidays to tell me she had committed suicide. We agreed to meet that afternoon to talk about what had happened. Distraught beyond words, he pleaded for answers. "Where did we go wrong? We loved her so much and we gave her everything." Shattered by words I never expected to hear, I hesitated, weighing my thoughts carefully before responding. Finally, I said, "Perhaps where you went wrong was in giving her everything." He stared at me but said nothing.

Year after year the children of privilege roll through my classroom. Many are both very intelligent and quite talented. From the time they were born, their parents, eager to secure their future, have given them everything and thereby conveyed the sense of privilege and entitlement that comes from always having been on top. When things come too easily for young people, when they encounter no resistance, when they do not learn to do without or even to fail, when they never hear the word *no*, they are not prepared to face life. What well-meaning parents all too often fail to realize is that to give a person everything is to leave him or her empty-handed. Sometimes the greatest gift we can give the person we love is not giving—this is the gift of withholding.

TWENTY-FIVE

A.M.

Letting Go

AARON'S THINKING CAP

Autumn breeds mixed emotions for a teacher. It is a time of ending and a time of beginning. Unfinished projects must be set aside as I face the demands and opportunities created by classrooms full of new students. This is a rhythm I have known my whole life, first as a student and son of teachers, now as a teacher and father of students.

But this fall has been different—Aaron has left for college. The sense of ending and beginning, for him as well as for me, is more profound this year. He had, of course, been leaving for many months, perhaps years. But there was a certain point at which quantitative change became qualitative difference; increments became a leap. It happened so slowly that I hardly recognized the change. As late summer days waned, rules became requests rather than laws; curfews became pleas rather than demands. One day, I am not sure exactly when, he was gone before he had left home. As this realization grew, a sense of loss began to linger like the fading browns that haunt the splendor of autumn's hills. Aaron was teaching me a lesson—I must learn to let go.

It is a lesson I have often tried to teach others. For many years I have told my students that one of life's hardest lessons is to learn to let go. "Letting go" is a phrase that carries many meanings. From fun and play to sickness and death, "letting go" registers the inseparability of loss and gain. Sometimes it is hard to learn that to cling is to lose and to let go is to gain.

For me the future after Aaron's departure is both the same and different. In the faces of my students, I see the face of Aaron. It came as something of a shock to me when I realized that Aaron is closer in age to my students than I am. Because I started teaching when I was twenty-seven, my students seemed more like my colleagues than my children. I demanded of them what my graduate school professors had demanded of me. Sometimes the results were productive, sometimes destructive. Every parent is an educator and every educator is, in some sense, a parent. A teacher who tries to be a brother or sister to his or her students does not have much to teach. And yet the longer I teach and parent, the clearer it becomes how much I have to learn from my students as well as my children. It is a difficult lesson that takes at least a lifetime to understand. There is some consolation in knowing that what I have been telling my students for years is true—learning to let go *is,* indeed, one of life's hardest lessons.

An unfinished manuscript sits on my desk. It is not like me to leave tasks incomplete. For the past several months, however, I was reluctant to refuse Aaron's occasional requests to hike, cycle, or run. I knew time was running out, always running out.

ECONOMICS LESSON

P.M.

Dinnertime

Call me old-fashioned but I believe dinnertime is a sacred ritual. The time must be precise, the order invariable. Country time, not city time—early, not late: 6 P.M., always precisely 6:00. Except on Sunday when it's 12:30. Everyone present, no excuses, no distractions—no phone, no TV, no music—nothing, nothing but community and conversation. That's the way it's always been and that's the way it will always be—at least in our home.

When Aaron and Kirsten were growing up, it was not, I must confess, always easy to tell the difference between the dinner table and the seminar table. We would talk about the day and what everybody had done. I would ask them what they were doing in their classes and what they were reading on their own time. We would also discuss what was going on in the world and what they thought about it. Dinny and I would press them about their ideas and opinions, and we would debate, often heatedly. The point was never agreement but responsible analysis and reasoned argument.

Over the years many friends and colleagues gathered around our family dinner table: Jacques Derrida, Jack Miles, Sara Suleri, Peter Eisenman, Tom Krens, Cornel West, Tom Altizer, Michael Govan, Mark Tansey, Stanley Tigerman, Edmond and Arlette Jabès, and others, many others. Whenever possible, we included Aaron and Kirsten. I was often gratified by the sincere effort these distinguished visitors made to draw Aaron and Kirsten into the conversation by asking them about their interests and ideas. I remember one particular night when Dinny and I had Derrida to our home for dinner. Kirsten was about five, and Aaron was out with friends so it was just the four of us. When Dinny needed help in the kitchen, I left Kirsten to entertain Derrida. As I fixed the salad and poured the wine, I could not help overhearing bits and pieces of their conversation. Kirsten was chattering away and Jacques was responding patiently, when I heard her saying, "Well, then, would you like to see my bedroom?" The next thing I knew,

Derrida was sitting on Kirsten's bed listening to her stories about her books and toys. This simple gesture has always been as impressive to me as any book Derrida ever wrote. It would, of course, be many years before either Kirsten or Aaron understood just how unusual our dinnertime conversations had been. One of the mysteries of teaching, writing, and parenting is never knowing whether the seeds you plant will take root and, if they do, how they will grow.

When Aaron graduated from high school in 1990, he was selected to give the commencement address. Though it was difficult to restrain myself, I resisted the temptation to offer to help him formulate his ideas. As is his wont, Aaron kept his thoughts to himself, and we did not know what he would say until he spoke publicly. When I heard his words that hot June afternoon, I realized he had indeed been listening to our dinnertime conversations.

Fellow students, faculty, administrators, families, and friends.

Looking back on the past six years, I have learned something more, something other than the chemical formulas for ammonia or the elements of style. I have discovered how fundamentally important it is to stress differences between individuals and how dangerously simple-minded it can be to try to cover those differences. In the words of the French poet Edmond Jabès, "to imitate means to betray and to betray oneself. One cannot be the other. All real closeness comes from difference."

While each individual in our class has a unique and special background, there are some aspects we all have in common. Our origin, in one way or another, is our school, Mount Greylock, but it is also the hills and the streams of northern Berkshire County. And while some may curse the hills for sheltering or hiding us from the real world, I thank the mountains for protecting us, for just long enough, from the pitfall presented by the so-called real world: the pitfall of conformity. The hills have shielded us from many of the pains that drive people into groups or gangs; groups where the individual is lost. At the same time, however, the hills have given us the space and the time to observe the world, to see where we stand in it, and to develop our own identity. It is this identity, granted to us by this mountain land, that we must carry forth and never forget.

The world into which we venture is a world of great opportunity and, at the same time, a world that harbors a great possibility for failure. This extraordinary year has seen walls crumble, some hostilities fade, and others reappear. Eastern Europe is tenuously clinging to democracy, South Africa is slowly making progress in overcoming apartheid, China lies in a state of bloody terror, Israelis and Arabs clash in the Middle East, South America struggles with the violence of the cocaine mobs, famine and starvation plague places as distant as Ethiopia and Haiti, and our own Native American population continues to suffer under the burden of misguided government policies. Finally, and perhaps most important, our natural world is barely able to sustain us anymore. These are some of the challenges we face.

Our problems are no longer limited by the boundaries of nations or states, they have become international or global. There are hundreds of different cultures and races in today's world. The solution to our problems, however, does not lie in the continued struggle of people against people because of their differences. Instead of trying to eliminate our differences we must learn to celebrate them, in an attitude that says, "You are different from me, I respect your uniqueness and your individuality and I will help you, work with you to cultivate what makes us distinct." We must look for differences among people and appreciate the richness they offer. Then, and only then, can we face those difficult questions.

As we pass into this world of differences, we cannot lose that which makes each of us unique, that which we have found in the mountains. If we do, the differences will fade and the creative friction will die. Never forget the mountains that sheltered us so well and yet let us peek over their rim at the world outside. Never forget the values you hold dear that you found along the road and paths of Berkshire County—and, in the halls of Mount Greylock. Always return to the mountains, to the roots that nourish you. Even after having reached the highest branches, return to your roots, remember your origin, your uniqueness, and regain your strength. If the races and cultures of the world are to come together and solve our difficulties, we must each hold firm to our own identity and celebrate the differences among them. Before you go over the mountain pass, perhaps you will permit me a word of caution: we will find conformity much easier, for our sedate society tempts us to follow the well-traveled road. Let us not accept the lure and comfort that blending in presents. To be different is to be alive, to be thinking—always thinking. Conformity dulls everything and eventually leads to failure. Celebrate your differences, my friends, celebrate your differences.

Prescient words for a seventeen year old in 1990. As Aaron concluded, I knew it was time for me to let go, and, perhaps for the first time, I was sure he would be fine, even though I was not so sure about myself.

TWENTY-SIX

A.M.

Compassion

AARON AND KIRSTEN ON TOM'S MOTORCYCLE

How do you measure compassion? The word holds clues. Deriving from *compati—com,* with + *pati,* to suffer—compassion is sharing another person's feelings or suffering. As such, compassion seems to require empathetic identification in which two somehow become one. While such a union does not necessarily presuppose familiarity or proximity, compassion tends to create a sense of closeness even when it is between or among distant strangers. Well-intended compassion can, of course, be exploited for political purposes and economic gain. When it is genuine, however, compassion can get you through the darkest night. But how can we ever be sure compassion is genuine? What if compassion can also be expressed in ways that are opposite to its customary appearance?

I began to suspect this possibility almost four decades ago, when my father, brother, and I gathered to try to figure out what treatment to approve for my mother, who had suffered a cerebral hemorrhage. Her condition was critical—she was on life support, and we did not have much time to make our decision. In the days immediately following a stroke, it is common for patients to suffer a second episode, which is almost always fatal. The day after she was stricken, we met with a neurosurgeon, who had been recommended to us by my father's physician. The meeting took place in a small dismal pale yellow cinderblock room with a gray metal desk and three matching metal chairs. Nothing hung on the walls—not even the ubiquitous doctors' diplomas or platitudinous sayings designed to reassure. We sat in silence while waiting for the doctor to appear. When he burst into the room, he seemed hurried but not distracted. With no chair available he perched on the edge of the desk as if ready to rush out as soon as his beeper went off. He brusquely introduced himself, quickly described my mother's "case," and then proceeded to tell us what he was going to do about it. This was not a discussion in which we explored different alternatives and came to a consensus about the best approach. Rather, it was a lecture in which he was the unquestioned authority and we were the unknowing students, although my father was a biology teacher and my brother a veterinarian. To make matters worse, the procedure he described was new and quite risky. He had performed this operation only three times but still expressed what seemed to be unwarranted confidence about a favorable outcome. He emphasized that there was no time to waste and told us we had to decide by noon so he could schedule the surgery for the next morning. He then left as suddenly as he had arrived.

We were all furious. At this moment of extraordinary stress, the doctor had shown absolutely no compassion. To the contrary, he had been abrupt, impatient, and, above all, arrogant. There was not a hint of caution or doubt in his words or demeanor. We realized, however, that we could not let our reservations about the man cloud the important decision we faced. With time running out and no other neurosurgeon available, we agreed, with many reservations, to accept his recommendation.

The next time we saw the doctor was when he emerged from the operating room after six hours of surgery to tell us that things had gone very well.

He had clipped the aneurysm and there had been no additional bleeding. The next twenty-four hours would be critical, but he was confident she would be fine. Though the edge was gone, either from exhaustion or relief, his self-confidence seemed stronger than ever. Unlike most doctors, who always seem to be looking over their shoulders for lurking lawyers, he did not qualify his prognosis with words of caution. He told us she would recover all her physical and mental capacities—no doubt about it.

In the weeks that followed, we saw the doctor only two more times. Our conversations were brief and to the point. No warm greetings, no small talk, all business. There was no getting close to this man. But as I watched him respond to my mother and deal with us, my attitude toward him changed. As she gradually recovered just as he had predicted, I began to realize that his abruptness, distance, self-confidence, and even arrogance might after all actually be expressions of compassion. A brain surgeon cannot serve his patients or their families if he has any self-doubt; nor can he perform effectively if he gets too close to them. Paradoxically, empathetic identification sometimes requires the insistent cultivation of distance rather than intimacy. In certain situations—and surely there are others—to be compassionate one has to be dispassionate.

Or so it seemed. I realized, of course, that we might have been right the first time—perhaps he actually was an arrogant son of a bitch, who was interested in nothing but himself and his career. Whichever it was, he had saved my mother's life, and for that we were forever grateful.

P.M.

Suffering

The most excruciating suffering is not physical, nor is it suffering that I must undergo. Rather, the suffering that is insufferable is the suffering of the other, which I can never bear. No matter how deep it runs, compassion cannot overcome the distance suffering creates. I can never really put my-self in the place of the other, and thus the principle of substitution always fails.

I learned this lesson in a foreign land. We had been in Denmark only five weeks when Aaron, who was five at the time, woke up one morning unable to walk. He had excruciating pain in his right leg and screamed when he put any weight on it. We were living in a working-class suburb outside Copenhagen and did not yet know anyone in the neighborhood. Since Dinny's Danish was better than mine, she knocked on a stranger's door and tried to explain the situation. Somehow the neighbor understood what she was saying and wrote down the name, address, and phone number of the nearest doctor. We did not have a car so we borrowed a child's wagon to take Aaron to the doctor's office.

As we sat in a crowded waiting room, our concern rose with Aaron's fever. When the doctor eventually had time to examine him, he was puzzled by the symptoms but had no doubt that Aaron's condition was quite serious. Picking at a scab on his knee that showed only minor signs of infection, the doctor muttered in broken English, "It might be scarlet fever; we must get

DANISH LESSONS

him to the hospital immediately." I doubted the diagnosis but knew Aaron needed to see a specialist as soon as possible. The problem we faced was that the Danish health-care system is socialized, and if you do not have private insurance, you have no choice of hospital or physician. We were fortunate to be sent to Glostrup Hospital, where the care turned out to be excellent.

That afternoon Aaron's temperature rose even higher, and by evening it reached 106, where it hovered for a week. As his temperature went up, so did the pain until he screamed continuously, even while lying in bed. The doctors still had no diagnosis and were not even sure which specialists to consult. Until they knew more, they refused to give him any medications—not even to relieve the pain—for fear of masking the symptoms. Coping with a seriously ill child is always hard but never more so than when you are in a foreign country. The doctors and nurses knew English rather well, but much still got lost in translation. The words were often right but the nuance wrong. We quickly discovered how many critical decisions hinge less on what is said than on how it is said—a slight shift in tone or unintended gesture can quickly change everything.

It was immediately clear that one of us would have to stay with Aaron all the time. There were not enough nurses and attendants to monitor him continuously, and many of those who were available could not speak English so he could not tell them where it hurt or what he needed. The first nights and days were filled with tests and more tests: X-rays, MRIs, urine tests, blood tests, … and needles—so many needles that his little veins were perforated and his thin arms black and blue. Through it all, the pain persisted and he rarely stopped screaming, crying, and sobbing. He never smiled and rarely slept; neither did we. Finally one morning a doctor we had never met came into the room and announced that they had a diagnosis: "Osteomyelitis, a severe infection in his tibia." He was a specialist in this condition and had never seen such a severe case. The danger, he explained, was that the infection would become chronic, and Aaron would not be able to walk again for years, perhaps for life. The only possible treatment involved at least a month of hospitalization and heavy doses of intravenous antibiotics, followed by weeks of oral medication and prolonged inactivity. He would also need surgery to drain the pus from the bone. Aaron was too sick to travel so we had no choice but to stay in Denmark and follow the doctor's orders. In the end things turned out well, and he eventually recovered, but it was a very, very long haul.

Such an experience leaves scars that are more than physical. What I most remember about those endless nights when Aaron was burning up with fever and screaming in pain was wanting nothing—absolutely nothing—more than to put myself in his place, to take his suffering from him by undergoing it for him. Night followed night until they all flowed together to become that dreadful night beyond night. In the darkness that knows no light, I discovered that the doctrine of vicarious atonement, which I had learned as a youth, studied in graduate school, and sometimes taught my students, is a vicious lie. No one can suffer for another—we all must suffer alone—absolutely alone. Physical pain is the dark shadow of the mental anguish of knowing you cannot assume the suffering of those you love most deeply.

TWENTY-SEVEN

A.M.

Clouds

TACONIC MOUNTAINS

On certain summer days the atmosphere is so clear that the line where sky meets mountain is crisper than any artist can draw. As morning gives way to afternoon, clouds gradually gather—not dark clouds that portend approaching storms but light, fluffy clouds that constantly change their shapes. From time to time I attempt to capture these clouds with my camera but always fail. Their forms are too transient, their movement too fleeting for the lens to record. What most intrigues me is the way these clouds drift—even when moving in a straight line, they seem to wander. I follow their movement by tracing their shadows dancing on the mountains. These clouds and the shadows they cast are always light—unbearably light—and the lessons they teach defy all gravity. The hours I spend gazing at summer clouds are as pointless as their drifting. This is what makes them priceless.

But it is winter clouds that most enchant me. These clouds are not celestial but appear between earth and sky. On clear and frigid winter days after a heavy snow, the wind often blows ferociously from the distant mountaintop across the valley and up the hill. Bursting gusts sweep up the powdered snow in clouds of unknowing, where the material somehow becomes immaterial and yet remains impossibly voluptuous. It is as if an invisible hand were passing over the void of the white surface, creating evanescent symmetries that appear by disappearing. The vision is instantaneous, no more than a blink of the eye, not so much a fraction of time as a fissure in it.

> For the listener, who listens in the snow,
> And, nothing himself, beholds
> Nothing that is not there and the nothing that is.

P.M.

Waiting

There are other clouds that are neither celestial nor immaterial but are darker than the darkest clouds on a stormy day. These are the billowing clouds of man-made infernos where the highest hopes and aspirations are vaporized. As they drift heavenward, these toxic clouds leave in their wake the unforgettable stench of burning matter and flesh. It was one of those clear cloudless days that make fall in the Berkshires special when the morning calm was shattered by a call that came with a suddenness as jarring as the disaster it announced.

"Mark, this is Nathan. Is Aaron OK?"

"Sure, I guess so. Why?"

"Haven't you heard? A plane crashed into the World Trade Center, and I think he was supposed to be there."

I had not heard because I was in the barn writing and was farther away from New York City than miles can measure.

"I'm not sure where he is. His classes the entire month of August were on the top floor of the World Trade Center, but I think they are over, and he was supposed to start his interviews at 9:00 this morning across the street in the American Express Building."

"That's right across the street. I'll try to call him."

Rushing into the house and turning on the TV, for the first time I saw the now unforgettable images of clouds of smoke coming from the towers. Over the years the endless looping of videos of that scene has done nothing to diminish the horror. As I watched incredulously, I tried to call Dinny, who was also in the city and was staying in midtown. The lines were jammed and I could not get through.

Shortly after the second plane crashed, Nathan, a friend of Aaron's from Yale, called again. Somehow he had gotten through to Aaron on his cell phone.

"He's OK. He was in the American Express Building and after the second building was hit, he figured he'd better get out. He's safe now. He said that two weeks ago he would have been taking the elevator to the top floor at the exact time the plane exploded."

Relieved, I thanked Nathan for his concern and for calling me. After I hung up, I tried to call Aaron and Dinny but still could not get through. I continued to gaze at the TV as I waited. While I was watching along with millions of others, the unthinkable happened—the towers collapsed. I had no idea whether Aaron had stayed or left, and there was no way I could find out. Had he stayed, there seemed to be little chance he would have survived. I could do nothing but sit watching the horrifying events unfold and wait. The endless waiting was excruciating, and the beauty of the day made it seem all the more cruel.

Nathan called again and wanted to know if I had heard from Aaron yet. He reported that he had been able to contact some of their mutual friends from Yale but could not reach Aaron. I said I couldn't either, and we both promised to be in touch as soon as we heard anything. Another hour passed, and Dinny finally called to report that she was fine but the city was in chaos. She had heard nothing from Aaron. And so we both waited and waited, calling each other regularly to offer empty reassurances. Few things make you feel more helpless than waiting for an urgent telephone call and not being able to do anything to hasten its arrival.

Another hour passed—it now had been more than two hours since Nathan's first call and my concern was growing. Yet another half hour and still nothing. When the phone rang again, I hesitated before picking it up—I was no longer sure I wanted the news for which I had been so anxiously waiting. It was Dinny. I immediately knew from the tone of her voice that the news was good—she had reached Aaron and he was safe. With thousands of others he was walking slowly north along the Hudson River, and he wasn't sure how long it would be before he got back to the apartment.

It was another two hours before Aaron called me from his apartment; he was OK but was obviously badly shaken. He explained that he and the others from work figured something was really wrong after the second plane hit. They could see the towers from the window in the office where they were meeting and decided they should leave the building. As they were waiting outside until it seemed safe to return to the office, Aaron saw people jumping from the towers to their deaths far below. He could not bear the sight and decided he had to leave. He told his colleagues he was taking off; they stayed behind and he didn't know what had happened to them. After surveying the mayhem, he decided to head west until he came to the Hudson River and then turn north. Along the river he joined the dazed crowd walking together in silence. When he was about thirty blocks from the towers, he heard the explosive sound of their collapse and saw clouds of dust and debris rising into the cloudless sky.

At that moment he realized that the people jumping from the towers to their deaths had actually saved his life. If they had not jumped, he never would have left the site and in all likelihood would now be dead under thousands of tons of debris. He was deeply troubled that he would not have survived had not others jumped to their death and was not sure whether he should feel thankful or guilty. I tried to explain to him that the tension created by this experience will never go away. When the price of life is death, thanks and guilt are inseparable. I do not know how deep the scars are; Aaron keeps his own counsel but often speaks by his silence.

A.M.

Freedom

RELIC FROM HEIDEGGER'S HUT

There is no freedom without terror. To spread freedom is therefore to increase terror. In the instant of freedom, the power of creativity appears as "the fury of destruction, which knows no limit." What makes freedom so terrifying is that it reveals an unfathomable abyss "within" that exposes as groundless every ground believed to be secure. This unfathomable abyss is the whiteness of the whale—the "never-to-be imparted secret, whose attainment is destruction." It is the nothingness that haunts being as its impossible condition.

Those who cannot bear to face this void define freedom as self-determination and even autonomy. To be free, then, is to be determined internally, by oneself, rather than externally, by another. The free individual is, in other words, self-regulating and self-legislating. But what if the line between inside and outside is obscure? What if there is an outside, an exteriority, at the heart of what appears to be "our" interiority? What if I am never one but am always already torn, sundered, split? What if I am not the origin of deeds deemed free because the *I* is forever after a Not that lets being be?

Freedom occurs in an instant that is not a moment—an instant that is neither temporal nor eternal but repeatedly returns as the outside that is forever inside in a way that keeps time flowing. In this instant, which can never be glimpsed because it occurs in the blink of an eye, I am what I am not and am not what I am. Freedom is the vanishing trace of a subjectivity without a subject. Rather than being the origin of free actions, the *I*, which is never properly my own, originally emerges again and again in the instant of freedom that dispossesses every subject. There are always two sides to freedom. On the one hand, freedom involves the deliberate realization of clearly conceived and carefully defined possibilities. Through this process I become, for better and for worse, what I am and am not. Herein lies my responsibility: I am what I become through the decisions I make during my lifetime. In making these decisions, I am guided by the rules of society and the principles of morality. This freedom, however, is secondary to a more primordial freedom that cannot be conceptualized, determined, or regulated. I am not only responsible *for* myself but am also responsible *to* something other that freely gives the self I must nonetheless freely become. This abyssal freedom is the indeterminacy from which all determination emerges. Such radical freedom is the trace of an infinite beyond that renders every subject finite and unknowable to itself. In the shadow of this freedom, the subject is truly sub-ject.

Before the beginning, I am not free because the *I* is given through a freedom that cannot be my own. My beginning repeats while displacing this originary freedom in the decision by which I choose myself as a freely choosing being. Having accepted responsibility for the freedom that is and is not my own, I must, then, proceed to make the decisions that will transform me into the person I am. Every particular decision presupposes the antecedent decisions in which I first choose to choose and then choose the rules that guide my life as well as the norms and principles by which I make specific decisions. Paradoxically, this originary decision must be repeated every time I choose. What makes it so terrifying is that there are no rules to choose the rules by which I choose. In the instant of decision, freedom is necessary—I *must* choose freely, and this decision is *necessarily* a blind leap. Insight into this blindness fills the instant of decision with dread.

The awareness of freedom as well as the nonknowledge that it inevitably entails provokes irreducible ambivalence—freedom simultaneously attracts and repels. There is nothing comforting or reassuring about freedom; to the contrary, the gift of freedom involves a dreadful responsibility we can never escape. To accept responsibility for freedom, which is never our own but nonetheless lets us be what we become, is to embrace not just the possibility but also the necessity of a terror we can never avoid. The bottomless depth from which freedom emerges is the inverted image of the whirlwind from whose infinite height the lofty voice of God freely raises us up by thrusting us down.

P.M.

Terror

Crossing the police barricade at Canal Street and walking past the courthouses and city hall toward Ground Zero, we entered an uncanny world that was both completely familiar and totally strange. Though street signs and landmarks remained unchanged, axes of orientation no longer lined up as they once did. It was not just the absence of people and traffic or the haunting silence; something else, something palpable yet difficult, perhaps impossible, to articulate was loose on the streets.

I crossed that barrier with Aaron two days after the attack. I felt it was important for him to return to the scene of terror and knew he should not go alone the first time. As we turned the corner on Broadway at St. Paul's Chapel, we caught our first glimpse of the American Express Building through the clouds of smoke still rising from the rubble. We both froze instantly. Standing but a stone's throw away, the building where Aaron had been looked like it had suffered repeated mortar attacks. Between us and the World Financial Center, the twin towers had stood just two days before. Now their absence had become an overwhelming presence.

A few blocks farther on, there was an opening through which we could see the true scope of the devastation. With dusk falling, bright lights illuminated a scene that was both profoundly unsettling and disturbingly sublime—the ruins looked like an otherworldly sculpture created by some unknown artist. A small crowd had gathered and was gazing at the smoldering ruins in stunned silence. We had repeatedly heard that TV and film could not do justice to the scene and that was right. It was not merely that screens are too small and camera angles too limited; rather, the reality confronting us was not only visual but, more important, visceral. The only word to describe my response to what we saw: *awe*. Contrary to every expectation, a strange religious atmosphere pervaded Ground Zero. There had been much talk about the role of religion in this conflict but very little understanding of what religion really involves. There are, of course, many gods and many faces of gods believed to be one. While religion often gives people a sense of meaning and purpose in times of personal and social crisis, its symbols, stories, and rituals also carry people to the edge of life, where unmasterable power always threatens to erupt. Throughout history, religion has been associated as much with terror and anxiety as with love and peace. For a few brief moments on September 11, the veneer of security was torn to reveal a primordial vulnerability that neither defense departments nor advanced technologies can overcome. For me and, I believe, for Aaron, the encounter with this awesome power was a religious experience that left nothing unchanged.

I don't know how long we lingered—in the strange realm of elsewhere, time stands still. Eventually, we roamed up Broadway past Trinity Church, whose graveyard was more haunting than ever, to the Wall Street subway station. Descending under ground, awe gave way to dread. For more than a century, philosophers have been telling us that dread is more distressing than fear. In contrast to fear, whose object is always specific and thus manageable, dread is provoked by something so indeterminate that it cannot be precisely named, defined, or located. Dread is the response to what is there by not being there. Like the webs and networks that now hold us in their grip, terror is everywhere yet nowhere. Individually and collectively, we sense the danger of things slipping out of control and are not sure how or where to respond. As Aaron and I waited for the train in dark silence, dread settled as thick as the poisoned dust enveloping us, and it still has not lifted.

TWENTY-NINE

A.M.

Forgiveness

GRANDPA COOPER'S POCKET WATCH

I am sometimes willing to forgive but am never willing to forget. To those who say, "Forgive and forget," I say, "Forgive but remember." The point is not that I hold grudges and seek revenge, though in all honesty sometimes I do. Rather, my refusal to forget reflects my respect for the past and insistence on the abiding significance of human decisions and deeds. Clichés sometimes become clichés because they are true: What has been done really cannot be undone. The fitting response is not to forget it and move on. There are few phrases in the contemporary lexicon of pop psychology and culture I loathe more than "It's time to move on." To forgive and forget in order to move on undercuts the importance of history—personal and otherwise—and minimizes the seriousness of our actions. Some things cannot and should not be forgotten—taking a human life, violating the innocent, betraying a loved one. There are, indeed, wounds so deep that they should never be allowed to heal, even if they could.

To forgive but remember is much more difficult than to forgive and forget. Forgiving and forgetting is a once-and-for all event—do it, get it over with, and move on. Having wiped the slate clean, it seems possible to start over, but erasure always leaves traces even when they are denied. What is forgotten does not disappear but remains, often festers, and sometimes returns when least expected. By contrast, when you forgive but remember, forgiveness is never over, which is not to say it remains incomplete. Forgiveness must begin anew every time certain decisions are made. The lingering pain of transgression is what makes forgiveness so hard for both the one who forgives and the one who is forgiven. In the moment of forgiveness the life of the transgressor becomes double: he or she is not merely forgiven but becomes a forgiven transgressor.

This is the lesson Luther teaches in his doctrine of forgiveness. If God forgives me, I am not simply redeemed; rather, I am a forgiven sinner—simultaneously justified and sinner. Sin, in other words, does not disappear but remains a part of my very being. Moreover, Luther insists that justification is not my own but is alien—the righteousness of another, Jesus Christ, is imputed to me. Having transgressed, there is nothing I can do to merit forgiveness—repentance cannot do away with transgression but can only sorrow over it. As every unfaithful lover knows, the more I struggle to gain forgiveness, the faster I discover my inability to do so. Forgiveness, if offered, is always the free gift of an other. It is not necessary to accept Luther's theology to appreciate the depth of his psychological insight into the complex dynamics of forgiveness.

Who has not transgressed? Who is not in need of forgiveness by an other? Who has not felt the anguish of being unable to do anything to win the acceptance for which he so desperately longs? The gift of forgiveness is difficult, if not impossible,

GRANDPA COOPER'S MONACLE

to understand. Though often overlooked, accepting forgiveness is perhaps even more difficult than granting it. In the moment of forgiveness, I affirm myself by denying myself. This contradiction exposes a split, fissure, fault at what I had believed to be the very core of my being. Receiving forgiveness doubles this contradiction by superimposing yet another opposition on the divided self: I am guilty yet forgiven. To live the ambiguity of such duplicity is to give time its due by admitting its irreversibility.

The act of forgiveness is not without its dangers. If the person who forgives does not see himself or herself mirrored in the eyes of the other, forgiveness itself becomes a transgression. I hold myself above the other and, by declaring innocence, actually admit my guilt. I can therefore forgive the other only by confessing my own need for forgiveness. Word and deed meet on the cross of forgiveness. Granting and accepting forgiveness are not outward acts but are speech-events that change our very being. When forgiveness is graciously offered and freely accepted, two become one in a shared confession: "I am not what I am and I am what I am not." These words are as transformative as any deed. God forgives but does not forget because he respects me and takes my actions with ultimate seriousness. For me to do less for myself as well as other human beings would be to deny the value of the lives I am attempting to affirm. In the moment of forgiveness, I become as paradoxical as the act of forgiveness itself.

P.M.

Cruelty

The gods are cruel—crueler than mortals because their powers are greater. The cruelty they inflict can be physical, mental, or an intense combination of the two. While the pain of such cruelty can be overwhelming, there is another cruelty—a cruelty beyond cruelty, which is often suffered but rarely discussed openly.

For more than thirty years he had been a friend and my closest colleague. We talked every day, usually at length, about current issues as well as the books we were reading and ideas we were exploring. Though he did not write, he read more widely and deeply than most of the people who write books but have nothing to say. Everything I wrote between 1973 and 1997 took shape during those conversations. When he retired, we talked less frequently and almost always on the phone. The rhythm of our dialogue had been interrupted and it just was not the same. In the absence of our exchanges, my thinking became more solitary than ever.

He had long been looking forward to spending summers and falls by the sea on his beloved Cape Cod. After he retired, he continued to begin each day by religiously reading the *New York Times*; only then was he prepared to turn his attention to serious fiction and nonfiction. Afternoons and evenings he would roam the dunes and beaches of the outer Cape. We would occasionally visit him on the Cape, and I have many fond memories of our seaside conversations.

Late one August night shortly after he stopped teaching, his wife called to tell me he had suffered a stroke and had been rushed to the hospital in Hyannis. I called to check on him repeatedly, but it was several days before doctors could determine his condition. When it finally arrived, the news was mixed: there was no physical impairment, and most of his mental faculties were still intact, but he could not remember some words and had difficulty connecting ideas and words. He clearly knew what he wanted to say but often could not find the words to express his thoughts. Our many discussions over the years about the complex relationship between signifiers and signifieds suddenly took on a brutal reality neither of us ever could have anticipated. Most devastating of all, however, he could no longer read—he was able to see the words on the page but the letters were hopelessly scrambled. This is a man for whom reading was more than a job—it had been his life. Indeed, his entire identity was wrapped up with words and the effective, often excessive, use of language. Words had made him who he was, and now language had betrayed him.

The first time I saw him after he had been stricken, I was surprised by how well he appeared to be. Indeed, for long stretches he seemed to be the same person I had known for so many years. But then all of a sudden he would stumble on a word, and the frustration simmering just beneath the surface would boil over. No longer able to discuss questions we once had probed for hours on end, neither of us was sure what to talk about. For the first few years I scrupulously avoided telling him what I was reading or sending him what I was writing. But we both knew what we were not saying. Eventually, we had to confront what we too long had been avoiding.

"It must be terribly difficult," I stammered.

"You have no idea how hard it is," he responded with a faint quiver in his voice. "The darkness is overwhelming—especially at night. I can't sleep and I cannot stop thinking. Never could but now it's a curse."

What was so excruciatingly painful for him was not only being unable to do what he once had done so well but the fear that he would never again be able to do what he so loved. He needed to say nothing more because he knew I understood. As I left him that afternoon, I realized more than ever that his loss was also my own.

The cruelty beyond cruelty is taking what a person most loves and cannot live without and leaving him no hope for recovery. Such cruelty serves no purpose, teaches no lessons, and promises no redemption. It can never be forgotten and should not be forgiven even, perhaps especially, when it is inflicted by the gods.

THIRTY

A.M.

Daughters

DINNY HORSING AROUND

My mother often said that one of the primary reasons the prospect of dying was so disconcerting was that she would never see where her only granddaughter, Kirsten, would end up. Such thoughts are not uncommon, but I suspect there were several reasons she expressed this feeling so often. Kirsten became the daughter she had lost at birth. In the quiet of my mother's endless melancholy, how could she not have asked what Baby Girl Taylor might have become had she not been strangled? There is no worse fate for a parent than to outlive a child—and then to have it happen not once but twice is cruel beyond words.

There were, however, other reasons as well. She saw in Kirsten her own fierce will, which she had passed on to me. My mother frequently repeated the story of bringing me home from the hospital on Christmas Day, almost two weeks after I was born. The nurse, she always recalled, said to her, "It will not make your life easy, but never, never break that child's will." When Kirsten was born thirty years later, she developed infant jaundice and for several days had to be placed under ultraviolet lights with bandages protecting her eyes. When she was finally released, the nurse who had been attending her said, "I've been doing this for thirty years, and I've never seen a baby more determined to tear off the bandages." Little did we know what that determination implied. As Kirsten grew older, her mother frequently repeated words my mother might have spoken about me: "If we can just get through these years, that will will serve her well." When my will and Kirsten's will clashed, as they often did, it was Dinny's resolute determination that enabled us to negotiate our differences.

A strong will is a gift that is a burden. During the depths of the Depression, my mother and father were both teaching high school in a small Pennsylvania coal-mining town. When they decided to get married, the school board informed my mother that she would have to resign. She refused and eventually forced the board to back down; she went on to a rewarding career of teaching the literature she loved so much. The same determination enabled her to survive twenty-two hospitalizations before life finally wore her down. She sought to instill in me the same discipline and determination she valued in herself, and, though I have not always been grateful, she was more successful than I would like to admit.

Will, however, like genes, comes from both parents. It takes a strong mother to raise a willful child. Strength is measured by the willingness to say no when others say yes and, no less important, to say yes when others say no. Dinny usually knows better than I when to hold and when to fold. This is perhaps the most valuable lesson she has taught Kirsten.

There is an admirable fierceness to Kirsten's will even when it seems to be tempered. Every time she runs a marathon or becomes incensed at incompetence and injustice, I see in her a resolute will that brings with it an impatience that is both a virtue and a vice. When a strong will accompanies a quick mind, conflict becomes inevitable. Though I don't think my mother expected her granddaughter to become a corporate lawyer in New York City, I doubt she would have been surprised to learn that Kirsten is impatient with the distorted values she finds around her. What would surprise and greatly disappoint my mother would be learning that boards and firms whose members are still mostly men continue to find subtle ways of controlling women and forcing the resignation of those who are the strongest. A strong will does not make life easier; to the contrary, resolute determination usually makes life much more difficult. Having torn the bandages from her own

KIRSTEN—MARATHON WOMAN

eyes, Kirsten forces others to see what they would rather ignore. My mother would be proud, as Dinny and I are, that Kirsten sees through tactics of deception and avoidance and has the courage to know when to say no.

P.M.

Obsession

The only writers worth reading are writers who cannot not write. They are obsessed, though they know not by what. Indeed, if they knew what obsesses them, they would no longer have to write. For genuine writers writing is neither a job nor a profession—it is nothing less than life itself. If asked why they write, they can only echo Luther standing before the Diet of Worms: "I can do no other." They do not write to earn money or in the hope of becoming a tenured professor; writing without why, they write because they *must* write. Their work requires no research other than life itself. The true writer obsessively pursues the sentence that will make his life worth living. Scholars who cannot write are granted tenure for their books about writers who can.

There are, of course, many other reasons to write. I recently called one of my former professors, who had just turned eighty-two, to congratulate him on the publication of his latest book. Offering what I intended as a compliment, I said, "Your ability to remain intellectually active and to continue writing are admirable." He responded dismissively, "There is nothing admirable about it. What else would I do?" I understood what he meant but was not saying directly. After the death of his wife of more than fifty years, he was lost and did not know how to go on. Slowly, very slowly, he began reading and writing again. Writing was the way he tried to fill his days when he was faced with the void created by his wife's absence. But writing to pass time by distracting us from what we feel compelled to avoid is not really writing. The writing that matters neither comforts nor reassures but relentlessly turns us toward what turns us away.

The obsession that allows—no, requires—one to write is as much a curse as a blessing. Ordinary writers confronted with a blank page fear words will not come; obsessed writers dread they will never stop. Day and night, night and day, words leave the writer no rest. They arrive when and where they will, crowding out other thoughts and interrupting sleep that is never sound. Once they start, no distraction will stop them—they flow faster than the hand can record them. Ask the writer where they come from and she will in all likelihood confess she does not know and is not even sure it is she who writes. Writing seems to emerge from a fathomless elsewhere. Though more interior than the most profound inwardness, the elsewhere that is the whence of writing is where I am by not being there. When the writer signs books, she knows her name is doubled by an anonymity that speaks pseudonymously in words that are not her own.

I have been fortunate enough to know two real writers—one now dead, the other still living; one a philosopher, the other a theologian, though such labels do not really fit. Both were preoccupied with the question of originality—one denied there is any such thing, the other insisted there is no genuine writing without it. Regardless of these conflicting opinions, their writings were undeniably original. Like all great art, their works take you elsewhere by allowing you to think what you have never before thought and, indeed, did not even know was thinkable. The works of such writers must be read slowly because they free the imagination to roam without any sense of direction. The point is not so much what these writers have actually written as where they allow readers to travel and what they enable them to think.

Watching my two friends age has been both painful and instructive. As true writers, they really cannot not write, for they actually believe that writing is life and thus are convinced that not writing spells death. Their obsessions make it impossible for them to stop writing, even whey they should do so. With the passing of the years, they continue to accumulate titles but have little new to say; indeed, I invariably know the argument before I read the book and no longer know how to respond. Reading a great writer who cannot stop when his time has passed is like watching a great ballplayer who continues to pitch after he has lost his fastball. Such players claim they continue for the love of the game, but everybody knows that is not why they are unable to stop. As works proliferate, their currency is steadily devalued. From time to time I have tried to find ways to suggest to my friends that perhaps it's time to write less, but my words have always been ignored. For a long time I was frustrated by their inability to let go but gradually came to realize that what makes it impossible for them to

KIERKEGAARD GRAVE RUBBING

stop writing is precisely what made it possible for them to write such extraordinary works. Without obsession nothing great is accomplished.

The writing that matters is not a choice—it is a gift that imposes burdens that cannot be refused. The obsession of writing often carries a high price: Kierkegaard collapsed on the streets of Copenhagen at the age of 42 and died a few days later; Nietzsche slipped into madness at 46 and lingered for a decade; Poe fell into a drunken stupor on a Baltimore street and died alone and unknown when he was 40; Melville faded from the public eye when he was only 33 and lived in solitude and anonymity for decades. There were others, many others. Often the more intensely the flame of writing burns the more briefly it lasts. For the serious writer the tragedy is not going mad or dying young but continuing to write when he has nothing left to say.

THIRTY-ONE

A.M.

Failure

Teaching is more about raising questions than providing answers. For many years I have told students on the first day of class, "If you do not come out of this course more confused and uncertain than you are now, I will have failed." They usually chuckle because they do not realize how serious I am. In most classes I fail. Many students who attend elite liberal arts colleges and Ivy League universities consider their four years either a ticket to future wealth and success or an enjoyable interlude before getting on with the serious business of life. All too often successful teachers are accomplished entertainers who do not push too hard or probe too deep. I also tell my students that no matter what they think, they do not really know what they want or, more important, what they need. They are, of course, too young to understand what I mean.

As the semester unfolds, a moment invariably arrives when the writings we are studying lead me to tell my students: "Regardless of how well intentioned you are or how hard you try, you will always fail. One of the most difficult dilemmas you will face in life is deciding what counts as success and what is failure *for you*." I proceed to explain that for this question, as for so many others, I have no answer to offer them. And then I add, "I will, however, say that in my experience—for whatever it's worth—what the world tells you is success usually turns out to be failure and what others see as failure is often your greatest success." Diligent students take notes; most do not.

Teaching undergraduates is a strange business. During four of the most formative years of their lives, you are deeply involved with them as they probe important issues they may never again consider. Teachers invariably become counselors who help students through crises they cannot confide to their parents. Then, as suddenly as they arrive, they disappear and in most cases you never hear from them again. An occasional note, call, or e-mail, perhaps even a glance at the alumni magazine brings some news but it's never what you really want to know. Did they understand what I was trying to tell them? What did they take away? Do they even remember taking the course? Are they successful or have their lives been a failure? And do they ever ask themselves, what is success and what is failure for me? So few write me that I will never know whether I have succeeded or failed.

P.M.

Success

Fear, unlike any I had ever experienced, was loose on the Street and in the classroom. It had been triggered by something so unreal that it was almost nothing, and yet the fear was palpable, even visceral. Though the cloud of fear began to gather in late summer, August doldrums in New York City and Washington diverted attention from the looming crisis. When the titans of Wall Street returned from Martha's Vineyard, Nantucket, Aspen, and Jackson Hole, they could no longer deny that the global economy was rushing toward a perfect storm. Within the short span of a few weeks, trillions of dollars disappeared, venerable financial institutions vanished, time-tested economic assumptions crumbled, and millions of people lost their jobs.

Analysts and commentators sought to calm fears by searching for historical analogies, but there were none. This crisis was unlike any other.

What made the situation unique was not only its unprecedented scale but the threat it posed to the current form of capitalism. Since the late 1970s a new form of capitalism has emerged—finance capitalism. In previous forms of capitalism (i.e., industrial and consumer capitalism), people made money by buying and selling labor or material objects. In finance capitalism, by contrast, wealth is created by circulating signs, backed by nothing but other signs, in a regression that for practical purposes is limitless. Financial markets have become a sophisticated confidence game, and the people at the helm are latter-day versions of Melville's wily Confidence Man, decked out in designer shirts and Armani suits, duping passengers on an April Fool's Day voyage down the nation's great tributary, the Mississippi, on the riverboat *Fidèle*.

A week before the failure of Lehman Brothers, which marked the tipping point for the collapse of financial markets, I began teaching my undergraduate course at Columbia University, "Religion and the Modern World," by declaring that it is impossible to understand the current financial crisis if you do not understand the complex relationship between Protestantism and capitalism. Always underscoring the contemporary relevance of abstract philosophical and theological ideas, I explained that, by privatizing, deregulating, and decentralizing religion, Martin Luther began a communications revolution that prepared the way for the Internet. By enabling a new global infrastructure, the Internet and the worldwide web created the conditions for finance capitalism. In addition to this, Luther showed that not only religious but all social, political, and even economic institutions are grounded in faith. When the social contract is broken, trust erodes and confidence disappears. More than a matter of finance, the economic crisis is really a crisis of faith.

The students seemed puzzled; this was not what they expected in a course on religion. They were blissfully unaware of the financial maelstrom swirling around them and were clueless about its implications for their future. As the crisis deepened that fall and the news grew worse day by day, the mood in the classroom changed in ways that are difficult to describe. It was not so much that the students became more serious and sober, though they did; rather, it was that they seemed stunned by the prospect of making their way in a world that was falling apart. One day I decided that I could longer avoid addressing their concerns so I asked them what was bothering them. Though hesitant at first, they eventually opened up and spoke frankly. In all my years of teaching, I have rarely heard such fear, anger, and hostility from students. What they most felt was a profound sense of betrayal. One of the most insightful students effectively expressed the feeling of others: "From the time we were born, our parents and teachers have been telling us that if we work hard and get a good education, we will have a bright future. Now this! You guys screwed it up and we're paying the price. Everything we've been taught is bullshit." A crisis of faith, indeed.

Perhaps it was chance, perhaps not, but when I returned to my office after class, I had an e-mail from a former student with whom I had stayed in close touch. She was one of the best students I have ever taught—bright, sensitive, and creative. After college she worked with a private foundation dedicated to improving public education. Her experience led her to conclude that the changes society needed could not be brought about without new policies and regulations at every level of the public and private sectors. Committed to working for these changes, she decided to attend law school. We kept in touch, and I encouraged her to follow the course she was pursuing. As she approached the end of law school, her advisers told her that regardless of her eventual goals, she should work in a major New York law firm for several years. When she decided to take their advice, she reassured me that she knew the difference between the real and the fake and would find her way back to education. I wasn't so sure.

All these memories came rushing back to me as I read her e-mail that morning. The depth of her insight about what was going on around her did nothing to allay her fears; to the contrary, her understanding of the magnitude of the problem made her all the more aware of the implications of the crisis.

Not to state the obvious, but this atmosphere is unlike any I've ever experienced. Firms are starting to lay people off with increasing frequency. We just learned that we aren't having our holiday party this year. Everyone is sitting around having conversations about who would go if there were layoffs. It's really remarkable what comes out in people (including myself, although I am trying to be cognizant and aware of what I'm saying and thinking). Everyone is full of speculation, and no one, probably not even the partners, has answers. It's almost as though we are in a bad social experiment where you see how long it takes people to turn on each other and focus just on themselves. The anxiety is overwhelming. None of this is shocking but the problem is that there's no resolution. We will continue to be anxious until something happens, so it's almost as if you want anything to happen to alleviate the anxiety. But the "thing" that would most likely happen in any sort of immediate future is layoffs, and no one wants that. Even if you survive, uncertainty doesn't stop in any real way until things get very busy and you are reassured that you can once again feel secure. Until, of course, it all happens again. It's a strange sensation -- a very different kind of waiting—almost like the world has stopped this month—when will it start again?

Perhaps a (not so pleasant) wake-up call for our generation ...

The world in which these young people were raised *did* stop, and it will never start again. These young people were raised in an era of excess and with the highest expectations for a secure and comfortable future, and it never occurred to them, or to most of their parents, for that matter, that the future they imagined would not materialize. Students now found themselves facing a strange territory for which there were no maps. Though none of this was their fault, they inevitably experienced a sense of failure.

As I read my erstwhile student's e-mail, I realized that even in the midst of the frenzy of Wall Street, she actually had remembered the lessons I had tried to teach her. She acknowledged that she was caught up in a confidence game and was at least in part responsible for the suffering it was causing. She also understood that the failure was not merely her own but was the failure of a system that had lost all sense of what is real and what is not. When confidence men are stripped bare, the only way to recover is to restore the faith they have destroyed.

The students' sense of urgency, which bordered on panic, was so profound that I had not known how to respond. By chance, the text for the next class was from Adam Smith's *The Wealth of Nations*. I decided to teach the class as if nothing had happened. The students nodded knowingly as I explained how Smith's notion of the invisible hand was first invoked by Calvin to explain the machinations of divine providence. For today's true believers, the market, which is omniscient, omnipresent, and omnipotent, has become God. With our discussion drawing to a close, I returned to the previous class. "While it was difficult, I'm glad you expressed your fears the other day. I want you to know that I understand and appreciate the dilemma you face. You have every right to be angry at your elders and anxious about the future. I did not know how to respond and so said nothing. When I returned to my office, however, I had an e-mail from a former student and I want to share what she said with you."

After reading the e-mail, I continued:

For more than twenty years, many of my best and brightest students have wanted nothing more than to achieve great financial success. First it was the dot-com boom and then Wall Street. For a child of the sixties for whom the world of business was the dark side, all this has been incomprehensible.

As my students rushed toward a future they thought they owned, I urged them to keep reading and never to stop thinking. Some did but most did not. As I followed their careers, I was surprised how many became extraordinarily successful with seemingly little effort. Sometimes they would write to report their accomplishments, but their words often were hollow. It was as if they were trying to convince themselves more than me about the value of what they were doing. Though I never told them, I regarded their uneasiness as a promising sign that they had understood what I had tried to teach them.

There is no denying that the times are dark. You might not realize it, but you are actually fortunate to be facing these hard questions at a young age; many others realize too late that they never asked life's most important questions. The world that awaits you is not the world you expected—it rarely is. The failure of the system crumbling around us was inevitable—houses built on nothing cannot stand. It is far better for this unreal world to collapse now than for you to achieve success by devoting your lives to gods you eventually realize are false.

The challenge you face is to find in the failure now surrounding us new opportunities to create more just and effective institutions and to live lives whose richness is more than net worth. Life is going to be less certain and more unpredictable than you ever expected. But you should welcome this uncertainty, because it might open the possibility of a freedom that will enable you to take the chances upon which your future, as well as that of the planet, depends. If you do take those chances, you will be a success, no matter how often you fail. My final warning is that time is short, shorter than you can possibly realize.

THIRTY-TWO

A.M.

Balance

I have always been wary of balance because I fear it will take the edge off. I prefer things off balance, slightly out of kilter, just a little bit edgy. When things seem settled, I get unsettled; when people get comfortable, I am uncomfortable. I value disagreement more than agreement, resistance more than compliance. As a parent I am demanding, as a colleague, difficult, and as a teacher, tough. It is because I respect others—because I want for them what they often don't want for themselves—that I try to keep them off balance.

GRANDPA COOPER'S BALANCED BOOKS

On the face of it, she could not be more different from me. She is balanced, I am not; she seeks the middle ground I avoid. She does not get unsettled when things seem settled, nor does she become restless when things slow down. To others it appears that she balances my imbalance. This is not completely wrong because my obsession with imbalance can, I confess, become excessive. Sometimes pushing things as well as people to the limit crosses the line. When this moment approaches, she pulls me back by insisting that I must restore a semblance of balance. I often resist but usually know she is right.

In daily negotiations large and small, her strategies and tactics are more effective than mine. Without repressing disagreement, she is able to win acceptance; without overwhelming resistance, she is able to gain compliance. She understands that balance and imbalance are inseparable—each simultaneously promotes and subverts the other. When regularly anticipated, the insistence on imbalance inevitably loses its edge. Predictable tactics of resistance become ineffective and can quickly be dismissed as simply more of the same. At this point it becomes necessary to change tactics and switch directions by resisting resistance and insisting on maintaining a semblance of balance. With this reversal the prospect of settlement becomes unsettling for those who had anticipated agreement to be impossible. Compliance, paradoxically, becomes a tactic of resistance. At the very moment when everything seems to be settled, no one is sure what to expect next, and thus everyone remains warily off balance. Far from stabilizing, equilibrium can be disruptive and balance edgy.

P.M.

Simplicity

Simplicity is complex—it is metaphysical, religious, political, psychological, and aesthetic. As long as human beings have thought about the world, they have searched for simplicity in the midst of complexity. The ancient Greeks, whose ideas echo silently in many of today's most sophisticated scientific theories, reduced everything to the appearance of one of four primary principles: earth, air, fire, or water. Religions west and east are monotheistic—Yahweh, God the Father, Allah—and monistic—Brahman, the Oversoul, Spirit. Though chaos might seem to reign and nothing make sense, if God is one, things somehow hang together and life holds the promise of coherent meaning.

Devotion to simplicity always poses the threat of simplification. As the world becomes more complex, people long for simplicity that clears the mind and purifies the soul: plain talk, plain clothes, plain folks. Such longing for simplicity can lead to fundamentalisms secular as well as sacred. Their profound differences notwithstanding, the Word of God, law of Allah, unified field theory, human genome, universal grammar, algorithm of all algorithms are different versions of the same book. The most influential versions of the belief in simplicity are based on the logic of either-or: either one or many, us or them, simple or complex. In today's tangled world this logic of exclusion is not only dangerous but is, in the final analysis, self-defeating.

Simplicity, however, is not always so simple. Consider a Shaker chair, Mies building, Brancusi sculpture, Rothko painting, or Zen rock garden. They are all astonishingly simple yet incomprehensibly complex. Indeed, it is their very simplicity that makes them so complex. Consider the rock garden outside my study window. Its simplicity is not exclusionary but inclusive—simplicity emerges in relations. The placement of rocks in the empty garden is simply complex. It is impossible to say what makes it right but you know when it is wrong. The distinctive way in which each rock relates to the others is what sets it apart and makes it distinctive. In this web of relations, many become one in a way that enriches rather than represses their differences. When relations shift, the rocks change. The garden, of course, has always been regarded as the ideal image of the world. In the subtle play of seemingly inert rocks in an empty garden, the real and the ideal meet. Gazing at the garden, I can almost believe that the world as it is is the world as it ought to be. Cosmic rhythms frozen in time by an immobile garden that never remains still. The world is neither simple nor complex but is complex in its simplicity and simple in its complexity. When you get it right, the complex simplicity of rocks reveals the way the world works. Perhaps that is why Eckhart said, "God and a rock are one."

One of the greatest challenges of teaching is to convey the complexity of simplicity and simplicity of complexity in a way that is accurate but understandable. Too many students want clear answers, and readers all too often look for quick fixes and simple solutions. But not everything can be boiled down to basics; there are no twelve-step programs for life's most pressing problems. For explanations and examples to be effective, they can be neither too simple nor too complex, neither too concrete nor too abstract. The real, I believe, is not found on one or the other side of any divide but always lies in between. Learning this lesson is never easy—it requires time and patience. If teaching and writing are to trace the fine line of life, they must follow the elusive boundary where things simultaneously come together and fall apart—like chapters of a book that are not fragments yet do not add up to a whole.

SIMPLE BALANCE

THIRTY-THREE

A.M.

Face

GRANDPA TAYLOR

What most intrigues me about the face is not skin but bone. Nothing is more personal than my face, yet it always remains strange to me. I never see it directly but only indirectly in reflections cast by mirrors and windows as well as the eyes and sometimes the voice of others. In the faces of others, I glimpse my own mortality, and others read things in the lines of my face that I do not know about myself. Efforts to the contrary notwithstanding, faces betray by exposing what we would like to keep secret.

I have long preferred rough to smooth and wrinkled to unwrinkled. Surface becomes profound in the beauty of a deeply lined face. Such beauty harbors wisdom that only time can bring. In a world of airbrushing and cosmetic surgery, however, this wisdom is not merely forgotten but is actively repressed. When was the last time you saw a wrinkled face on television? As lines are erased and wrinkles smoothed, surfaces become merely superficial. With the lines go the years of wisdom they trace, and we are left to listen to the babble of people who look like they have never lived.

But something else disappears with those lines—the very traits that make each person different vanish without leaving a trace. Modeled on the virtually identical models that appear everywhere, everybody begins to look the same. Choosing a face is like designing jeans or running shoes from a menu. As people become more virtual and the virtual becomes more real, a disturbing inhumanity begins to appear in our midst. On the screens that are becoming the world, I am no longer sure when I am watching a person and when I am looking at an avatar. Faces become virtually indistinguishable until I have trouble telling one news anchor or actor from another. And to make matters even more confusing, I see the same faces in magazines, on the street, and in my classes. In the search for customized individuality, anonymity becomes the norm.

This superficial anonymity, however, masks one that is more profound. When I gaze at wrinkle-free faces designed to deny age and with it time, skin melts away and I see bone. Though disconcerting, this insight is not necessarily morbid. While rarely appreciated, bones are remarkably beautiful; they are, indeed, works of art by an anonymous artist. Unlike superficial beauty, profound beauty is horrifying because it is inhuman. Though many struggle to deny it, our unique individuality is only skin deep—strip away skin and all you are left with is bone. Imagine, just try to imagine, holding in your hands and pondering the skull of the person you love most dearly, and then imagine finding beauty in that skull. No matter how skilled a detective you are, you will never see in the lines of bone the face of the person you once loved. If, however, you reflect long enough, eventu-

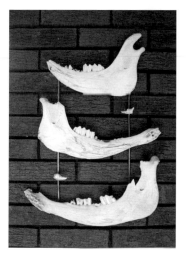

MYSTIC BONES

ally you will be forced to see yourself in the vacancy of her eyes. Beneath the surface of my face, individuality disappears and I too become anonymous. The faces of others reveal by concealing the anonymity from which we all come and to which we all return. In the horrifying beauty of bone, we are no longer face to face because two become one. The strange ecstasy of death.

P.M.

Aging

As I watch my family and friends age, I often ask myself: What do I fear more—losing my mind while my body stays strong, or the failure of my body while my mind remains clear? A false choice, you might say, but in some cases the mind-body dualism is insistent no matter how hard you try to explain it away philosophically. I have seen both these frightful conditions close enough to know that I am not sure which alternative I would choose.

On the one hand: Taylors live long but my father's brother Charles outlived them all—he did not die until he was 104. A high school teacher like all his brothers and sisters who were not farmers, Charles was multitasking before multitasking was cool. He was a sports addict, and no matter what time of year we visited him, he was watching games and horse races on two TVs and listening to two more events on his radios. His commitment to sports was so deep that when his only daughter was born, he named her after his favorite racetrack—Laurel. If you could ever get him to stop listening long enough to

MY FATHER'S MASONIC TROWEL

talk, he could always tell you what was going on in every game or race. He continued to live alone in his own house until he was one hundred, when failing eyesight finally forced him to move to a Brethren home at the intersection where his daughter-in-law had been killed and his son critically injured in an automobile accident years earlier. By that time he could no longer watch his beloved ballgames and races on TV, and, when his hearing began to fail, he was unable to listen to them on the radio. His mind, however, remained crystal clear. Our visits with him during his last year of life were excruciating—he was deaf and blind but still could think and talk. He was frustrated beyond words and wanted nothing more than to die. Though he had never read Plato and never heard of the Gnostics or Manicheans, he surely knew that his body was a prison from which he longed to be released. There was nothing we could say to him to relieve his desperation and, even if we tried, he could not hear us. Trapped in his own body, he was alone— absolutely alone—and all he could do was wait for a release he did not believe would bring deliverance.

On the other hand: John became college president the year I began teaching in the department he had created. He is one of the most remarkable people I know. A native North Carolinian raised in an orphanage because his parents were too poor to support him, at eighty-three he still conveys a graciousness that puts you at ease immediately. His wonderful wife, Florence, combined southern charm with a self-effacing wit. This allowed her to put in their place the faculty members, men and women alike, who belittled her for being "nothing more than a wife and mother"—and she did so without their even realizing what she had done. During the years of his presidency, John and I grew quite close. He and Florence took so great an interest in our children that when Aaron and Frida were married, they asked John to perform the ceremony.

I usually do my best to avoid faculty meetings but, after John had been president for twelve years, rumors of his resignation were circulating, so I decided to attend the monthly gathering. The meeting that September afternoon turned out to be one of the most distressing rituals of transition I have ever observed. John was devoted to the college and loved his job but knew that, even though he was in excellent health and had many productive years ahead of him, it was time for him to leave even though he wanted to stay. His parting words were, as always, gracious, but he obviously was very shaken. We never talked about that day; indeed, after his departure we did not see each other often. He moved to Washington, D.C., where his national influence in higher education continued to grow. By the time he retired again, he was primarily responsible for the appointment of more than forty college and university presidents as well as countless high-level administrators.

One day six or seven years ago, John called to tell me that Florence was in the early stages of Alzheimer's disease and they were moving back to Williamstown, where he felt it would be easier to deal with the problem. They settled in the retirement home just down the road from where we live. Since his return we have become even closer and now have lunch together at least a couple of times a month. During the early years after his return, I would always ask about Florence and we would discuss her condition. It was clearly good for him to have someone to talk to about the ordeal. Not until these discussions did I begin to fathom the true horror of losing your mind while your body remains strong.

I remember one conversation especially vividly. Florence, he reported, had become convinced that they were once again teenagers in their North Carolina high school. When he visited her in the nursing home, she transported him back in time to be with her. To the best of John's recollection, her memory of that time was accurate down to the slightest detail: the clothes they wore, the friends they visited, the formals they attended, the arguments they had, the plum jam her mother made. And yet Florence had no idea where she actually was or who John really was. At first he tried to explain that she was confused but, realizing it was futile, he decided to play along with her and become a teenager once again. As he recounted his experience, his dismay about Florence did not completely mask the pleasure he took in reliving their past together. Though it was impossible to be sure, Florence might have known more than either of us realized at the time. Sometimes I suspected she was preparing him for her excruciatingly long good-bye.

Gradually, her condition worsened and she steadily sank into silence. When she became unable to care for herself, the nursing home was not equipped to meet her growing needs. Overwhelmed by guilt, John resisted moving her to a specialized facility as long as possible. As the situation became desperate, our roles reversed—the trusted counselor to whom I had turned for advice so many times now turned to me for guidance and reassurance. It was as if he were asking my permission to let her go. I told him he was physically and emotionally unable to continue caring for her by himself and that he would do her no favor by endangering his own health. Finally, he relented and agreed to permit her to be moved twenty miles away. During this whole period I never saw Florence again; indeed, I cannot honestly remember the last time I saw her.

After the move we talked about her less and less often—he didn't offer and I didn't ask. After all, what could either of us say? We both knew a dark cloud of guilt was hanging over us. For the past five years, she has been completely unconscious, but her body continues to function all too well. Florence seems determined to go on living even if she does not know why. Summoning strength and determination I greatly admire, John has begun

MY FIRST BIKE

to live again. University administrators from across the country regularly seek his advice, and he remains active on several important boards. Most remarkable, however, he is once more taking courses and has begun teaching again, and the students genuinely appreciate his courses. We continue to have lunch every other week, and he is always eager to hear what I am reading and writing. Our roles, however, have returned to their proper order, and he once again has become my mentor. Though he would never say so, John is quietly teaching me how to age gracefully. We both know he is living with unspeakable horror every hour of every day and especially of every night. And yet we never mention it to each other. In a strategy devised to confront rather than avoid, we talk about what we need to talk about by not talking about it.

As I ponder the dilemma these two tragic cases pose, my questions proliferate. For an intellectual little is more terrifying than the prospect of losing one's mind. Nevertheless, given the choice between Charles and Florence, I suspect I would choose body without mind rather than mind without body. But I must confess that I am not sure because, watching John, I realize that even though I would have no idea what was going on, my choice would condemn those I most love to unbearable suffering.

THIRTY-FOUR

A.M.

Stigma

Disease stigmatizes but not all stigmas are the same. Some are visible, others invisible; some are more threatening, others less. I bear the stigma of several diseases. A stigma, I have discovered, singles out, sets apart, creates a distance. Once stigmatized, you become other, always other. This othering is not so much my own activity as it is a process of distancing that others deploy as a strategy of containment and control in their relations to me. In declaring the other other, people claim, "I am not that."

When I was diagnosed first with diabetes and then with cancer, I thought long and hard about what to tell and not to tell others about my condition. Since there were no visible symptoms in either case, it would have been possible to keep my illnesses secret. The longer I pondered my dilemma, the clearer it became that hiding is a tactic of denial to oneself as well as to others. You do not really accept illness until you are able to say publicly, "I am sick." This confession carries additional weight when the diseases are chronic because you must then add, "and I will never again be well." Once these words are uttered, nothing is ever the same and others always look at you differently.

After considerable reflection I decided to be as honest as I could be with myself as well as others about the illnesses I suffer. I have long believed that if you can't live it, you should neither teach it nor write it. So when disease befell me, I knew I had to try to live the tears I had long written about, and

I realized that how I lived these nots might be the most important lesson I could leave students and readers. The delicate balance of confession is to find the fine line between flaunting and fleeing. Having dreaded admitting to others what I found so hard to admit to myself, I was completely surprised when confessing illness brought a strange sense of freedom. At one level or another, everyone knows that some day he or she will also have to say, "I am sick and there is no cure." Anticipating this moment can be so dreadful that it transforms life into ceaseless denial and endless flight, but when the time arrives, the experience can actually be liberating. Suddenly you become free to enjoy whatever time remains in ways that are impossible as long as you believe disease is distant.

Not all confessions, however, are greeted the same way. When I first told people I had diabetes, their responses tended to be a mixture of sympathy and incredulity: "How can this be true? You look great, you are in good shape, and you even run every day." Expressions of support were invariably followed by questions that seemed to carry hints of self-interest: "Does it run in *your* family?" implied "it doesn't run in *mine*." More often than not, the parting words of consolation were: "Well, it could be worse; at least it's not cancer. After all, diabetes is manageable."

When it *is* cancer, everything changes—words of sympathy are invariably shadowed by intimations of fear. In my presence others see what they dread they might become, and that future is terrifyingly unmanageable. While apparently comforting me, friends and acquaintances often seem to be struggling to reassure themselves: "They are making great progress on your type of cancer." "You are lucky, you caught it early." "Once they cut it out, it's gone." As word of my illness spread, many friends called once, but few followed up, and fewer still visited after surgery. When we happened to meet in the library or on the street weeks later, they would say that they would have stopped by but had not wanted to disturb me. I knew, as did they, that this was not the reason for their avoidance.

When you suffer a chronic disease, things never get back to normal; indeed, you finally realize what you have long suspected—there is no such thing as normal. Disease is *never* gone, they *never* get it all, it's *never* over.

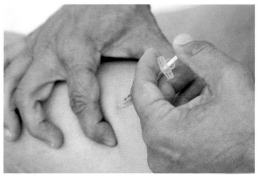

SHOOTING UP

Things are always unmanageable and we are never in control—and yet we must go on. Chronic disease teaches us that the challenge that life poses is not to find a cure but to learn to live with the impossibility of cure.

P.M.

Autoimmunity

My body is a body politic that is always at war with itself. *I am* has become *I war*. The enemy is not external—a menacing other or invading alien—but internal—I am the other of myself and thus am alien to myself. The threat deemed without is actually within. My body does not know itself, does not recognize itself, and therefore miscalculates by reading the same as an other to be attacked. In this way my body produces the other it then proceeds to destroy and in destroying the "other" destroys itself. In this struggle the clash between self and other is transformed into a conflict that marks self as other. If allowed to rage unchecked, this disease becomes fatal and there is no cure. At best, the end can be delayed, deferred.

The logic of autoimmunity operates at all levels of life. If microcosm reflects macrocosm and vice versa or, in less poetic terms, if the cosmos is fractal, then the same patterns recur in different contexts. Shifting from the individual to the universal, the logic of autoimmunity exposes the structure and operation of today's global body politic. Social, political, and cultural systems mistake productive differences for fatal oppositions and precipitously rush to war rather than resorting to deliberate negotiations. Like my diseased body, societies, cultures, and religions produce the other they then seek to destroy. When this occurs, *we are* becomes *we war*. By creating the other it then resists, the system, however it is construed, marshals its forces and consolidates its operations—at least for a while. In the clash of civilizations, for example, identity is negative because it is resolutely oppositional. For conflicts to be violent, both sides must accept the same rules of engagement: I am *not* that … we are *not* they. When autoimmunity becomes the governing logic of world systems, the body politic becomes diseased. If allowed to rage unchecked, this disease becomes fatal and there seems to be no cure. In defeating the ostensible alien deemed menacing, the system destroys the very other it needs to be itself. It is therefore necessary to produce another other, which, in turn, can be opposed and eventually overcome. This process must go on endlessly; the logic of autoimmunity, in other words, involves the eternal return of the same as difference in the guise of opposition. Such a strategy, however, is both short-sighted and misguided—victory is defeat and complete success is total failure—in destroying others we tear ourselves apart.

There is, however, an alternative logic hidden in the logic of autoimmunity. If I need the other to be myself, then the other is not merely other but is also a moment in my own being. I cannot be who and what I am without the other who cannot be who or what he or she is without me. When I mistake difference for opposition, I misread the other in a way that is finally self-destructive. If the logic of autoimmunity gives way to the logic of mutuality, the body politic is transformed, perhaps even healed.

What if today's body politic is a global organism in which every member is a cell and every organization an organ? Just as my body becomes diseased when my killer T-cells misread cells in my pancreas as alien invaders, so the body politic becomes diseased when other individuals, societies, cultures, and religions are misread as alien invaders that must be destroyed. In these misadventures the price of success is high; I cannot live without the cells my body kills any more than the body politic can survive without the rich diversity it struggles to repress. When disease becomes chronic, the condition becomes terminal. The only way to heal the body politic is to interrupt the seemingly endless cycle of violence by subverting the self-destructive logic of autoimmunity. Then, and only then, might *we war* become *we are*.

SHEIKH SULTAN BIN TAHNOON AL NAHYAN AND HIS FALCON, ABU DHABI

THIRTY-FIVE

A.M.

Patience

GRANDFATHER'S GRANDFATHER CLOCK

Patience is a waiting that is not an awaiting. The patient who suffers disease, pain, or anguish awaits relief, perhaps even cure. The promise of research, a phone call with the diagnosis, the test results with an answer, the prescription for a pill. Awaiting is an active response to suffering through which the patient attempts to master time by making the future apprehensible as well as manageable. Even when it appears dark, the future can lend the present meaning and direction if there are strategies to negotiate it. As long as a condition remains unnamed, it provokes anxiety. By naming a disease, diagnosis transforms anxiety into fear, which can be dealt with. No longer abandoned to waiting, the patient can begin doing something about her condition. Unless, of course, the diagnosis names the unnameable that can be neither managed nor controlled. The prescription promises relief, if not cure, even when the therapy is long and arduous and the drugs are *pharmakons* that are worse than the disease. Though one must be patient, at least something can be done—for now. Such active patience is, however, really impatience, which is often an expression of the will to power designed to avoid rather than confront mortality.

There is a patience beyond this (im)patience, which emerges with the confession that time and with it life are finally unmanageable. The activity of awaiting struggles to control the uncontrollable by circumscribing the future. Waiting, by contrast, is a radical passivity that is more passive than the passivity that is the opposite of activity. The patient—and who is not a patient?—who waits expects the unexpected and therefore remains open to the opening of the future. There is nothing reassuring about waiting; to the contrary, patience is profoundly unsettling. This patience beyond patience exposes us to a future that sometimes is monstrous. Even when the future appears promising, it harbors an uncertainty that renders life inescapably insecure. Though research might be productive, the prognosis good, and the pill effective, the unexpected is always looming just over the horizon. Forever awaiting the arrival of what does not arrive but only approaches by withdrawing, the patient finds that every moment becomes both more and less urgent. Far from providing reassurance, patience arouses the anxiety that is inseparable from life itself. The insufferable openness of the future is the pathos at the heart of all suffering. Knowing he does not know, the patient who is truly patient realizes that nothing remains . . . nothing remains but waiting.

P.M.

Chronicity

Chronicity—the word is not proper but, then, nothing ever is. Far from one, time is always many—its layers are convoluted in such a way that they overlap and fold into each other, sometimes seamlessly, sometimes exposing fissures that tear everything and everyone to pieces. Rather than living one time at a time, we live multiple times simultaneously. This simultaneity does not lift us out of time in a way that allows us to overcome its passing but, to the contrary, deepens temporality by complicating its contours.

Different diseases disclose alternative temporal rhythms in life: some have a beginning and an end, others do not; some can be cured, others cannot; some require purposeful discipline, others do not. While every disease poses its own difficulties, none is more challenging than chronic disease. When you suffer a chronic disease, you are exposed to the most debilitating and inescapable dimension of temporality.

I did not understand the time of disease until I developed diabetes in what I had always assumed would be midlife. Though it struck suddenly, this disease invariably involves hereditary factors and thus must have been inscribed in my genes before birth—indeed, even before my conception. I have traced family lines back to the eighteenth century but have found no trace of diabetes, and yet I have always already been sick even though I did not know it, because my end was inscribed in lines of code long before my beginning.

Coping with chronic disease takes you places you have never been and forces you to do things you never imagined doing. I remember all too well (how could I ever forget?) the first time I suffered by my own hand the wound of a syringe. It was not the pain I feared, though there was that, but the violence, the violation of my body. Its wounding, puncture, bleeding— the injection of a foreign, synthetic, artificial agent into my own flesh. I felt I was betraying my body, which had betrayed me. Wound upon wound, betrayal upon betrayal. I drew the syringe slowly, carefully, deliberately and watched the mesmerizing trickle of the chemical substance. Numbers and lines, fine lines that must not be crossed. When the agents reached the proper line on the syringe, I paused long enough to forget what I had to do. Then, with a suddenness that startled me, I sank the needle into my flesh, deep into my flesh, and emptied the contents of the syringe into my body. Much to my surprise, I felt *nothing*, absolutely nothing—no pain, no pleasure, no relief. Nothing but a slight trace of blood marked the flow of time. As I pondered what I had done, I realized that this ritual would be a part of my daily routine as long as I live.

What is most difficult about such diseases is their sheer chronicity. Diabetes never takes a holiday—it must be monitored and managed hour by hour, day by day, year by year. Coping with this disease requires extraordinary discipline, which involves not only daily blood tests (at least six a day) and insulin injections but also a tightly controlled diet and a rigorous daily exercise regime. It is as if you were always training for a marathon you can never finish. In time, it all becomes ritualized, which is not to say regularized. The pulse of life as well as disease: fluids flowing in and out, out and in. Insulin in, blood out; codes and numbers in, codes and numbers out. This ritual, like most others, turns on the tension between excess and control: too much and/or too little, never enough, never equilibrium, never harmony. And all this must be sustained over time with no prospect for a cure. It often becomes too much—the sheer relentlessness of the disease inevitably wears you down and discipline inevitably falters. In such moments it all seems so pointless, so hopeless, and you wonder, should I go on or stop? But what does it mean to go on? And what would it mean to stop?

When in the throes of chronic disease, its temporality seems more primal than the others I also experience. The forms of time that have an identifiable beginning, middle, and end, as well as a narrative structure that joins them in ways that lend life meaning and purpose, seem to have been artificially constructed to repress the inescapable chronicity that shatters continuity in repetition without renewal. Needles punctuate the lines of the stories we tell ourselves to get us through the night … leaving ellipses that mark tears that can never be mended—tears that can never be wiped away. There is no doctoring such a rift once it opens. No matter how disciplined I am, nothing ever balances … *nothing ever balances*. Cure remains impossible and, in the end, time always triumphs.

THIRTY-SIX

A.M.

Technology

We are always already posthuman. Indeed, the line that simultaneously separates and joins what is human and what is not can never be drawn precisely. Culture and its extension in technology are the supplements that *originally* constitute the human as such. Far from opposite, nature and artifice are codependent and coevolve. The natural is artificial because the artificial is natural. The distinctive trait of humanity is an originary lack that makes prostheses, implants, and transplants necessary for survival. Nevertheless, many critics today—from the supposedly sophisticated to the apparently naive—insist that rather than enhancing humanity, technology threatens the "authentically human." Technophobes on the left as well as on the right want to flee the present by turning the clock back to a pretechnological era that never existed. Campaigns to "preserve nature" and "protect human life" actually hasten the demise of the so-called natural and death of the so-called human.

Though a committed technophile, I do not wear technology on my sleeve; rather, I carry it on my belt. It is a small computer no one ever notices—like

INSULIN PUMP

the purloined letter, its conspicuousness makes it inconspicuous. Everybody assumes it is a cell phone or a pager, but it is really an insulin pump without which I cannot live. I am literally plugged in 24/7/365. The pump is both prosthesis and implant—a computer with twenty-one programmable screens and a small plastic tube inserted through a needle into my leg. Through this tube flows "artificial" insulin that substitutes for the "natural" insulin my body is unable to produce. The pump is, in effect, a digital pancreas, though it cannot—at least not yet—function on its own. This artifice, which supplements the human, must itself be supplemented by the human to close the salvific loop. The body is, among many other things, a cybernetic system in which a semblance of equilibrium is maintained through negative feedback signals. In my body the loop linking glucose intake to insulin production in the islets of Langerhans cells in the pancreas is broken, and I must complete the circuit by first calculating numbers and then programming the computer to release the required dose of insulin. My calculations, unlike those my body should make by itself, are never precise and so I am always off balance. This situation can be dangerous, and there is not much room for error: Too little insulin creates hyperglycemia, which can lead to kidney failure, and too much insulin can induce coma. Both conditions can result in death. Far from destroying life through the will to power expressed in the will to mastery, technology—at least for now—allows me to maintain the control of my body necessary for survival.

Though not everyone wears a pump on his or her belt, no one can live without technology. My pump is a manifest sign of the latent connections that form the worldwide web without whose inputs and outputs life is impossible. The extent of these connections will become explicit in the next iteration of the insulin pump. Researchers are now perfecting technologies that will take human beings out of the loop and make the pump a self-regulating apparatus. This will require the patient to wear yet another mechanical device that tests blood sugar at regular intervals and feeds this information to the pump, which in turn calculates and administers the precise dosage required. Where wireless networks are available, the data can be sent to a computer that records and stores blood sugar levels and insulin doses. If the system detects a problem resulting from either excessive or insufficient insulin or sugar, a message is transmitted to the health-care provider as well as the individual's pump, which sets off an alarm. This functionality will be available anywhere in the world where there is access to the Internet. It is worth pausing to consider the implications of this technological innovation: The insulin circulating in my body and the biochemical processes it enables are monitored and regulated by global information and communications networks. The mechanical and digital devices that now function as my pancreas are, in other words, nodes in this worldwide web, and my body has become a prosthesis of a prosthesis.

In the posthuman condition boundaries and borders that once seemed secure become fuzzy. What is inside and what is outside? What is natural and what is artificial? What is an organism and what is a machine? What is human and what is nonhuman? My blood is regulated by servers that can be located anywhere in the world; my eyes expand to screens distributed globally, my memory is downloaded in data banks that are instantly accessible. When outer is inner and inner is outer, self is world and world is self. We become both metamind and metabody—cells in an intelligent global organism whose lifeblood is information. The networks that sustain life are the current embodiment of what once was named the divine Logos. In today's divine economy, to be is to be connected and to pull the plug is to die.

P.M.

Addiction

What is so insidious about addiction is its secrecy and the suspicion and mistrust this creates. The life of the addict becomes a prolonged exercise in hiding from others as well as himself. No matter how close the relationship, once you suspect addiction, the person becomes a stranger.

Words that once revealed now conceal, deeds that once were expressive now dissimulate. When nothing can be taken at face value, every gesture must be read like an enigmatic text that has no key.

The call came on a beautiful summer evening. We were enjoying a cookout with friends we had not seen for a long time, and everyone had had enough gin and tonics to be in a good mood. The ringing of the phone interrupted us. When I picked it up, I knew immediately there was a problem. The familiar voice of my long-time friend's wife said, "He's overdosed again and this time it's real bad. He's in the hospital, you'd better come fast. I'm scared, very scared." He was unconscious and she was not sure he would survive. One of our friends with us that evening was a physician and when I explained the situation, she agreed, "She's right; you should get there as soon as possible." This was not the first time he had faced such a crisis. It had begun when we were college roommates in the sixties. He always lived on the edge and sometimes went too far. Something told me that this time was different so I quickly threw a few things in a suitcase and began the five-hour drive to Maine.

It was late when I arrived at the hospital, but they let me see him in the intensive care unit. He had regained consciousness but was in very bad shape. Sweating profusely and shaking violently, he was suffering a severe case of the DTs. The doctors wanted to give him methadone but he refused. When I spoke to him, he had trouble responding. His wife explained that he had suffered a seizure and his teeth had sliced his tongue in half. The tongue is quite sensitive and cannot be stitched; the wound was excruciatingly painful and would take weeks, perhaps longer, to heal. I stayed at his bedside throughout the night, while doctors and nurses constantly monitored his vital signs. The dose he had taken was so strong that his body was in danger of going into shock, which could be fatal. It was a small country hospital, and I was not sure how much experience they had had with severe drug cases.

By morning, however, his condition had begun to stabilize, and he was coherent enough to begin considering treatment options. The doctors said there were only two alternatives: rehab or a methadone program. We had been down this road before—he had tried rehab several years earlier and it had not worked. Since he knew more about biology and psychology than the doctors and counselors, he had not taken anything they told him seriously. A few months after he was released the last

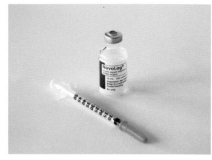

SYRINGE

time, he started drinking again and soon was back on morphine. He wasn't going to try what had not worked in the past. Methadone, he insisted, was not an option because he didn't have time to drive to the clinic. I told him he didn't have time not to.

As we talked over the next two days, he admitted that he would not live if he didn't stop using drugs. When he told me that he had decided to go cold turkey, I was skeptical. In retrospect I think it was the seizure and sliced tongue more than anything else that convinced him he had come to the end of the line. Since my classes did not start for a while, I stayed with him during the difficult first weeks. During those long nights we talked more candidly than ever before—or so it seemed—about his problems and much else. We both realized, however, that some secrets are so deep that we can never be sure we are telling the truth to ourselves or to others. We knew all too well that addiction is a chronic disease for which there is no cure.

I also developed a chronic disease several years later, but society was kinder to me than to him because people did not think I was responsible for falling ill. My disease, like his, involved needles and drugs, injections and fixes. As my fear of needles gradually gave way to perverse fascination, I was able to understand his condition much better. Late one night he said, "There is something hypnotic, even addictive, about the syringe: the care for the instruments, the deliberateness of the preparation, the solemnity of the administration of the drug. It's not just the drug—you get hooked on the ritual." I now know just what he meant. As in any ritual worth repeating, there is a moment when death approaches—one line too many and the dose is lethal. Every time you load the syringe, death draws near. Before I began shooting up, what I never expected is that, far from making addiction terrifying, the approach of death is part of what makes it so attractive.

Having become an insulin junkie, I was not sure his addiction and mine were so different. I was, however, sure that in such matters secrecy is destructive and so I decided to be completely open about my addiction. Rather than hiding in the privacy of bedroom or bathroom, I would shoot up in public, where people would have to confront what I am and what they one day might become. Though people are often taken aback, no one has ever left the room or excused himself or herself at the sight of the syringe. In most cases the act of injection has led to discussion of the disease and the problems as well as the opportunities it poses.

As days turned into weeks and weeks into months, my skepticism about his decision to forgo methadone began to fade, and I was both surprised and delighted by his resolution and discipline. He has now been clean for more than a decade but, having seen the power of addiction, I remain vigilant. Whenever I listen to his voice or observe his gestures, I try to detect hints of concealment. Far from a betrayal of confidence, doubt has become an abiding obligation.

That summer night many Augusts ago, his life literally hung in the balance and there seemed to be no way out. His determination against seemingly insurmountable odds taught me that the impossibility of cure does not mean that life cannot go on. At the time I could not have known how important this insight soon would become in my own life. It is difficult to convey how trying chronic disease becomes and how tempting it sometimes is to OD. Going through his ordeal with him also taught me another unexpected lesson: the suspicion and mistrust that often destroy relationships can, in certain circumstances, be the most profound expression of love.

THIRTY-SEVEN

A.M.

Pain

Pain is not the same as suffering. There can be suffering without pain and pain without suffering. Nor is pain primarily physical. Indeed, physical pain is but the aftereffect of a deeper pain, which is always a matter of knowledge or its impossibility. Pain and secrecy, it seems, are bound in a knot that can never be undone. Both betraying and guarding secrets can bring pain. When some secrets are told, everything changes in the twinkling of an eye. Revelation transforms knowledge into ignorance by exposing as pernicious lies truths that long seemed certain. Pain is knowing that you did not know, even when you were sure you had figured it out. The experience of pain is fleeting, though its effects linger—perhaps forever.

However, an other pain is more profound because it is more elusive, more evasive, more obscure. This pain is not the result of betraying a secret but is the effect of confessing that some secrets can never be betrayed. After all is said, if not done, what remains most telling, I have come to believe, is precisely what I cannot tell. I did not begin to suspect this secret until I attempted to tell it all to someone I thought had withheld what he should have revealed. Far from a shadowy preconscious or unconscious waiting to be exposed, this secret is, as Freud inconspicuously notes, something like the navel of the mind, which reveals the unknowable by concealing it. This point of contact with what cannot be contacted is the trace of a recessive origin that gives birth to thinking by leaving an ungraspable residue that can never be erased. The pain of suspecting that I do not know what is most intimate—for how can I ever again be sure?—casts a shadow over everything I tell myself as well as others. Perhaps it's not really the way I think it is. Perhaps it didn't happen the way I remember. Perhaps I'm not who I believe I am. Perhaps. Perhaps. Perhaps. It is because I suspect I do not know that I must write and because I can never be sure whether I know that I cannot stop writing. The more I think I know, the less I realize I know, and the more I show, the more I hide.

P.M.

Intimacy

Things too intimate to be said sometimes can be written. Since the beginning of philosophy and perhaps before, speech has been associated with the presence that breeds intimacy, and writing has been deemed dangerous because it engenders an absence that incites errancy. Presence and proximity, however, should not be confused with intimacy. Indeed, it is often the presence of the other that actually discloses how distant we are or have become. Staring at each other face to face, we encounter a void that can be neither closed nor covered. In the presence of this breach, even "I'm sorry" seems too little too late.

Distance, by contrast, permits an intimacy that speech interrupts. Absence relaxes inhibitions that presence imposes. When the other is not here but elsewhere, I am free to write what all too often goes unsaid. The written cannot be translated into the spoken without infinite loss. Words that bear weight on the page often ring hollow when uttered. That is why we are so often embarrassed to say what we most want to write: "Forever." "I love you." "Nevermore."

But not all writing is intimate and not all distance creates closeness. Sometimes writing is calculated to destroy those who are closest to us, and

LA CARTE POSTALE

sometimes distance exposes an emptiness that cannot be filled. In today's world ever-expanding networks draw us closer together in ways that make the distance separating us more evident. When messages are instant, intimacy becomes impossible. Intimacy takes—and gives—time. You cannot be intimate on the fly or when you are in a hurry. There is a rhythm to intimacy: to be intimate with another, you must pause, linger, reflect. The moment of intimacy is almost nothing in which the not-yet is already.

I once had a friend who understood writing better than anyone I have ever known. Over the years we exchanged many letters. I would always type my missives, and he invariably would respond with handwritten notes and letters. His handwriting was almost illegible, and usually I could understand no more than half the words on the page. But I never asked him to type his letters because I knew that, for all his insistence on the absence that haunts writing, he knew his hand was the trace of an intimacy he was unable to give voice. That is why I never asked friends who know French far better than I to help me decipher his text. I would rather his words remain incomprehensible than violate the confidence his hand extended to me. We both realized, but never actually said, that his letters were, in a way, love letters.

Many years ago Dinny and I decided to burn our love letters. There were many letters—I have long forgotten how many—because there were times when we had written to each other daily. It has taken me many years to understand why personal visits and phone calls were never enough to sustain our intimacy. Writing, I have learned, allows intimacy to be shared by figuring what spoken words cannot capture. I still remember the style of her monogram, the blue of the paper and ink, and the quirky curves of her script. While there have been moments when I have wished I could reread those letters, I have never regretted our decision to reduce them to ash. Intimacy must always guard its secrets.

I am writing these words with pencil on paper. That is how I always write what I regard as most important and most intimate. Everything else I write on the computer—no drafts, no rewriting—straight in, straight out. As storage capacity expands and memory becomes virtually infinite, intimacy is forgotten. When is the last time you wrote or received a love letter? Words that matter cannot be processed.

WRITING PENCILS

THIRTY-EIGHT

A.M.

Blindness

Sometimes the literal is figurative, though the figurative is never literal. From ancient myths and scriptures to contemporary psychology and critical theory, the gift of blindness, we have been taught, brings with it irreplaceable insight. Prophets and visionaries who are blind reveal truths to people who cannot see what is staring them in the face. Throughout the history of the West, the metaphysics of light, which associates knowledge with vision, has always been shadowed by an epistemology of darkness in which knowing is shrouded in a cloud of unknowing.

The obscurity of vision, which is not the same as the vision of obscurity, began so gradually that I did not see it coming until it was almost too late. One morning as I began my daily ritual of pondering the day's first light, the clouds veiling the mountains did not lift as they usually do. At first I assumed my glasses were dirty, but no matter how many times I cleaned them, my vision remained dark. As the day gradually dawned, the cloud in my right eye moved back and forth as if it were drifting lazily in the early morning breeze. I told myself it was nothing but really knew otherwise. Ever since I have had diabetes, I have feared blindness. When people ask me, as they often do, why I have not written about music, I tell them, "I'm waiting till I go blind to study music." They usually laugh dismissively, thinking I am kidding, but in truth I am not.

This was not the first time I faced blindness. Eight years earlier I developed cataracts and underwent surgery to replace the lenses in both eyes with plastic implants. I was conscious during the surgery and still have vivid memories of how the world appeared in the brief moments between the removal of the natural lenses and the insertion of the artificial lenses. The light was very bright and completely dispersed. I could not, of course, focus and thus could see no objects. Light and shifting shades of darkness oscillated in fluxes and flows where nothing was distinct or determinate. When the surgeon implanted the plastic lenses, it was as if Marduk once again had slain Tiamat and the world had been created anew. Lying help lessly on the operating table with my eyeball sliced open, I recalled something the man who first taught me Kant had said many years earlier. When I once asked my professor why he had become a philosopher, he responded through a haze of pipe smoke, "Because I have worn glasses from the time I was a child." "Glasses?" I said, "What do glasses have to do with philosophy?" "Everything," he insisted. "It has always been obvious to me that the world is not as it appears to be." A complex insight parading as simplicity itself. How are we to understand the world? Is it light or dark? Diffused or focused? One or many? Dionysus or Apollo? Or is it, perhaps, the ceaseless altaration between (the) two? It is impossible to answer such questions with any degree of certainty because we all wear glasses even if we do not know the prescription.

GRANDPA COOPER'S SPECTACLES

The darkness now clouding my vision is different from the bright light that rendered everything obscure. I realize, of course, that the fog lurking along the corner of my eye is the shadow of death, which I can never escape. As the days pass, nothing becomes clear and my vision grows worse. Doctors have told me that yet another technological fix might solve the problem for a while, but they cannot promise that there would be no complications or that I will not face further difficulties in the future. The possibility of blindness, it seems, is no longer an idle fantasy.

For a person whose life is devoted to reading and writing, there is little more terrifying than blindness. No matter how long I might listen to music, there would remain a void left by not being able to read the books I love and gaze upon paintings that expose me to mysteries I cannot comprehend. The longer I ponder the blindness that one day will come, the more I realize that my fear of losing my sight harbors a more profound dread, which is nonetheless strangely liberating. As vision fades, I have fewer distractions and more time to think. Darkness becomes illuminating when it reveals that what once seemed to be insight is blindness and that what now is blindness makes it possible to see through what for so long had seemed real.

P.M.

Aura

My insulin reactions usually occur between 12:00 and 2:00 A.M. When blood sugar levels fall below 80, the body needs to restore its balance. If readings drop below 60, the situation becomes critical, and at 40 coma or even death can occur. In response to an insulin reaction, my body produces adrenalin, which, at least for now, rouses me from sleep in time to correct the situation. The most common symptoms of low blood sugar are perspiration, light-headedness, and cognitive dissociation. When you have diabetes, it is necessary to learn how to read your body with as much care and insight as the most challenging book. In this case textual misinterpretation can prove fatal. During the day I can feel reactions coming on and head them off; at night, however, things are different and the risk is much higher, especially when I am alone.

By the time a reaction awakens me, my blood sugar is usually very low. As the level continues to drop, something very strange happens—I begin to have visual hallucinations. When I hit 60—and this number is always precise—light begins to shimmer. It is as if I were gazing through a translucent scrim that is fluttering in a gentle breeze. I once described my experience to Oliver Sacks. He had never heard of anything like it but speculated that it might be similar to the aura that accompanies migraine headaches. This well-known condition is caused by the constriction of blood vessels in the brain. But this is not all that happens. When my blood sugar drops to 50 and below, which is very dangerous, something even stranger occurs. An image appears that is always exactly the same: I see a solid black rectangle with a half bagel or donut floating above it. All the lines are crisp and edges clear except the open ends of the bagel or donut, which are jagged. As soon as I glimpse this image, the bagel begins to close. When I see this moving image, I know I am in trouble and have to get orange juice as quickly as possible. Though I have never seen the gap in the bagel completely disappear, I have come close enough to calculate that from the time the image first appears, I have approximately forty-five seconds before I lose consciousness. I have consulted leading endocrinologists and neurologists, but no one can explain how or why this happens.

While I am not a doctor, the function of this vision is clear to me: the closing bagel is a timer that tells me exactly how long I have to get the sugar fix I need to prevent the onset of a coma. Coping with disease has taught me that the body is an incomprehensibly complex network of chemical reactions and information processes. The more I learn about the body, the less I know. One thing, however, is certain: even when life seems stable, our bodies always teeter on the edge of collapse. Life and death hinge on a difference as slight as a blood sugar of 40 or 39. To make matters even more perplexing, prescriptions are never unambiguous: what is poison at one moment is medicine the next. The sugar that threatens my life during the day saves my life at night. Nothing ever balances, and equilibrium is deferred as long as life continues. Sometimes life hangs by a thread as thin as a baffling hallucination or a fleeting aura.

THIRTY-NINE

A.M.

Cancer

Nothing—absolutely nothing—prepares you for the words, "I'm sorry, you have cancer." No matter how long you have anticipated the news, no matter how sympathetically it is delivered, the world stops the moment the message arrives. The future, which is never secure, suddenly seems blank—plans, projects, programs are immediately suspended. A broken relationship never mended, a book almost complete left unfinished, an unborn granddaughter never met. Even if the prognosis is "good," cancer exposes a fragility that is the inescapable trace of the future's uncertainty.

Cancer is unlike other diseases. Neither my mother nor grandmother ever uttered the word. Even when close relatives were dying and everyone knew why, the word *cancer* was banned. It was as if saying "cancer" were a magical incantation or performative utterance that spread disease by word of mouth. Earlier generations seemed to believe that the prohibition of the word would contain the disease. *Cancer* does, in fact, reveal the power of language, albeit in a different way than those who forbid it intend. Illness functions metaphorically and different diseases convey different values. Tuberculosis, for example, has long been associated with heightened aesthetic sensibility and exceptional spirituality. While some writers suffered TB, many more, as Susan Sontag pointed out, romanticized the disease—Novalis, Tolstoy, John Keats, Charles Dickens, Franz Kafka, Thomas Mann, Thomas Wolfe, Baudelaire, André Gide, Ingmar Bergman, Eugene

O'Neill—the list goes on and on. Cancer, by contrast, is never idealized and there is nothing either romantic or redemptive about this disease. While tuberculosis supposedly etherealizes, cancer materializes by making the most rudimentary bodily processes painfully inescapable. Rather than releasing untapped abilities, cancer is utterly debilitating. The remarkable advances of modern medicine notwithstanding, the word *cancer* remains so threatening that it has become the metaphor for the incurability of disease that everyone finally suffers.

Though its chemistry is extremely complex, the mechanisms by which cancer operates are relatively simple. Unlike many diseases, which are caused by hostile agents invading the body, cancer results when processes necessary to life go awry. Though deadly, cancer is, paradoxically, the embodiment of life's uncontrollable exuberance. The body survives through a process of continuous regeneration in which billions of cells are replaced every day. For both internal and external reasons, normal cells self-destruct after they have replicated themselves a predetermined number of times. Unlike silicon copies, carbon copies eventually degenerate and become defective. In cells that are cancerous, the replication mechanism turns on but does not turn off. Growth explodes until it becomes effusive and finally excessive. At this point life overflows its proper bounds and becomes death.

When life spins out of control, only three things can be done: gene therapy, which is designed to flip the cells' off switch to stop replication; radiation or chemotherapy, which destroys cancer cells; and surgery, which removes the tumor. Every "cure" is, however, also poison: tampering with one gene influences others; drugs kill cells they are supposed to protect; knives inflict wounds whose scars never heal. Though significant advances have been made, there is still no cure for cancer. Malignant cells are elusive and can always slip away and remain undetected for years. Cancer, like addiction, is forever.

Most of these lessons I learned in a class I taught with my friend and colleague in the chemistry department. Intentionally echoing Erwin

Schrödinger's famous book, Chip and I titled the course "What Is Life?" Our goal was to create a dialogue between science and the humanities by considering the philosophical and theological implications of the most so-phisticated contemporary scientific accounts of life. Recalling Heidegger's insight that the function of a tool is not evident until it breaks, I suggested that we devote part of the course to the study of disease. Because autoim-mune diseases and cancer are spreading so rapidly and are so intellectually fascinating, we decided to concentrate on them. Little did I know how poi-gnant those classes would be. Since I was more familiar with diabetes than I wanted to be, I assumed responsibility for the discussion of autoimmune diseases, and Chip, who devotes much of his research to cancer, focused on the biochemistry of different forms of this devastating illness.

I talked openly with students about the personal experience of wres-tling with diabetes as well as the biochemical complexities and philosoph-ical implications and conundrums of autoimmune diseases. I am always surprised by how few people suspect my illness before I tell them about it. Like others, the students said they had assumed the pump on my belt is a cell phone rather than a lifeline. They obviously appreciated my candor, which allowed them to talk more openly about their own experiences with disease.

I was not, however, completely honest with the class. As we finished our discussion about diabetes, I did not tell them that I was going to do some fieldwork before we met again. By the next class, I would have had a second biopsy, which I suspected would be positive. Unfortunately, I was right; the evening before Chip's first lecture on disease, the doctor called to tell me I had cancer. The initial shock fades, but you never fully absorb such news, even with the passage of time. Needless to say, I did not sleep much that night and by the next day my head was spinning with thoughts I could barely comprehend and surely could not communicate. That morn-ing's class was the longest I have ever endured. As Chip showed colorful animations of interacting molecules and explained the intricacies of the chemical reactions involved in cancer, which, I now realized, was rampaging through my body, I sat silently trying to absorb what he was saying. At least for a while, the word *cancer* had become unspeakable for me, as it had been for my mother and her mother before her.

P.M.

Surviving

SKULL SCULPTURE, STONE HILL

Surviving is not the same as recovering. Recovery takes you back to where you were so you can once again get on with life; surviving takes you someplace you have never been and makes it impossible to go back to where you once were. The survivor not only cannot but does not want to get back to normal, because he now realizes that nothing remains what it was. Recovery conceals the very wound the survivor wants to keep open. This insistence on lingering with the negative does not reflect morose preoccupations but expresses the determination not to forget the lessons learned during the ordeal. Those who simply recover are not really survivors.

The most profound lesson the survivor learns is seemingly simple: life is frightfully fragile. This hardly seems to be a great revelation until you realize that knowing is not always understanding. While riding in an ambulance through midtown traffic when a few seconds might be the difference between life and death, when struggling through an endless night when life turns on calculating the precise dosage of an experimental drug that itself might be fatal, you begin to understand just how tenuous life truly is. Survivors are never cured; at best their disease is controlled or goes into remission, but it does not go away. The morning after the crisis seems to have passed, the survivor sees in the unknowing eyes of others who appear to be healthy the terrible truth he has just learned: disease and death are not out there waiting to befall us but are always in our midst, even when life seems untroubled.

For survivors the acceptance of life's fragility can actually be liberating. If the future everyone dreads has already arrived, there is no longer any reason for it to hold us in its grip. Once you realize that the end is near, even when it seems distant, time unexpectedly slows down. There is no longer any need to rush because whatever you think must be done quickly doesn't really matter. Though suffering alone, survivors form a community without communion. They do not need to wear bracelets or T-shirts while marching in parades or participating in demonstrations to identify one another. Inconspicuous in any crowd, survivors recognize each other by their slower gait, which is not quite leisurely but never hurried. They pause to give lost strangers directions and take time to play with a child. No longer sure what is coming next, they hesitate slightly before responding to serious questions. Those who recover always think they have more important things to do—survivors know they do not.

Though I am still living, I am not yet a survivor; I will not reach that goal for another year, and even then there will be no certainty about the future. But, of course, there never is. Though I now know, in a way I never before have, that time is short, the appreciation of just how uncertain the future is has given me more time than I ever knew I had.

FORTY

A.M.

Trust

WINTER ON STONE HILL

Life often hangs by a thin thread, and sometimes you really do have only one quarter to make the call. When that moment arrived for me, I never could have anticipated the person to whom I would turn. Our worlds could not be more different: his is Wall Street, mine the university; he is very wealthy; I am not; he is midtown, I am uptown; he is East Side, I am West Side. A child of the sixties, I had grown up suspicious of wealth and wary of businessmen. When our worlds intersected, I was therefore very surprised to discover that I share more values with him than with many people with whom I have lived and worked my entire professional life.

We live on opposite sides of town in the city and opposite sides of the hill in the country. When we first met, he had just given the college the largest gift in its history for the construction of a center for the performing arts. His extraordinary generosity was met with deep mistrust and vocal opposition by both faculty and the town. Around this time he had heard about some of my classroom experiments and invited me to breakfast to discuss what I was doing. While most of my colleagues resisted my efforts to reform the curriculum and introduce new technologies in the classroom, he immediately understood the importance of these initiatives and, much to my surprise, offered to support my efforts. Since the college was not interested, we formed a company and during the next six years worked together very closely to provide high-quality education on a global scale by using new information and network technologies.

We failed but our endeavor was a great success for both of us. Our collaboration proved to be an memorable experience during which I discovered many things I never imagined learning. Being allowed to peek behind the curtain of his world, which is usually closed to outsiders, proved to be something like a sojourn with a foreign tribe. As any good anthropologist could have told me, upon returning I found that I had learned more about my own tribe than the other I thought I was studying. It gradually became clear to me that he is in fact one of the most powerful people in the country and as such is able to surround himself with exceptionally intelligent and talented people. As I got to know many of his associates, I was startled to discover that their knowledge of the world is much more thorough and sophisticated than that of most academics who fashion themselves experts working at the so-called cutting edge. Moreover, many of his friends and business colleagues are genuinely concerned about social problems and are at least as interested in education as academics. With absolutely no expectation of financial return, his colleagues willingly contributed considerable time and energy, as well as enormous financial resources, to our effort to promote global education. When our venture failed, it was not because of the bankers' lack of commitment but because of the mistrust and suspicion of college and university faculty members. As I literally looked at my world from his side of the table, I did not like what I saw.

Over the years I also learned something else important about him—he is completely trustworthy and intensely loyal. He makes judgments about people quickly and stands by them, often with little or no consideration for his own self-interest. Furthermore, in an age of celebrity he avoids the front page and works quietly with both the powerful and the powerless. Though he claims he is not religious, he faithfully follows the biblical maxim of not letting the left hand know what the right is doing. Indeed, he prefers his gestures of generosity to go unnoticed. He is an adviser to leading business people throughout the world as well as influential politicians across the globe, and the source of his power is not only his experience and wisdom but also his complete trustworthiness. When people ask or tell him something, they can be absolutely sure he will keep their confidence. While critics can, of course, always explain away such trust, they invariably fail to recognize in themselves the ulterior motives they think they see in others.

After we became better acquainted, I turned to him several times for counsel and advice, and every time he responded generously, thoughtfully, and helpfully. No occasion was more critical, however, than the day I unexpectedly was forced to confront a matter of life and death. When I needed to find the doctor to perform the operation upon which my survival depended, I had no doubt about whom to call. As we spoke, I had not finish my sentence, when he interrupted, "Don't worry, I'll take care of it." A few days later I was in the hands of the surgeon I so urgently needed. What is even more remarkable than his response to me is knowing how many other people powerful and not so powerful would have used their last quarter to make the same call I made. He would have done for each of them exactly what he did for me, and he would never have told anyone about it. Even if I had wanted to offer a token of appreciation, there is nothing I could give him. I incurred no debt and he expected no repayment. A rare friendship indeed.

P.M.

Bitterness

Bitterness gradually erodes the soul from within until nothing is left but a hollow shell. As I watch friends and colleagues grow old, I see two kinds of bitterness. In one, the person is bitter because life did not give him what he thought he deserved. His talents were not recognized and his achievements were unappreciated. He complains that others with far less ability, who had not done nearly as much, enjoyed the accolades and received promotions. In the face of such harsh realities, his only hope, which admittedly is slim, is that future generations will recognize what the present one does not.

In the other form of bitterness, a person to whom life seems to have given everything discovers he has been left with nothing. His talents were widely acknowledged as he quickly climbed the ladder of success. With everyone singing his praises, he reaped all the rewards, financial and otherwise. But no matter how great his accomplishments, the day inevitably arrives when it is time to let go. He dreads this moment because at a certain age moving on is no longer moving up. All the toys in the world cannot ease the frustration of a player who is no longer in the game. People who once hung on his every word do not seek his advice and, indeed, do not want to hear what he has to say. His calls, which were always promptly answered, are no longer returned, and visitors rarely seek him out. No longer receiving the attention and deference he believes he deserves, he becomes bitter. No matter how luxurious, his apartments and houses become a prison from which he cannot escape. Having spent his entire life busily running away from himself by running toward what he thought he wanted, he is finally forced to admit that he never took the time to learn how to do nothing. If he lives long enough, he gets his wish and moves out of the houses few could afford. But his new address is even more depressing than his old. In the assisted-living facility he confronts another harsh reality: at the end of the day, everybody lives on the same hall.

In both cases bitterness breeds resentment, and resentment isolates one from others and finally turns one against oneself. Resentful of a world that does not give what seems to be owed, the bitter person becomes locked up within himself. Then something strange unexpectedly happens. Though he once would have done anything to be free of bitterness, his torment becomes the object of his passion and source of his identity until he eventually comes to love bitterness and resentment more than life itself. Unable to let go of what is undeniably tormenting, his condition becomes fatal and he slowly withers away, destroying others as he destroys himself. The only cure for bitterness is accepting that life owes us nothing—absolutely nothing—not even life itself.

FORTY-ONE

A.M.

Hands

MY BASEBALL GLOVE

MY FATHER'S BASEBALL GLOVE

Either you have hands or you don't. If you do, you can't explain it; if you don't, there is nothing you can do about it. While hands obviously differ, nothing visible distinguishes good hands from bad hands. What, then, is it about hands?

To understand hands, it is helpful to look at arms. A friend once asked me, "If you could be a star professional athlete in any sport, what would it be and what position would you want to play?" Though I had never con

MY FATHER, PITCHING

sidered the question, my response was immediate: "Baseball. Pitcher." Perhaps it was because my father had been a gifted pitcher, who once had been offered a professional contract by the then–Philadelphia Athletics and during my youth had coached our high school baseball team. I played baseball from the time I could walk and in elementary school would regularly skip class to accompany my dad as the team batboy. I never knew if he told my teachers the real reason for my absence. When I began to play, I found my proper place at first base—good bat, no arm. I did, however, try pitching once but that experience was brief. With the bench empty and the bases loaded in the eighth inning, the coach switched me from first base to the pitcher's mound. After I proceeded to walk four straight batters, he mercifully switched me back.

I have always been puzzled about my inability to throw hard. My arm looks just like kids' who could throw much faster than I could. Indeed, our best pitcher in high school was so skinny that people rarely took him for an athlete. But could he ever throw! About a year ago a local kid, once an outstanding pitcher widely touted by pro scouts as a sure bet for the big

SLUGGER

leagues, was helping me move into my apartment in New York City. I asked him, "How many guys can throw a 90 mph fastball?" "Surprisingly, quite a few," he answered. "But not many can throw 91 mph. I could throw 90, but no matter how much I trained or how hard I worked, I could never throw 91. My kid brother could throw 92 mph without even trying. That's why he's pitching for the Pittsburgh Pirates and I'm running the family moving business."

Surgeons are like pitchers. By the time I met Peter Scardino, I had decided he was the surgeon I wanted to operate on me. It was not irrelevant that he had been a religious studies major at Yale and, like me, had been introduced to the field in a course entitled "The Quest for the Historical Jesus." But the real issue was hands. I had done my research and had no doubt that surgery rather than radiation was the way to go. Though I had read his book and knew his position, I wanted to hear Scardino make the case for traditional surgery rather than the much less invasive and traumatic robotic or laparoscopic alternative. Like an experienced teacher, he began with a visual aid—a graph with the number of operations on the horizontal axis and the cancer cure rate on the vertical axis. From 1 to 300 surgeries the curve ascends sharply, showing a rapid improvement in the success rate. After 300 the curve levels off but continues to ascend gradually. In other words, even someone who has performed three thousand operations continues to improve. Scardino explained that a more fine-grained analysis showed that there is still considerable variation in the cure rates of surgeons who have operated thousands of times. This is exactly what you would expect—repetitions count, but the skill of the surgeon is even more important. Scardino said that he was conducting a study for the American Cancer Society, whose aim was to develop a program that would increase the success rate for the most experienced surgeons. I told him I thought the study was a waste of time because, even though you might be able to teach an average surgeon to be better or help an experienced surgeon improve, it is no more possible to teach a good surgeon to be great than you can train a pitcher who can throw 90 mph to throw 91 mph. Discipline, yes … but also grace, always grace.

Either you have hands or you don't. No matter how thoroughly the genome is decoded, the reason some pitchers have arms and some surgeons have hands will always remain a mystery. Without in any way dismissing the importance of rigorous research and training, when life is on the line, I put my faith in that mystery. Scardino has hands and that's why I decided quite literally to put my life in his hands. As we shook hands when parting two days before surgery, I could not help but think that his hands look just like mine.

P.M.

Will

I have always believed in the power of will but have always doubted the will to power. Nothing significant has ever been accomplished without the disciplined exercise of the will. People too often mistakenly regard freedom and discipline as opposites; they are, to the contrary, complementary—discipline provides the parameters of constraint within which freedom can be effectively exercised. The disciplined will solicits resistance without which neither development nor growth is possible. The athlete tagged a natural, the artist who creates spontaneously, the writer who writes effortlessly could not do what they do without years of training and practice. The power of will makes me what I am by making me other than what I have been.

When the power of will becomes the will to power, however, the goal of life becomes less self-mastery than the domination and control of others. Rather than respecting resistance, the master strives to overcome all limits by crushing the opposition. Rejecting freedom within constraints, the will to power seeks freedom from constraint. The will that would be absolute eventually becomes self-destructive by destroying the very other without whom it cannot be itself. At this point the will to power becomes a fury of destruction, which is the will to death.

My belief in the power of the will was put to the test in a most unexpected way. My collapse occurred with unimaginable suddenness, and initially the prospects for recovery were slim at best. The urgency and confusion of the emergency room and CCU left little time to comprehend the gravity of the situation. Indeed, when my family left at midnight, we still did not fully realize just how critical my condition really was. As the frantic activity of the CCU doctors and nurses subsided and I was left with two very young physicians for the night, I gradually began to grasp what I was up against. While I did not know at the time that none of the doctors expected me to survive, I did realize I was on the border between life and death and that things could go either way. In the early morning hours, there was a moment—a strangely clear and calm moment—when I knew I had to decide whether I wanted to live or die. The experience was not anything like others have described—there was no light, no long hallway or tunnel, no vision of a pure and perfect world beckoning me. Nothing but the brute reality of doctors, nurses, tubes, wires, machines, ceaseless white noise, and the inescapable glare of fluorescent lights. The choice was simple: life or death. I was not yet weary of the struggle and without an instant's hesitation chose life. Even at that moment, however, I realized that my decision—if, in fact, it were my own—was only the beginning of what would be a very long process. To come back from the edge of that abyss and regain my strength would require exceptional will power and great discipline. Fortunately, I did not know at the time just how hard it would be or how long it would take. I sometimes wonder whether my decision would have been different if I had known.

Refusing to sleep the rest of the night, I watched those charged with keeping watch over me. The doctors' English was broken, and they spoke to each other in Spanish, thereby compounding my confusion and uncertainty. By morning the numbers had improved slightly but still were far from what they should have been. That was when I knew I had reached my limit and that will alone would not be enough to bring me back from elsewhere. Though I was able to control my diabetes with resolute discipline, no amount of willing would make my kidneys and liver start working again. There was nothing more I could do but lie there and wait. As minutes passed into hours and hours into days, I slipped into that night beyond night and learned again what I already knew and often presumed to try to teach others: the dream of control is always an illusion—we are not even the masters of the bodies we mistakenly believe to be our own.

The lessons of those endless nights and days are not simple—nothing ever is. While I could not will my body to do what it was not prepared to do, I believe I would not have lived through that night and returned from elsewhere had I not chosen life. Nor would I have recovered without months of vigilant monitoring and disciplined activity. The will is most effective when it respects its limits and constantly pushes itself to the edge but never further. When deliberately disciplined, will is the power of life itself.

FORTY-TWO

A.M.

Secrets

Are you still reading? I often wish I could step off the page to explain things better by talking with you directly. But, I realize, this is an idle fantasy because all discourse is destined to be indirect. Sometimes I wonder if I've said too much or too little about myself as well as others. We live in a world obsessed with exposure where privacy and, with it, interiority are disappearing. Art has become political in unexpected ways: the modernist aesthetic ideal of clarity has become a political ideology of transparency in which everything is turned outside in and inside out. The disappearance of interiority issues in the death of the self as we have known it since the time of Saint Paul. Encountering what he took to be the risen Christ on the road to Damascus, Paul discovered the interiority of human subjectivity that ever since has defined the history of selfhood in the West. Is saying as much as I've said a symptom of the death of that self and the end of that history?

Protests to the contrary notwithstanding, endings are rarely final. Even in a world of tell-all memoirs, reality TV, and global surveillance, secrets remain and not everything is transparent. After all these pages, I have a confession to make: There are some things I am not telling you. In all honesty, I am not being completely honest with you. Though usually dismissed as hopelessly old-fashioned, reticence and a sense of propriety are still virtues well worth cultivating. Dignity—but this too seems to have disap-

MOTHER

peared—requires it. I am not sure whether what I have left out is the least or the most important. As I have suggested, what is even more baffling is that I don't know whether I really know what I am not telling you. If we are honest with ourselves, we must admit that we all harbor secrets of which we are unaware. But, then, can we ever really be honest with ourselves or with each other? Perhaps honesty is the grandest of all deceptions. As always, this seemingly inconsequential *perhaps* transforms every period into a question mark.

The issue is complicated and is not simply a matter of telling what I have not told or what I could tell you if I realized it. There seems to be—but again I cannot be sure—a more profound interiority that haunts us. I can describe it only as an unfathomable abyss within that opens us to an outside that is not precisely exterior. I do not so much refuse to reveal this interior exteriority from a sense of modesty or propriety as it resists revealing itself. It never appears in the light of day but always slips away, leaving even the surest certainties uncertain. Whenever I speak, it speaks through me whether I realize it or not. It is precisely in my effort to tell you everything that I discover that all cannot be revealed. Then and only then do I realize that the person I mistake for myself is but a mask through which something else always echoes. And so I give myself to you withholdingly.

But this withholding, dear reader, is not merely my own. Even when I try to tell it straight, things get twisted. I am hiding—always inevitably hiding—from myself as well as you. And, in all honesty, I don't know what or from what I am really hiding. Indeed, if I did know, I would stop writing and, I suspect, you would stop reading.

P.M.

Tripping

When you're tripping at the edge of the abyss, and perhaps even when you're not, visions are real. They do not sneak up slowly but suddenly overwhelm, transporting you somewhere you have never been and, indeed, have never even imagined. The so-called known world does not disappear but remains both as it is and transformed. People continue to speak and listen as if nothing had changed, and no one seems to notice that you are no longer really there but now are elsewhere.

The first time was completely disorienting. I was lying in bed in the CCU with my family, two doctors, and several nurses gathered to discuss matters they thought I was prepared to hear. All of a sudden I was not precisely there but was on the ceiling looking down on the scene from above. It was the same room but now it looked like an early version of a virtual reality game: Colors had lost all shading, and three dimensions were flattened to two. Something resembling a joystick floated around the room, always eluding my grasp. I could hear voices but could not understand what they were saying. Though the experience was not exactly otherworldly, I knew I was no longer in the world I had for so long taken for granted. Sounds, shapes, and colors shifted in synchronous rhythms. It was not so much synesthesia as something like colored hearing. My gaze was fixed and would not change even when I vigorously shook my head. Then, as quickly as it appeared, my vision shifted once more.

As I stared at family and doctors, something equally baffling occurred. What appeared to be thousands of tiny black beads began oozing from the shirts and blouses of the people gathered around me. When I turned away, I saw the same beads seeping through the window and emerging from all corners in the room. They seemed to flow from every gap and crack. After spilling onto the bed and floor, the beads came to life and slowly began to organize themselves into a horde of grotesque creatures that seemed to have escaped from a third-rate horror film. As these monsters continued to grow, they seemed to take over the entire room. Their legs became entangled and surrounded me until I was imprisoned and could only gaze out at others who could not hear my screams. Metamorphosis, indeed—everywhere I looked I thought I glimpsed Gregor Samsas.

Every now and then one of those little black beads floats across the edge of my field of vision, reminding me that what we call normal is constantly changing. We see by not seeing, hear by not hearing, but then everything shifts in the blink of an eye, and we can no longer be sure what is normal and what is not. It is impossible to know where brain ends and mind begins—and, of course, vice versa. The worlds in which we dwell are formed as much as found, figured as much as discovered. Order emerges from disorder by filtering the disruptive noise of perception. But noise is never simply noise, for it can always be figured otherwise. Disease, like peyote, mescaline, and acid, takes us elsewhere by altering consciousness. Far from reassuring, ecstasy is terrifying. Once you have seen harrowing noise, nothing sounds quite the same again. What were those beads I heard and where did those grotesque creatures I saw come from? Was it the infection raging in my body? Was it drugs—the drugs that were supposed to kill the bacteria that were killing me? Was it the dosage—a milliliter too much or too little? Was the vision a delusion? Was it a revelation? If so, of what? Or was it nothing—the nothing that is not there and the nothing that is?

FORTY-THREE

A.M.

Strangers

At the end of the day, our lives depend on strangers. Late one night, after she had awoken me to take my vital signs, she told me that she had prayed for me the day before. I was ashamed to admit that I barely remembered her face. I inquired where she worshipped and she told me she attended a megachurch near Times Square. She had been born and raised a Catholic in the Philippines but had converted to Protestantism after coming to this country. After talking about faith for a while, I asked her, "How can you continue to believe when you see so much suffering and death day after day and night after night?" She replied, "How could I not?"

From the moment someone responded to the 911 call, many strangers were responsible for saving my life. During the days I was in the hospital, I saw more than forty doctors, and only three were from the United States. The others were from countries all over the world: Russia, China, India, Rumania, Mexico, Argentina, Peru, Ukraine, and Kazakhstan. At first I was unsettled by these strangers. I live in a world where pedigree counts—not biological but intellectual: college, graduate school, medical school, residency. Where had these people studied? With whom had they trained? I knew nothing about them yet my life depended on them.

I was surprised how quickly they gained my trust. The first night proved decisive. I knew the situation was critical, though for several months I would not realize exactly how critical it had been. It was probably better that way. After all the tubes were inserted and all the machines hooked up, attendants, technicians, and, finally, family left for the night. The CCU is never dark and rarely quiet. When the other physicians had departed, the two young doctors—one from Peru, the other from Argentina—remained behind. In broken English they explained that they would monitor and adjust the medicine dripping into the tube that had been inserted into the artery leading from my heart. There was a machine beside my bed registering numbers whose significance I did not understand. I did not sleep a wink, nor did the doctors. The image from that night seared in my memory is of those two young doctors, dressed in green scrubs, with their masked faces inches from the machine, intently staring at changing digits flickering on the screen. They never left the room, never sat down, never took a break, never broke their gaze. Occasionally, they would mumble something to each other in Spanish, but they never again spoke to me. By morning I thought I had turned the corner but I had not. They had given of themselves well beyond what their job required; indeed, theirs was a generosity that knew no bounds. I realize now that I would not have survived that night without the vigilance of strangers—and perhaps without the prayers of the night nurse. And yet I do not know their names and will never be able to say thank you.

P.M.

Tips

Though a practicing Christian, he is the stingiest person I know. He likes to pass himself off as sophisticated and worldly, but the clothes never quite fit the man. While depending on the gifts of others to advance his career, in his own life he regards generosity as an excess that must be strictly controlled. This is not always obvious to others because he has mastered the art of distraction and deception with all the skill of an experienced magician. I was never fooled by his sleights of hand because I have long believed that the measure of a man is what he does when he assumes no one is looking.

As is often the case, small gestures are the most revealing. Behind closed doors, he seemed to reverse the biblical maxim by taking away with his hidden hand what he had given with his public hand. He is one of the few people I know who can provoke resentment while doing you a favor. His irrepressible need to exact expressions of thanks, which in most cases would have been given anyway, destroys the very gratitude he seems to need so much. The issue is not, of course, gratitude but power—his power and others' weaknesses. He does not realize that there can never be generosity as long as the cycle of indebtedness is repeatedly reinforced. I gradually came to understand that our differences are not so much personal as theological: his God is not my God.

A seemingly insignificant episode: One day he called and invited me to lunch. When he picked me up, he asked where I wanted to go, and I suggested a funky place I adore but he avoids. We had a pleasant lunch during which he asked me about my work. I tried to explain the book I was writing in which I was arguing that Protestantism had led to the death of God, which in turn issued in late twentieth-century popular culture and network technologies. Perhaps as the result of the Catholicism that held him captive, he had trouble catching the drift.

As our conversation neared what I thought was its end, he called for the check. When I reached for my wallet to pay my share, he seemingly graciously declined my offer and paid the bill, leaving a four-dollar tip on the

TIP

table. Instead of getting up to leave, he continued the conversation but for some reason seemed agitated. After almost an hour, while trying to be as inconspicuous as possible, he furtively picked up one of the four dollars he had left for a tip and replaced it with three quarters. A few minutes later he finally got up and we left. I had trouble believing what I had just seen.

It's a small town, and we both knew the server and the struggles she was going through. His gesture left me incredulous and I felt guilt by association. I still regret not having left a few more dollars on the table.

FORTY-FOUR

A.M.

Sharing

CLOCK THAT GRANDPA COOPER MADE

When I was transferred from the intensive care unit to the general ward, I shared a room—and, I would discover, much more—with Marty. I had not had a roommate other than Dinny since college. Marty was, in many ways, much more interesting than most of the people I met during my student days. He proudly claimed to be half Apache and half Italian—a volatile mix, to say the least. His present life was rough; he lived alone in the Bronx projects, where nightly gunfire made it impossible for him to leave his apartment. A social worker had brought him to the hospital, but he had no idea why he had been admitted. When nurses would come to check his vital signs, he would ask what his problem was and when he would be released; they said they did not know. A doctor finally arrived several days later, but he had never seen Marty before and had none of his records. He briefly examined Marty and left without answering any questions. No doctor ever visited him again.

The worlds in which Marty and I lived could not have been further apart. The only time I go to the Bronx is to attend a Yankees game, and Marty had absolutely no idea what an idyllic New England college town even looks like. But at night our worlds became one. The general ward in a large urban hospital is not a place anyone would choose to spend much time. Rooms were full and patients spilled into the halls. Well-meaning nurses and attendants were overwhelmed and could barely maintain order. If you were not strong enough to fend for yourself, help rarely arrived in time. Families seemed bigger in the general ward. Hordes of visitors crowded into the rooms and roamed the halls nightly. Since no one ever asked them to leave, many stayed long after visiting hours were over. Though the time between lights-out and the predawn visit by nurses was brief, the hours seemed endless. Neither Marty nor I could sleep and so we talked or, more accurately, he talked and I listened. Our conversations reminded me of late-night talks with college roommates. There was, however, a critical difference: when you are young and healthy, nighttime chatter is a luxury, but when you are older and sick, it's a necessity.

Marty was a great storyteller, and I often wished I had been able to record the tales he spun. He first told me about his family or lack of family. His wife of many years had died the previous Thanksgiving, and he had not talked to his daughter for so long that he did not even know where she lived or if she had any children. When he turned from the present to the past, he really came alive. He had been a sailor, or so he said, until he injured his foot and could no longer work. His naval career had begun during the Second World War, when he was assigned to a ship responsible for tracking German U-boats. He claimed to have had more than one close call, and I was not about to doubt him. After the war he joined the merchant marine and traveled all over the world. He had a story for every port: orgies in Bangkok, hashish in Istanbul, jail in Baghdad. As the nights wore on, the tales grew wilder until I had no idea where fact ended and fantasy began. Nor, I suspected, did Marty, but neither of us cared. When you're lying awake in a hospital in the dead of the night, truth is not the point.

One morning a few days before I was released, a social worker came in to tell Marty he was going home. She gave him a prescription from a doctor he had never seen. He asked what it was for; she told him it would make him feel better. He told her he could not get it filled because the nearest pharmacy was several blocks from his apartment and he could not walk that far. She told him to call a friend; he told her he didn't have any friends. Two hours later she returned and wheeled him out of the room. We said good-bye, knowing we would never meet again. It was one week before Christmas.

The nights after Marty left were much longer. We had become friends, and I missed him and his stories. It pained me to imagine him home alone on Christmas Day, but I had not asked for his address or phone number. Nonetheless, I felt we were somehow still in touch with each other. Though our daytime worlds were totally different, what Marty and I shared was the need for stories to get us through the night.

P.M.

Fatigue

My mother used to call it tired blood. I never knew what she meant until one summer I simply ran out of energy. As I searched for a way to describe my condition, the only word that seemed to work was *fatigue*. Fatigue is not the same as tiredness. Being tired can be enjoyable and refreshing—after a long day of manual labor or physical exercise, muscles often ache to the point of pain. There is something pleasurable in this pain, and so we often push ourselves to the limit, sometimes even a bit beyond. Asceticism has always involved the search for pleasure, though in our society the gym has replaced the cloister and exercise has become a religious ritual. It is as if long hours of sweating cleanse the body of poisons collected during extended sedentary periods. When you are really tired, sleep comes easily and you awake refreshed and renewed—ready to begin again. Being tired is, then, a symptom of health and renewal.

There is nothing pleasurable or healthy about fatigue. Not only physical but also mental, fatigue neither refreshes nor renews; it pollutes rather than purifies. Never overcoming you suddenly, fatigue creeps up and invades gradually by insinuating itself throughout your system until one day you realize you have had little energy for weeks, even months. As fatigue waxes, concentration wanes. While listening to others, you become distracted and don't really hear what they are saying. When you sit down to read a book, your eyes grow heavy and you quickly fall asleep. But when you go to bed at night, fatigue makes it impossible to sleep—strange though it seems, fatigue creates insomnia. Sleep comes when you don't want it and won't come when you most need it. Insomniacs drift into the night beyond night where rest is impossible.

If sleep finally arrives, it does not revive. There is little that is more frustrating than waking up fatigued and knowing you face a long day that will only make you feel worse. Fatigue becomes chronic rather than episodic—like a low-grade fever that won't go away. Eventually, it leads to exhaustion, which creates a sense of weariness that casts a pall over everything. When weariness becomes world-weariness, life loses all sense of meaning and purpose. Beckett was wrong, perhaps because he still believed too much: when you can't go on, it is foolish to insist you must go on. A symptom of persistent disease and approaching death, fatigue allows those who no longer can hang on to let go without regret.

FORTY-FIVE

A.M.

Idleness

Nothing is harder for me to do than nothing. The issue is not merely psychological—it is metaphysical, ethical, even religious. I guess my problem with doing nothing shows how deeply Protestant I remain. I have never been able to forget my grandmother's severe warning to me when I was a child: "Idleness is the devil's workshop." For her the idle person was not merely lazy but shiftless, useless, worthless. As the work of the devil, idleness, I was taught, is sin and sin, of course, breeds guilt. Even today I never feel more guilty than when I am doing nothing. I doubt I will ever completely overcome this sense of guilt and, indeed, sometimes I'm not even sure I want to do so.

What makes idleness so dangerous and thus so tempting is its purposelessness. Idleness, like play, has no end other than itself. If you can explain why you are idle, you are not idling. Redemption from this sin, my grandmother drilled into me, comes from work. That is why she always kept me busy—sometimes working, sometimes playing, or what she thought was playing. The problem was that my grandmother never really understood how to play. Forever suspicious of idleness, she had the remarkable ability to transform play into work, and she somehow managed to pass on this talent to her daughter, who in turn passed it on to me.

These are the reasons, I suppose, that even as a child I worked so hard at playing. It was impossible to know where obedience ended and rebellion began. Having swallowed the suspicion of idleness with my mother's milk, I always found the lazy, hazy days of summer less crazy than boring. It took many years and much reading before I began to understand boredom. Ever the dutiful grandson, I concluded that Roland Barthes was wrong—there is no bliss in boredom. And for once Kierkegaard did not have it quite right—"the rotation method" is not a solution when you are bored. Distraction doesn't distract when that is its aim because activity alone is not enough—it must be purposeful.

Or so I thought until I became critically ill. Illness teaches many lessons, the most valuable of which are unexpected. I did not really know how to idle before my illness, which gave me the excuse to do nothing. Indeed, I had no choice—doctor's orders: "You must remain idle for at least four to six weeks." For the first time in my life, I *had* to do nothing. As impatience gradually gave way to patience, idleness, I discovered, is not necessarily the result of physical depletion or a lack of energy and therefore is not the same as lethargy. When lethargic, you are drowsy, sluggish, and, above all, indifferent. Lethargy dulls the senses and creates a feeling of inertia, which seems to anticipate death. Idleness, by contrast, enlivens by sharpening the senses—you see what you usually do not see, hear what you usually do not hear, feel what you usually do not feel. While idling, you can be fully engaged without being purposeful.

If you are a patient patient, illness teaches the virtue of idleness by recasting the purpose of purpose. The journey to the edge of the abyss brings in its wake the transvaluation of values. So much of what had seemed purposeful begins to appear purposeless, and what once had a point suddenly becomes pointless. Like the frenzied activities it is designed to overcome, purposeful action all too often distracts

GRANDPA COOPER'S SKETCHBOOK

us from the inescapable gravity of our condition. Paradoxically, we fail to recognize this gravity for what it is until we learn to appreciate the sense of levity that idleness brings.

One of the most delightfully surprising lessons that illness has taught me is that idleness can actually be pleasurable—not quite blissful but pleasurable nonetheless. Doing nothing gives you time to think idle thoughts that often lead elsewhere. Though rarely productive, such thinking is valuable, perhaps the most valuable thinking of all. Eventually, the interlude ends and it's time to begin writing once again. But, having learned how to do nothing, I can freely admit that the world will not end if this book is not finished and thus for the first time I can enjoy the pleasure of the text, which (the) work always obscures.

P.M.

Guilt

The finality of time is never felt more poignantly than in the experience of guilt. While seeming to acknowledge that time cannot be reversed, the well-worn maxim "What's done cannot be undone" actually seeks to stem time's flow by encouraging the distressed person to move on. More often than not, however, moving on shows disrespect for the past by letting it slip into oblivion. But the past will not let go so easily; it holds us in its grip even—perhaps especially—when we try to forget it. Confessing the inescapability of time, I would rewrite what passes for common wisdom as "What has been left unsaid can never be said."

As is so often the case, the argument began over something insignificant. She asked me to visit a sick relative and I refused because I said I didn't have enough time. With the fall semester fast approaching, I still had work to complete and the trip would have taken a couple of days. She played the guilt card with her usual deftness, and I reacted angrily with words calculated to hurt. Hers was a tactic I had come to know all too well over the years. Guilt held her tight in its grip, and she was determined to pass her guilt on to me. I was equally determined that she would not. Overt conflict was rare but this time things spun out of control. In the heat of the moment, I said things I should not have said. The words I spoke cut to the bone by calling into question what she believed most deeply. She burst into tears, which was not unusual, though this time they seemed to come from deeper recesses than I had seen before. We were alone, there was no one else to whom she could turn, and there surely was nothing I could say to undo what I had done. I never regretted not visiting my sick relative, but I have always regretted having spoken those words.

Whenever I teach the theology of Luther and Calvin, I ask students whether shame or guilt is the more powerful experience. Shame, I explain, is regret for having done what you ought not have done, and guilt is regret for not having done what you ought to have done. The class is usually evenly divided between those who say shame is more powerful than guilt and those who insist on the reverse. My own experience leaves me little doubt—guilt trumps shame every time.

What I most regret about that event years ago—and there are, of course, many others—is not that I said what I should not have said but that I did not say what I should have said. I never said to her, "I'm sorry." True love means always saying you are sorry. We never spoke about the incident again, and I suspect that with time it faded from her memory. But it did not fade from mine, and in many ways my regret has deepened with the years. I always intended to apologize to her for what I had said and even imagined how our conversation would unfold. But then one day she died unexpectedly, and the words I had harbored so long will go unspoken forever. For not having said what I ought to have said, I will always feel profound guilt. What I now must confess is that in that guilt, she won (as always) by passing on to me the very heritage I was so determined to resist.

FORTY-SIX

A.M.

Driving

GRANDPA COOPER ON HIS INDIAN MOTORCYCLE

Something very odd has happened since I have returned—for some reason I have begun to enjoy driving. I had always hated to drive and have never had the slightest interest in cars. I regarded such matters in purely utilitarian terms. Driving seemed to be a waste of time because I always felt I should be doing something more useful or important. But since driving is unavoidable, I was forced to put up with it, albeit impatiently. In addition to harboring these misgivings, I find there is something terribly inefficient and even morally offensive about driving. Locked inside private cars burning far too much gasoline, people pollute the air and hasten the environmental catastrophe that surely is coming. There is, however, no practical alternative and so I packed my ethical misgivings in the trunk and drove on.

Why, then, has driving become pleasurable? While I am not exactly sure how to answer this question, I now realize that I had not really understood driving or perhaps had not understood the waste it inevitably involves. Driving *is* a waste of time and of much else as well, but waste is its point because driving as such has no point. Driving—real driving—is not, as I had thought, about getting from one point to another. Nor is driving simply utilitarian; that is to say, it is not merely a convenient means of transportation. Even if there is a destination and driving is the most efficient way to get there, for real drivers driving is not about getting from point A to point B; rather, driving is about driving. When the means is the end, straight lines become ovals where everyone drives in circles.

Going nowhere even when you have direction, you gain from driving the euphoria of lightness and repose. In this useless expenditure more than time is wasted. Driving, it turns out, runs on a solar economy that mimes the sun's self-consumption. When sunlight stored in fossil fuels burns a second time, the earth consumes itself. Sun and earth glow so brightly because they are burning themselves out. The hotter the earth, the greater the cost, and the greater the cost, the more we pay. Gas, trucks, cars (new on average every three years), tires—four, six, eighteen—bridges, tunnels, streets, and highways—no dig is too big, no price is too high. Spending, excessive spending, until everything is lost—even yourself. Senseless. But then you put the pedal to the metal and in the air rushing by you hear a whisper:

> I am the road. And roar.
> Here I go. Here goes. Not I.
> > Always

It's always so wasteful, impractical, and destructive that it's hard to deny that driving is immoral. But it is a mistake to invoke ethical imperatives because driving, like art, is beyond good and evil. With no purpose other than itself, its value is incalculable. For those who are not unduly driven, driving is (an) art. When "The Art of the Motorcycle" is on display uptown, high becomes low, and art literally takes to the street. NASCAR as potlatch—transport as tripping.

P.M.

Accident

We are more accident than substance. Nothing underlies the myriad experiences of life to provide a secure ground, firm foundation, perhaps even a certain meaning. Nor is there a plan, purpose, or program that both provides direction and pulls everything together. The egg is always cracked before anything ever hatches. Events are aleatory—they befall us in ways that can be neither predicted nor controlled. Resisting every schema designed to pattern them and eluding all structures constructed to organize them, accidents are unfigurable.

GREAT-GRANDFATHER AARON COOPER IN PENNSYLVANIA COAL MINE

Disfiguring had recently been published, and I had been invited to give a lecture at a college near my childhood home. The title of my presentation was "Representing the Unrepresentable." I left a day early so I could spend some time with my father. Since my mother's death he had withdrawn by turning inward, and I worried about him living alone. As was my custom, I went for a run late in the afternoon. It was dusk—that unsettling border where day and night join and separate—on a gray, rainy late winter day. I had been running for an hour and was nearing home when I paused at a busy corner I had crossed countless times since I was a child and waited for an opening in the rush-hour traffic. I checked left and finally saw a gap in the string of headlights, then checked right and thought I had enough time to beat the oncoming traffic, but I failed to check left again. With eyes cast down I started across the street, when I suddenly heard the loud noise of a car horn and screeching brakes. The next thing I knew, I felt the rending pain of metal against flesh. I never saw the car that hit me. I was thrown onto the hood, and my head smashed into the windshield. The shock of this initial impact crowded my mind with the thought of death; there was no flashback, no rapid replay of the tape of my life, nothing but the pale specter of death. There was, however, a light—not a celestial light or a light at the end of a tunnel but an instant of blinding white light in which nothing appeared. Rather than revelation, its absence, or, at most, the revelation of the absence of revelation—I saw nothing. Then, with a calculation that still baffles me, I realized that if I were to survive, there was only one way off that hood. If I fell to the left, I would be hit by oncoming traffic, and if the driver stopped too suddenly, I would be thrown off the front of the hood and would be run over. I had to get off to the right. I later calculated that the car was going about 35 mph when it hit me and carried me about two hundred feet; the whole episode could not have taken more than two or three seconds. In that brief time I somehow managed to maneuver my body in such a way that I was able to slide off to the right. In the split second that I was falling, everything shifted into slow motion. I saw my legs above my head and realized that if I did not tuck them beneath me, the car would crush them. Stunned but conscious, I hit the ground.

My first memory after the fall was of a woman's scream: "I hit this man! I hit this man! I hit this man!" She rushed from her car to make sure I did not try to stand up. I never saw her face—only her black shoes, black slacks, and the black fender of her Ford Taurus. I later realized that its aerodynamic design had saved my life by allowing me to slide over the hood like oncoming wind. Other cars stopped and someone called the police. As I sat shaking on the cold, wet, black road with my back throbbing and head splitting, I checked my limbs and concluded that nothing was broken. Eventually, sirens sounded above the din of the traffic and an ambulance arrived. Before answering questions, I told the police officer to have someone get my father, who lived only a block away. The paramedics examined me and wanted to take me to the hospital. I refused because I knew that getting out of a hospital is much harder than getting in, and I had to deliver a lecture the next day. I said I was going home and assured them that if I started pissing blood, I would call a doctor. Gathering my disfigured body, I leaned on my aging father and limped back home. We both were glad I was alive.

Accidents expose us to the sheer contingency of events. There is no more reason why I was hit by that car than why I survived the accident. Regardless of how carefully we plan or how deliberate we are, we are always wittingly or unwittingly collaborating with chance. To read purpose where there is none is to struggle vainly to cover the void that both gives and takes; to accept events as purposeless is to remain open to the wonder of "there is" as well as "there is not."

FORTY-SEVEN

A.M.

Imperfection

Perfection is the mark of death, imperfection the sign of life. Far from admirable, the pursuit of perfection blindly rushes toward the end of the only life we can ever know. If perfection were ever achieved, time would stop—having arrived, we would have nowhere left to go. The end of time is not life everlasting but eternal death.

And yet people remain obsessed with perfection: the perfect game, the perfect score, the perfect partner, the perfect style, the perfect moment, the perfect body, the perfect face. The contradictions involved in the contemporary obsession with perfection are revealed in the oxymoron that has become emblematic of our era: virtual reality. In the age of digital reproduction, realism paradoxically has become the standard of virtuality. The avatars' skin and hands, movements and gestures are measured against living originals. These originals, of course, are not actually original because they are modeled on the models modeled on them. The real, in other words, is itself becoming virtual and the virtual is becoming real. By collapsing the distinction between the real and the virtual, so-called reality TV reveals our emergent condition as one in which everything is preprogrammed. With blemishes removed and stutters eliminated, actors and anchors become indistinguishable from androids as well as from each other. Like bellies deemed too big and breasts believed too small, video and photographs are doctored, and if reality still doesn't measure up, it can always be reprogrammed.

The dream is as old as the human imagination: to eliminate imperfections and thereby triumph over death. The difference today, prophets tell us, is that what has always been mere fantasy now is becoming a technological reality. Permanent cure is on the horizon and the remaining challenge is to live long enough to live forever. By reprogramming the genome and rewiring the brain, we can overcome human imperfections and everyone can enjoy eternal life. This will finally be the arrival of what once was called the Kingdom of God on Earth.

I want no part of this kingdom because what I most love are life's imperfections—not necessarily what is wrong but what is not quite right, what falls just a little short. Rather than bloodless beauty, the slight blemish that cannot be airbrushed away, not wrinkle-free faces but lines as deep as the wisdom that age brings. In place of perfect balance, I prefer minor disruptions that throw everything and everyone off; rather than the perfect performance or game, the mistakes and errors that keep the game going. Sometimes to get it right is wrong and to miss the mark is to be on target.

The draw of imperfection is that it opens the space and time of *al most—always almost*. The imperfect is incomplete and, when things are incomplete, nothing is settled and there is always more to be done. Faults are openings, flaws chances—this is the beauty of imperfection. Beauty is never flawless, to the contrary, there can be no beauty without shadows, no harmony without dissonance, no figuring without disfiguring. Rather than fueling frustration, the eternal return of *always almost* arouses desire by holding the future open. While the person who longs for perfection seeks to escape time, the person who accepts imperfection embraces time as the only eternity there is. If there ever were a kingdom, its time would be future imperfect.

P.M.

Vulnerability

The dream of invulnerability is as old as the human imagination itself. Strategies for security range from physical to mental, offensive to defensive, local to global, and mythic to scientific. The most threatening aspect of vulnerability is psychological rather than bodily because what we most seem to dread is the loss of control.

Illness exposes the inescapable vulnerability that we usually try to repress. No matter how secure a fortress we build, it can always be undone by a single bacterium that resists our defenses, a single gene that won't switch off, a single cell that misreads a code. Sometimes I can do something about it, often I cannot. When facing my vulnerability, I remain absolutely naked even when clothed. As things spin out of control, I have no choice but to place my life in the hands of others—others I frequently do not even know. This requires a leap of faith more risky than any God ever demanded because those to whom I entrust myself are neither omniscient nor omnipotent. The more others realize what they do not know and cannot do, the more trustworthy they are. Confidence is not the lack of uncertainty but the willingness to accept uncertainty when it's unavoidable.

Even when deliberately planned and carefully reasoned, significant decisions are invariably surprising. Some things you can know only after you take the leap. What is most unexpected about the unavoidable yet free decision to accept vulnerability is the release it offers. Once you admit that things are out of your hands and there is nothing more you can do, you

MY FIRST CHRISTMAS

suddenly experience a strange feeling of freedom. And with this freedom comes something else: contrary to all expectation, the acceptance of vulnerability creates a surprising sense of invulnerability—not physical invulnerability but a deeper, far more important, invulnerability. You begin to realize that, after what life has already done to you, others can no longer hurt you.

What harm is a friend's betrayal when your own body has already betrayed you? What difference does rejection make when your body is rejecting cures? What damage can the sharp attacks of critics inflict when your body is attacking itself? Embracing rather than fleeing vulnerability exposes knowledge as ignorance and serious considerations as petty preoccupations. This acceptance sets you free to say what you have long left unsaid and to write what you have been withholding far too long. If others don't like it, so be it.

I was never particularly patient with bullshit, but having been elsewhere I am now far less tolerant of it and far more willing to let people know what I really think. Time is much too short to put up with those who still labor under the illusion of their invulnerability because they refuse to admit that one day soon they will be where I have been. By accepting the reality that others deny, I become invulnerable at precisely the moment of my greatest vulnerability.

FORTY-EIGHT

A.M.

A friend is the person who remains when everyone else has left. He knows when to call and when not to call because he is close enough to realize the value of distance. Though weeks, months, sometime years may pass between conversations and visits, when friends reconnect, it seems as if time had been standing still.

Friendship cannot be planned—it either happens or it doesn't. Like love, it is out of our control—a matter of grace rather than work. Genuine friendship is rare and thus truly precious. If you have four or five close friends in your life, you are one of the fortunate few. Because it is not at our disposal, friendship is unpredictable and often surprises us. Looking back, I never could have anticipated who would become my dearest friends. Sometimes in moments of crisis those you expect to call don't and those you don't expect to call do. When things settle down, it is important to remember who was there and who was not.

Contrary to popular wisdom, friendship is not reciprocal—it is beyond every economy of exchange. Friendship is a gift—perhaps a pure gift or as close to a pure gift as is possible in this life. This gift is offered with absolutely no expectation of return. No tit-for-tat, no quid pro quo. A friend acts without why. If asked for a reason, she cannot give one. Because a friend's deeds are never calculating, the value of friendship remains incalculable; though not precisely infinite, its worth is immeasurable. When it seems to be excessive, as it often does, friendship can appear unreasonable, even mad. Friendship can be so profound that it passes without leaving a trace. On occasion the left hand really does not know what the right hand is doing. A true friend often acts in silence without letting anyone know what he has done. Small gestures hidden from sight, generous acts carried out in silence. Cynics will always find ulterior motives and unconscious desires but friends know better.

BALLPLAYERS

The gift of friendship creates neither debt nor guilt—nothing is expected in return. How can you reply to such deeds? How do you accept such a gift without undoing it? Even "thank you" seems too much and, of course, too little. A friend neither expects nor wants thanks; no matter what I say, he responds: "Pas de quoi— it was nothing."

P.M.

Doubt

I worry about true believers and committed unbelievers much more than I worry about incurable doubters. True believers—even those who believe in unbelief—seek certainty and the security it supposedly brings. When belief overcomes doubt, everything becomes transparent and no question goes unanswered. The quest for such certainty, we are told, marks the beginning and end of modernity. As different gives way to same, reflection turns reflexive, and wherever you look, you see only yourself. Victory, however, becomes defeat when self-certainty leads to destruc-

KIRCHE WURZBRUNNEN,
ROTHENBACH, SWITZERLAND

tion, which in time bends back on itself and becomes self-destructive. In this looking-glass world, there are no rabbit holes through which you can slip to the other side and linger elsewhere. The more you see, the less you know, and the less you know, the more doubt creeps in at the very moment it was supposed to have been erased. If I can never turn around fast enough to see myself seeing myself, can I ever truly know myself? And if we cannot know ourselves, how can we know others?

Augustine, not Descartes, had it almost right—"Dubito ergo sum" rather than "Cogito ergo sum." Doubt is what makes us human; the lingering gap in vision is the opening for the doubt that saves. The only belief worth embracing is not the belief that overcomes doubt but the belief in doubt itself. In the moment of doubt, I suspect—but I can't be sure—that I do not know and this nonknowledge brings uncertainty and insecurity, which are undeniably deeply unsettling.

Who would really want it otherwise? Certainty is far more disturbing than uncertainty, transparency much more threatening than obscurity. Doubt tempers the soul by exposing its inescapable limits. These limits are not merely restrictions but are the condition of a creativity that does not have to be destructive. Since I forever doubt, nothing is settled and thus I can never rest; I not only can go on but must go on. Far from plunging me into despair, doubt is the breath of a future that remains forever open. "Dubito ergo sum" must therefore be rewritten as "Dubito ergo fio"—I doubt, therefore I become.

FORTY-NINE

A.M.

Love

GRANDPA COOPER'S RING SIZER

"I love you no matter what."

"No matter what?"

"No matter what."

"No matter what I do?"

"No matter what."

"No matter what I don't do?"

"No matter what."

We have heard the words so often that they no longer seem extraordinary. "No matter what? ... No matter what." How can such familiar words be made strange?

Love, it appears, is a matter of indifference. For love to be true love, it must be unconditional: I love the other no matter what. What the beloved does makes no difference to the lover, for love's only law is to be without return. This law is unlawful—it breaks (with) every legal economy. Like a rose, love is *ohne warum*—without why. This is what makes love and friendship inseparable. Love is beyond the law, it is a matter of grace, mazing grace.

Grace is indifferent. It is given, if at all, freely—without regard for what has been done or left undone. As such, grace is undeniably careless. Though it seems impossible, I care most deeply when I care not. The careless "no matter what" is awe-ful, truly awful. If it doesn't matter, who cares?

If no one cares, nothing seems to matter. And, in a certain sense, nothing *does* matter. In the profitless economy of grace, no one can afford (to) care. Care remains bound to and by the law; not just any law but the law of laws, which is the law of return.

"It doesn't matter."

"But—"

"No, really, it doesn't matter. It was nothing."

To give as if giving nothing is to give everything by giving not. Always unlawful, the indifference of grace involves boundless generosity. The generous deed is senseless: it is offered without reason and with no expectation of return. Generosity, in other words, must always be given freely. Absolute generosity, if such were possible, would not only give freely but would give nothing less than freedom. To give freely by giving freedom is to let go by letting be and to let be by letting go.

Love is indifferent. Indifferent to what the other does or does not do. I can love the other only by letting go, withdrawing, abandoning. Love does not rebind (*re-ligare*) but releases (*relaxere*), releases unconditionally. More than absolute, such love is the Absolute itself.

"No matter what?"

"No matter what. I don't care. Really, I don't care."

P.M.

Fidelity

Only a small part of fidelity is about sex—though this, of course, is not unimportant. Fidelity is more, much more, about death: "Until death do us part" and perhaps beyond. Death is not a moment awaiting us in the distant future but haunts the present like a shadow that permits light to be seen. Fidelity allows the sharing of what cannot be shared by always being there, especially in the darkest moments.

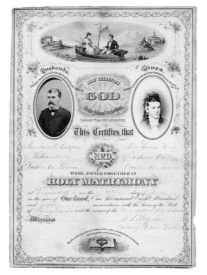

MY GREAT-GRANDPARENTS' MARRIAGE CERTIFICATE

When death stepped out of the shadows, Dinny was there even when I was not. After more than four decades, it is no longer possible to know where I end and she begins. Our thoughts need not be spoken to be communicated. When my mind failed, she took over and her decisions became my own. When I wasn't sure whether I should take the new drug doctors told me I needed to survive, she knew how to get the advice we needed. I had more confidence in her than the physicians attending me and finally declined to take the drug they insisted would save my life.

Whenever illness is serious, survival always depends on more than physicians and pharmaceuticals—it is a matter of faith and will. Faith that the future remains open and the will to move toward it. When illness holds you in its grip and won't let go, it can become overwhelming; fatigue leads to despair, and it all becomes just too much to bear. Enough is enough, no, more than enough, and the will can no longer summon itself—all you want is relief and release. When that critical moment arrived, we both knew it; Dinny would not allow me to give up and intervened to will what I no longer could will. Hers is no Pollyannaish confidence that things always work out for the best but is the tough-minded recognition that though the openness of the future is a gift, it must nonetheless be willed resolutely. Her will became my own, and I eventually left behind the night beyond night and returned from elsewhere.

When Dinny left the hospital, I remained surrounded by others, but, alone in a strange city, she faced an empty apartment. Night after night she was more alone than I. Phone calls and e-mails could not break the isolation she suffered. Through it all she broke down but once and then only briefly. In that moment I glimpsed the strength it took for her to pull me through by doing for me what I could not do by myself. Friends, preoccupied with how I was doing, did not realize the ordeal she was undergoing, but I did and I will never forget it.

FIFTY

A.M.

Hope

Honesty compels me to admit that hope is impossible for me. Once you have passed through the night and glimpsed the night beyond night, how can you hope any longer? It's not just the pain, suffering, and violence but their eternal return that make hope so hopeless. Whether we are coping with the suffering of a newborn baby with no prospect of normality or genocide that seems to know no end, any search for meaning and purpose is more of a travesty than the admission that it is all senseless. My problem with hope is that so often it denies the reality of our situation by telling just-so stories that simply are not true. Good does not always come out of evil, we do not always learn from our mistakes, suffering does not always make us wiser or stronger, and if there is a God, He [*sic*] does not always work for the best. Sometimes evil is what it is and nothing else, sometimes suffering has no reason. There is no pedagogy for the oppressed, and it is disingenuous to preach that there is. To suggest that there is light at the end of the tunnel and that all things work out for the best for those who believe is to deny the horrors that are undeniable facts of daily life. "Given what you describe, how can you go on with life if you do not hope for something better?" you ask. "How can you be honest about life if you do?" I respond.

And yet can I be sure that things are actually hopeless? Perhaps what I don't know rather than what I do creates the impossible possibility of hope. Nonknowledge, I believe, is coiled within knowledge as its necessary condition. While inevitably casting a shadow over all I do, the uncertainty that nonknowledge imparts implies that I cannot be sure that hopelessness is the last word. Such uncertainty is the abiding trace of a future that remains unknowable. While the openness of the future is a gift, which sometimes poisons, how we respond to this gift is our choice: hopelessness or hope. But how is it ever possible to decide?

As I have grown older, I have, contrary to all expectation, become more hopeful rather than less. Far from an accident, this has been my deliberate choice. As I look into the eyes of my children, grandchildren, and students, I realize that hopelessness is a self-indulgence I can no longer afford. Hope is a duty, an obligation—I owe those who come after me the gift of hope. But this hope must be honest—it must not explain away brutal realities that cannot be denied. I must therefore continue to insist that we can never be sure that tomorrow will be better than today or that the end will be richer than the beginning. Nevertheless ...

Nevertheless ... we must hope. When hope is authentic, it hangs by the thin thread of *perhaps*. I hope, not because I know but because I cannot know, and because I cannot know, I must always add "Perhaps—." Perhaps there is hope. Perhaps hope is the impossible possibility that helps us go on when everything seems hopeless. Perhaps.

P.M.

Despair

Over the years one of the ways I've known which way the wind is blowing is by listening to my best students. Like anxious horses who feel the storm coming before it appears on the horizon, creative students know where things are heading before the things that will get us there hit the market. During the 1980s and early 1990s, I began to sense that a tectonic shift was taking place. Students had not stopped reading—I would not let them—

but print was no longer their medium of choice. Having grown up with TV, computers, and video games, they were visual in ways I am not. The narratives that framed their world were from films rather than books. When the Internet took off a few years later, change reached warp speed.

Any good teacher must meet students where they are in order to lead them elsewhere. My problem was that I no longer understood exactly where my students were. I talked with them at length and read quite a bit, but reading in this case could help only so much. In search of help, I finally turned to my friend Hartley, who was one of the most intensely visual people I knew. Suffering dyslexia, which made it difficult for him to read, he had been forced to seek refuge in visual images at a young age. By the time we met, he actually thought in images rather than words. When he read theorists of visual culture, he understood them in ways I did not. Since his manner of thinking was similar to that of my students, he could help me bridge the gap separating me from them. Hartley knew film the way I know philosophy, and he made videos the way I write books. We talked long and often; half the time neither of us understood what the other was saying, but through it all I eventually came to a better understanding of image and he came to a better understanding of word.

Our conversations were suddenly interrupted when Hartley had to undergo heart surgery. The news of his condition surprised me because he was strong and in good shape. An avid cyclist, he would climb the Berkshire Mountains as if they were the Alps on the day of a critical stage of the Tour de France. The operation was serious, but his doctor was a leading heart surgeon and the prognosis seemed good. We had dinner the night before he left for Boston and he was in high spirits. We discussed the work we would do when he returned.

Two days later Linda, his wife and my close friend, called to tell me there was a problem. The operation had gone well but, while he was in the recovery room, he had suffered a stroke. He was stable but his condition was uncertain. The doctor insisted that the stroke was unrelated to the surgery, but none of us believed him. In the days that followed, Linda reported that Hartley's mind was clear but his speech was slurred; he was also paralyzed

DEAD EYE

from his waist down. Rather than coming home, he was heading for a reha-
bilitation center where, with much hard work, his speech slowly returned
to normal, but his dyslexia grew worse and increased the difficulty he had
reading. Fortunately, he could still process images effectively; his paralysis,
however, was permanent. When I finally saw him again, it was a shock to
see this strapping man confined to a wheelchair.

We began our conversations again, but they were not the same. Neither
of us could quite bring ourselves to discuss what we both knew we should
be talking about. One day he asked me if I would help him with his pool
workouts. I was, of course, eager to do anything I could but was not prepared for what I faced. I had not really understood exactly what Hartley
was up against until I labored to lift the dead weight of his body into the
pool. Once he was in the water, his arms flailed as he struggled to pull his
sinking body across the pool. His face was lined with a grim determination I deeply admired. As the weeks wore on and his condition did not improve, resolution turned to despair. Despair, Kierkegaard has taught us, is

the sickness unto death that comes when the future seems closed. Though Hartley never said so directly, I knew he thought the life ahead of him was not worth living, and nothing I said could persuade him otherwise.

One afternoon as we sat with our feet dangling in the pool, he told me that he had listed me as a reference when he recently had bought a hand-gun. When I expressed surprise, he explained that he and Linda were taking lessons at the local firing range. Since he obviously could no longer control his body and was unable to compete in anything requiring physical activity, he thought that learning to shoot might give him some sense of competence, however diminished it might be. I did not believe a word he said and called Linda as soon as I got home. "Linda, this is nuts. We both know what's really going on—you can't let him do this." She said she understood my concern but insisted it would be fine as long as she was there. I finally gave up but said, "OK, but you must lock up the gun and keep the key yourself."

My meetings with Hartley alternated between heady discussions and exhausting sessions in the pool. Though he made little progress, Hartley continued to work hard and rarely expressed frustration. By this time I knew him well enough to hear what he was not saying. I did not, however, know what to do about it because I understood the depth of his despair and realized that any hope I offered him would be a lie. Before I could call Linda again to express my growing concern, she called me. When the phone rang early in the morning, I knew the news was not good. "Mark, Hartley shot himself last night." Their son, Ivor, had found his body when he came home from work. After I hung up the phone and struggled to absorb the news I had feared, it was impossible to avoid a feeling of responsibility for what had happened.

While I was still wrestling with guilt, Linda called a second time and asked me to speak at Hartley's memorial service. I agreed to do so but had no idea what to say. As I pondered this impossible challenge, I finally concluded that I could no longer avoid saying what I thought needed to be said, even if I did not know how people would respond. When the afternoon of the service arrived, I concluded my remarks by saying:

I now realize that sometimes we are called upon to give the most difficult gift of all—the gift of death. *No* decision—absolutely no decision—is more excruciating than the decision to allow a loved one to choose death rather than life. But in giving the gift of death we also receive it. And when the gift of death comes back to us from the other to whom we have given it, that gift returns inverted and reversed. In this strange moment, the gift of death becomes the gift of life. In his death, Hartley has given *us* life—a deeper life, a richer life, a more complex life. What greater act of generosity can we ever imagine?

WILD WEST—*DOUBLE NEGATIVE*, NEVADA DESERT

FIFTY-ONE

A.M.

Happiness

SELMA IN TIMES SQUARE

Why is it so much harder to write about happiness than unhappiness and joy rather than melancholy? Happy eras, we are told, are the blank pages of history—and, so it would seem, of books. Perhaps it is because it takes more courage to write about happiness than unhappiness. Those who fashion themselves sophisticated dismiss people who embrace happiness as naive, simple-minded, and superficial. On the scales of criticism and scholarship, gravity outweighs levity every time. How many major writers' reputations rest on odes to joy?

My candidate is Nietzsche—no person has written more profoundly and eloquently about happiness and joy. Not just joy but "everlasting joy." What makes his words so poignant is that they were written from the depths of a suffering that never ended. Neither naive nor superficial, Nietzsche writes in the night beyond night from which few ever return. When others say nay, he says yea. Nevertheless, Nietzsche is remembered by friends and foes alike for his no rather than his yes.

And yet Nietzsche never enjoyed the happiness for which he so desperately longed. The gap between desire and fulfillment is the space of his writing. Had joy overwhelmed him, he would in all likelihood have fallen into a silence other than the madness that eventually consumed him. The title of his greatest work—*The Gay Science*—continues to echo as a desperate plea rather than a knowing affirmation. Intense unhappiness becomes bearable by imagining that things might be otherwise elsewhere. The writer *must* write this elsewhere to get through the night and the darker the night, the better the writing.

Happiness, by contrast, quells the urge to write by collapsing the future into the present. Joy is of the moment—that is why it is both so precious and so fleeting. Far from an alluring promise, the morrow becomes a looming threat to be deferred as long as possible. While the moment of happiness lasts, there is neither the desire nor the need to write; indeed, writing breaks the spell of joy. Rather than the symptom of lack, the blank page is the trace of fulfillment. This is why the writer fears that for which he nonetheless longs—happiness and the contentment it brings mark the end of writing.

But of course the moment always passes, and when it is gone, writing once again becomes possible, even if it is no longer necessary. Happiness untempered by unhappiness *is* trivial, and joy that forgets melancholy *is* superficial. True joy is not the happiness of the once-born but of the twice-born, who passes through without moving beyond the dark night of the soul. The person who can do nothing but linger with the negative never realizes that "midnight is also midday." Happiness is not found by fleeing the travail of temporality but by immersing oneself ever more deeply in it. "*For joy accepts everlasting flow!*"

P.M.

Melancholy

DIRT FROM KIERKEGAARD'S GRAVE

There is a melancholy of things complete that arrives unexpectedly. Fulfillment does not fulfill, and the end so eagerly anticipated proves disappointingly empty. The deal is closed, the book finished, the class graduated, the career complete, and it is finally time for celebration. When family and friends gather, there is, however, an uninvited guest. Melancholy disrupts the moment—the person in its grip can never be fully present. While others are immersed in the moment, the vision of the melancholic is split, his consciousness always double. The most profound melancholy is invisible to the eyes of others. The melancholic spirit travels incognito—while seeming to be absorbed in the moment, he floats above, watching from without, knowing the moment will pass and uncertain it will ever arrive again. In melancholy the present is never fully present but always already past—even before it arrives. This trace of this impending past is most haunting in precisely those moments that are supposed to be complete.

Melancholy is never a matter of will. It settles like a mist that cannot be dispersed and, as long as it remains, shades every corner of life. The color of melancholy is neither the black of bile nor the gray on gray of a winter day; rather, it is the glow of late August light playing on goldenrod. Melancholy reflects the beauty of summer's last flower, which is almost perfect because it is already fading.

For those devoted to living in the moment, there is a sadness about melancholy that inevitably leads to mourning. And yet … and yet, there is also something strangely sweet about melancholy. Far from prompting flight, melancholy has an allure that coyly attracts even the most resistant. That is why Kierkegaard called melancholy "my most faithful mistress." While undeniably disturbing, melancholy does not necessarily agitate; it often brings a sense of calm and serenity that allows pensive reflection—perhaps even contemplation. Though I often curse her for it, melancholy was the most precious gift my mother left me.

FIFTY-TWO

A.M.

Ordinary

IVY FROM HEGEL'S GRAVE

When you first receive the diagnosis of cancer, it is difficult not to feel singled out. Though I did not for a moment ask "Why me?" I did nonetheless feel exceptional in a way I never had before. In the days following that dreaded phone call, I watched friends and colleagues go about their business as if nothing had changed and realized that now I was set apart—I had become not merely different but other.

I had not, however, anticipated how much things would change when I crossed the threshold of the cancer ward. Forbidding from the outside, the hospital offers unexpected reassurance to those who know there is no certain cure. What I found most striking during the first days of this long ordeal was the way the brutal honesty of the hospital staff and people suffering transformed the extraordinary into the utterly ordinary. Everybody admitted to the cancer ward had received the same traumatic news I had, and we all were engaged in a life-and-death struggle whose outcome was far from certain. What was exceptional on the outside became routine on the inside. Doctors and nurses approached every crisis in a completely matter-of-fact way: "This is the situation. This is what needs to be done, and here is how we are going to do it." Their words were confident without being arrogant. Most doctors who treat cancer patients have seen too much inexplicable suffering to be certain about anything. Slowly, their honesty and calm assurance spreads to patients, and panic turns into pragmatism: "OK, what do I have to do to get from here to there? When do we start?"

Something else also begins to happen that is quite extraordinary. As patients become as matter-of-fact about their condition as their doctors, they begin to talk to each other. Strangers who do not even know each other's names, and who never would exchange a word outside the hospital, talk about intimate things they cannot discuss with their families or closest friends. The shared sense of crisis creates a freedom of expression unknown in the outside world. In the waiting room, the private becomes public without being obscene. When passion gives way to compassion, fleeting relationships deepen.

Kierkegaard was wrong—anonymity and community are not opposites; and Heidegger was wrong—the prospect of death not only drives us apart, it also draws us together. Though we rarely talk about it with those to whom we are close, disease and death are not really exceptional but are what we all finally share. In the hospital a unique community emerges among strangers. This community is all the more intense for its brevity—it might last no longer than a single conversation in the waiting room, an afternoon in the recovery room, or a few days in a hospital bed. Such relations end when the stay is over: what goes on in the hospital stays in the hospital. And yet these relations run deep and remain more memorable than many of the relations with others we think we know well. Anonymity and the awareness that relationships will not last allow people to become closer to strangers than they are to those they believe closest to them. In a world where intimacy is often cheap, the richest community might be found in the most unexpected place—the cancer ward.

P.M.

Extraordinary

BACCHANALIAN REVEL

An Ordinary Evening in Williamstown

The extraordinary is ordinary,
The ordinary extraordinary.
"The serious reflection is composed
Neither of comic nor tragic but of commonplace."
Lush, purple Concord grapes ripe on the vine,
Goldenrod glowing in the day's last light,
A monarch butterfly lighting on the silk of a burst milkweed pod.
"A permanence composed of impermanence."
Geese honking high above as they gather to leave once more.
High low, low high.
The sweet serendipity of the everyday.
A rabbit nibbling grass at the edge of the field,
The plunk of an apple falling to the ground,
Pears left half eaten by deer and crow.
Mountains whose "lineaments were the earth."
The glint of a turkey feather lost in the grass.
"Hallucinations in surfaces."
Shadows visibly growing longer.
Drooping black-eyed Susans dreading first frost.

"Obscure in colors whether of the sun
Or the mind."
Weeds—but why weeds?—grown tall waiting to be mowed.
Sun, moving south, slipping below the distant tree line.
"The instinct for earth," for Williamstown, where, unexpectedly,
"The real and the unreal are two in one."
The truth of incarnation.
Wisdom asks nothing more
Nothing more.

Notes

page 31 *One day there is life.* Paul Auster, *The Invention of Solitude* (New York: Penguin, 1982), 5.

page 46 *The cradle rocks* Vladimir Nabokov, *Speak, Memory: An Autobiography Revisited* (New York: Random House, 1989), 19.

page 71 *One day there is life.* Auster, *Invention of Solitude*, 5.

page 76 *The afternoon was well advanced* Paul Auster, *City of Glass* (New York: Penguin, 1990), 100.

page 78 *God and the imagination* Wallace Stevens, *Opus Posthumous: Poems, Plays, Prose*, ed. Samuel French Morris (New York: Random House, 1957), 178.

page 98 *How with this rage* William Shakespeare, Sonnet 65.

page 104 *exuberant, floating, dancing, mocking* Friedrich Nietzsche, *Gay Science* (New York: Vintage, 1974), 164.

page 112 *Never a borrower nor a lender be* Shakespeare, *Hamlet*, 1.3.75–77.

page 117 *I was just thinking* Jean-Paul Sartre, *Nausea*, trans. Lloyd Alexander (New York: New Directions, 1964), 112.

page 169 *For the listener* Wallace Stevens, "The Snow Man," *Collected Poems* (New York: Knopf, 1981), 10.

page 173 *the fury of destruction* Stevens, *Opus Posthumous*, 178.

page 286 *"For joy accepts everlasting flow!"* Friedrich Nietzsche, *Thus Spoke Zarathustra*, trans. Marianne Cowan (Chicago: Henry Regnery, 1957), 354–56.

page 291–292 My poem, "An Ordinary Evening in Williamstown," is indebted to and quotes seven lines from Stevens, "An Ordinary Evening in New Haven," *Collected Poems*, 465–89.

Acknowledgments

A life is, I believe, a complex web of intensive and extensive relations. Though things never quite come together, in retrospect patterns appear that were not obvious while they were emerging. The distinctive ways in which the trajectories of others intersect in the time and space that we briefly share make us what we are and are not. *Field Notes from Elsewhere: Reflections on Dying and Living* is, among other things, an extended acknowledgment of many debts I can never repay. It is simply impossible to single out some at the expense of others.

I would, however, like to express my gratitude to several people who have helped me translate life into words: Jack Miles, Sara Suleri, James Shepard, Paul Lieberman, David Miller, Gil Anidjar, Candice Olson, Fay Vincent, and Herbert Allen for their insightful readings and thoughtful criticisms; Margaret Weyers for everything she does; Stella Lee for her impeccable sense of design; Laurence Kirshbaum and Megan Thompson for their sage advice; Wendy Lochner, James Jordan, and Lisa Hamm for their enthusiastic support; Polly Kummel for her admirable attention to detail; Peter Scardino, Gordon Weir, Toby Cosgrove, Harry Wilson, and Erwin Steubner for medical care not limited to the body; and, of course, to my family —Dinny, Kirsten, Aaron, Frida, Selma, and Beryl—without whom I would not have made it.

Stone Hill

Also by Mark C. Taylor

After God (2007)

Mystic Bones (2006)

Confidence Games: Money and Markets in a World Without Redemption (2004)

Grave Matters, with Dietrich Christian Lammerts (2002)

Vito Acconci with Jennifer Bloomer and Frazer Ward (2002)

The Moment of Complexity: Emerging Network Culture (2001)

About Religion: Economies of Faith in Virtual Cultures (1999)

The Picture in Question: Mark Tansey and the Ends of Representation (1999)

Critical Terms in Religious Studies, editor (1998)

Hiding (1996)

Motel Réal, Las Vegas, Nevada, CD-ROM with José Marqez (1996)

Imagologies: Media Philosophy, with Esa Saarinen (1994)

Nots (1993)

Disfiguring: Art, Architecture, Religion (1992)

Double Negative, with Michael Heizer (1992)

Tears (1989)

Altarity (1987)

Deconstruction in Context: Literature and Philosophy (1986)

Erring: A Postmodern A/theology (1984)

Deconstructing Theology (1982)

Unfinished: Essays in Honor of Ray L. Hart, editor (1981)

Journeys to Selfhood: Hegel and Kierkegaard (1980, 2000)

Religion and the Human Image, co-author with Professors Carl Raschke and
   James Kirk, (1976)

Kierkegaard's Pseudonymous Authorship: A Study of Time and the Self (1975)